T0390348

The Mushroom Hunter's Kitchen

The Mushroom Hunter's Kitchen

A Culinary Homage to Wild and Cultivated Mushrooms

Chad Hyatt

Page 273 is a continuation of this copyright page.

Originally published by Chad Hyatt in 2018. First published in substantially revised form by The Experiment, LLC, in 2025.

The Experiment, LLC | 220 East 23rd Street, Suite 600 | New York, NY 10010-4658
theexperimentpublishing.com

This book contains the opinions and ideas of its author and food safety information and advice based on currently available information and best practice. It is not a foraging or mushroom identification guide. Readers are responsible for accurately identifying mushrooms before consuming them. Neither the author nor the publisher accepts liability or responsibility for any possible harm resulting from handling or consuming wild mushrooms. If you believe you have ingested toxic mushrooms, call poison control.

Library of Congress Cataloging-in-Publication Data

Names: Hyatt, Chad, author.
Title: The mushroom hunter's kitchen : a culinary homage to wild and cultivated mushrooms / Chad Hyatt.
Description: New York : The Experiment, 2025. | "Originally published by Chad Hyatt in 2018. First published by The Experiment, LLC, in 2025"--Title page verso. | Includes bibliographical references and index.
Identifiers: LCCN 2025003547 (print) | LCCN 2025003548 (ebook) | ISBN 9798893030648 (hardcover) | ISBN 9798893030655 (ebook)
Subjects: LCSH: Cooking (Mushrooms) | Edible mushrooms. | Mushrooms. | LCGFT: Cookbooks.
Classification: LCC TX804 .H937 2025 (print) | LCC TX804 (ebook) | DDC 641.6/58--dc23/eng/20250208
LC record available at https://lccn.loc.gov/2025003547
LC ebook record available at https://lccn.loc.gov/2025003548

ISBN 979-8-89303-064-8
Ebook ISBN 979-8-89303-065-5

Cover and text design, and illustrations throughout, by Beth Bugler
Cover photographs by Elena Feldbaum
Author photograph by Lenny Hyatt

Manufactured in China

First printing July 2025
10 9 8 7 6 5 4 3 2 1

For my pinche pinche, *Rosa—*
You make everything possible, and
I am eternally grateful for your
unflinching support. Life is so much
better with you in it.

Contents

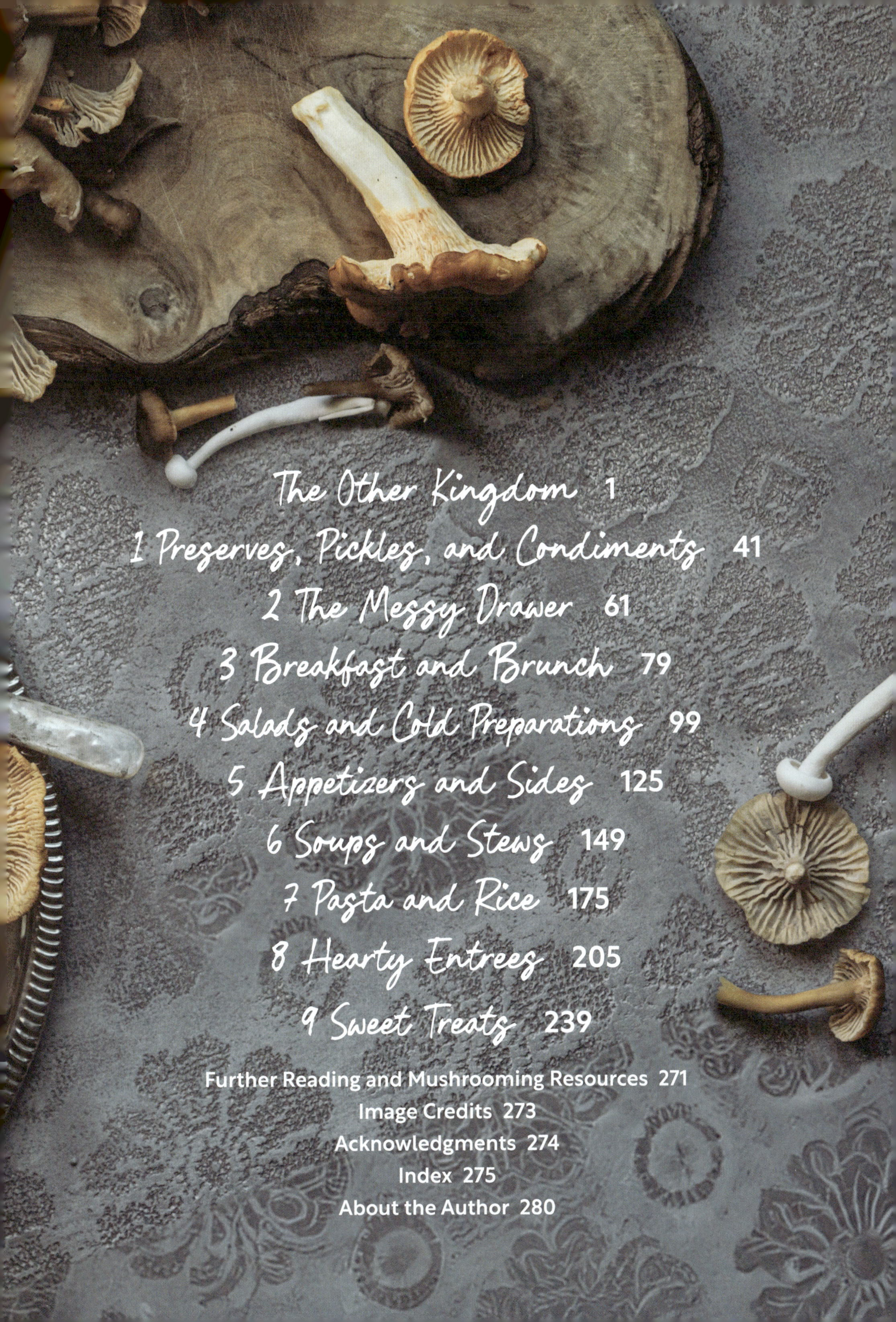

The Other Kingdom

It was Saturday night, almost midnight, on Thanksgiving weekend, and the excitement was palpable. About fifteen of us got up from our warm seats around the hearth, strapped on our headlamps, and wandered out into the deep darkness of Northern California's Mendocino coast. We could see almost nothing outside of the small, illuminated circle of ground in front of each of us. As we headed into the dark forest, we had a singular focus. We were hunting porcini!

Moments earlier we had been getting to know each other around the fire, laughing it up, enjoying the remains of good food and drink. We had met for the first time the day before, spending our time together looking for, learning about, cooking (my job), and tasting different mushrooms. The crew represented at least five different countries, and ranged in age from teen through senior citizen, and all of us were there to explore one common interest.

The leader of this ragtag band, and our host for the weekend's festivities, was David Arora, one of the most well-known and important myco-ambassadors and mycologists of the last few decades. The midnight porcini hunt had been David's idea. The utter silliness and seeming impossibility of searching for mushrooms in the dark made the entire exercise that much more fun.

We tried not to stray too far from the group as we delved into the dark forest. Even with the headlamps, we had to rely on the pack for a sense of direction, as there were no trails. I could hear lots of hooting, hollering, laughing, and general glee as I tried to stay near the other little circles of light moving between the trees.

Suddenly, someone screamed out in celebration. The first porcino had been found! Shortly after, another yell of success came from near the first. Now that we knew it was indeed possible to find porcini in the dark, the mood shifted from jovial to intense and focused. None of us wanted to go back empty-handed.

That Thanksgiving weekend marked my first mushroom event as a member of the staff. I was as giddy, excited, and awestruck as any of the paid attendees. I found one porcino during that midnight hunt, but the real discovery was the community and connection of the mushroom world. Friends I made that weekend are still among the best friends I have, and my own personal mushroom network has now spread over the entire country and beyond. That weekend also marked the beginning of my side career as a presenter, educator, and staff member at mushroom events around the country, and indirectly led me to write this book.

David often says the relationships forged between people are the most important things we gain from mushrooms, and I could not agree more—and I've always felt similarly about food and cooking.

The Joy of Eating Mushrooms

This book is for anyone interested in cooking mushrooms—not only mushroom hunters. Though a few recipes rely upon specific wild mushrooms, most translate with no problem to mushrooms you can buy at the store, and substitution ideas are available throughout.

I want to encourage everyone to expand their mushroom culinary horizons, and challenge even my most knowledgeable readers to think a little differently about mushrooms. In my cooking demos and classes, I focus on showing people ideas about mushrooms that they likely have not seen before, often in direct opposition to what they have heard or been taught. We do, in fact, submerge them in water. We use them in all facets of the meal, from hors d'oeuvres to salads, condiments to entrées, and even desserts.

I also encourage my more experienced audience members to cook with many mushrooms that have been generally dismissed as lousy edibles. I believe that much of what we think of as good mushrooms and bad mushrooms for the table is cultural. Many common, plentiful mushrooms that most Americans ignore, such as milk caps and slippery jacks, are prized edibles in other cultures. The more mushrooms you can identify and learn you like eating, the more opportunity you'll have for a successful hunt every time you are out. While everyone else is chasing just two or three different mushrooms, you'll have dozens of edibles in your sights.

The author enjoying a morel hunt

My Myco-Culinary Story

I discovered the world of mushrooms shortly before beginning my cooking career, almost two decades ago, and my growth as a mushroom enthusiast paralleled my growth as a culinary professional. While attending a wild mushroom-themed dinner at a local restaurant, I met Todd Spanier, who had supplied all of the night's mushrooms. Though fearful of collecting my own, I had a long-held culinary interest in wild mushrooms. Todd convinced me that the skill was easily learned with some honest effort. Through his recommendation, I bought a copy of David Arora's *Mushrooms Demystified*, a book that taught my entire generation of mushroom hunters everything we knew about mushrooms, including how to identify them.

Not too long after, I received an accidental tip about a porcini flush in the Lake Tahoe area, and a friend and I took the two-hundred-mile-plus drive there from San José the next morning. Thunderstorms had sent a flush of boletes up all over the place, and my first real mushroom hunt netted about ten pounds (4.5 kg) of perfectly pristine porcini buttons! Every mushroom we found seemed like discovered treasure, and came with all of the corresponding thrill and satisfaction. Further, having read up prior, I learned that I could easily recognize the porcini in the field. That day provided the first big step into a life-changing passion—I was hooked.

Soon after, when the rains started locally, I began nosing around the live oaks in the Santa Cruz Mountains, and my first chanterelle patches revealed themselves. As my fervor grew, I spent more and more time looking for the next great spot, often walking past countless mushrooms I didn't know.

The beautiful Painted Sullius

Some days, the prime edibles were not out, so I started learning to identify the other mushrooms that I had been ignoring. Exploring rarely appreciated edibles and encouraging others to do the same quickly became a passion of mine. Soon, I had collected and eaten ten new species, then twenty. I still enjoy trying new mushrooms any chance I get, but I stopped counting my conquests years ago, when they numbered well over three hundred.

Meanwhile, cooking became my career. Shortly after becoming interested in mushrooms, I gave up an unfulfilling, decade-long engineering career and went to culinary school. My first few cooking jobs were in locally well-known and well-regarded kitchens, including a Michelin-starred restaurant and a gastropub where local chefs would come to eat and hang out.

Eventually, I became an executive sous chef at an exclusive country club, where I began creating à la carte specials using the mushrooms I foraged on my days off. I loved the challenge of collecting enough mushrooms for the restaurant and then figuring out how to fit them onto the menu. By the fall of 2015, I had moved on to a corporate chef gig that left me with even more freedom to experiment with mushrooms at work, and was well on my way to becoming a regular member of my local mushroom hunting community. And by the time the fall mushroom season rolled around the following year, I'd started work on this book. Word gradually trickled out about this project, and I started getting calls to do more mushroom-related dinners and events. Those events went well, and they led to more events the following year, and the years after that, which led directly into my current career as a freelance chef focused on special (often mushroom-related) events.

Welcome to the Mushroom Hunter's Kitchen

My research for what became *The Mushroom Hunter's Kitchen* began years before I started to work on it consciously. The act of seeing it through has been a cathartic labor of love that has profoundly changed me. In turn, the process has shaped my career as a chef into something I could never have dreamed.

Every recipe in this book is about the journey I've been lucky enough to share with a friend or loved one, and about the myco-community that has shaped a big part of my life. It's about my many friendships and adventures that mushrooms have enabled, encouraged, and facilitated over the years. This book is my chance to share something with the mushroom world that has given me so much over the years. I hope exploring these pages will bring you as much joy as researching and writing it has brought me.

Porcini peeking through the grass

Getting To Know Edible Mushrooms

I cannot emphasize enough that this book is for anyone interested in cooking with mushrooms—not just mushroom hunters. But I do highly encourage everyone reading this to get out into the forest and go on a hunt, if you're able and at all interested in doing so. All you need to start collecting mushrooms is something to put them in and the motivation to seek them out. Learning how to identify different mushrooms and how to find the ones you want takes time and practice, but luckily, it's also a ton of fun. Building that skillset is a happy lifelong journey, so enjoy the process of getting there.

IN PRAISE OF TRYING NEW MUSHROOMS

For many years, I have made it my mission to expose myself and other mushroom hunters to new edibles and the sheer variety of mushrooms out there. Besides the joy of learning and teaching, pragmatism drives this mission. These days you can find many more mushroom varieties than ever before at your local market. These mushrooms have different textures, aromas, and flavors that can both inspire you to cook new dishes and fit into old favorites in new ways. If you are a mushroom hunter, there are even more possibilities open to you, and learning new edibles will also make your hunting so much more fun and likely to succeed.

The mushroom hunters in your area are likely competing for all the chanterelles, porcini, and other "choice edibles" they can find. More competition leads to a more challenging hunt. Yet even though species like milk caps (*Lactarius*), *Russula*, and slippery jacks (*Suillus*) are quite abundant, most hunters pass right by them without a second glance. Not only will learning to enjoy some of the less-appreciated edibles help you vastly improve your odds of a successful hunt, but some of them work even better in certain dishes than the standard "prime edibles." For example, I can't think of many mushrooms that work as well in stews as a milk cap or *Russula*. The more of these species you learn to enjoy, the more likely every hunt is to become a fruitful venture!

Additionally, if you live in the eastern United States, you rarely find large areas of forest dominated by just one (or even two or three) tree species. This makes hunting for edible mushrooms much more challenging if you know only a few types because, since most mushrooms have specific tree associations, few mushrooms show up continuously as you hike through large areas of woods. It's a far cry from the western United States, where fairly uniform habitat can be vast and you can follow seemingly uninterrupted trails of chanterelles, hedgehogs, matsutake, porcini, and other edibles for miles in good times. So, though eastern hunters can often get large quantities of a few mushrooms like black trumpets, hen-of-the-woods, or chicken-of-the-woods, most mushrooms can be found only in smaller patches where their preferred tree partners congregate. If you want better odds of coming home with a full basket, you need to learn about more mushrooms.

What *Is* a Mushroom?

What we call a mushroom is only a small, fleeting part of an otherwise mostly invisible underground network of fungus. The mushroom is a reproductive structure known as a fruiting body, the fungal analog of what in the plant kingdom would be called a fruit.

A Word about Safety

This book is filled with recipes, stories, and ideas for using wild mushrooms, but it will not teach you how to safely collect or identify them. Collecting and eating wild mushrooms or any other wild food requires skills and knowledge that take time and effort to acquire. When done with an appropriate amount of caution and attention to detail, collecting and eating wild edibles can be a perfectly safe pastime. However, doing so without appropriate caution and knowledge is extremely perilous and potentially deadly.

The only safe way to eat a wild mushroom is to know the species you have with 100 percent certainty and to know whether or not that particular species is edible. If you cannot confidently identify a mushroom, do not eat it. If you are interested in learning more about mushroom identification and sound foraging practices, see page 271 for resources you can use to get started.

Even when you are able to confidently identify a mushroom, you may still give yourself digestive troubles if you eat too much of it. Many mushrooms are perfectly edible in small amounts but can have laxative effects or cause digestive upsets when consumed in larger quantities. Eating large amounts of the same mushroom repeatedly over several days sometimes causes serious problems, even with species that normally give you no issues. Remember that variety is the spice of life, especially with food and even more so with mushrooms, and don't overdo it.

Amanita silvicola *(left), one of the dangerously toxic white* Amanitas *often found growing near or intermixed with the white gilled, white matsutake (right) in coastal California.*

SO, WHAT MUSHROOMS ARE GOOD TO EAT?

It depends on who you ask. Many mushrooms that one culture highly prizes get berated as inferior by another. Countless people base their opinions about which mushrooms are good to eat on field guides' lists of good edibles. For all but the most advanced mushroom hunters, you should absolutely trust your field guides to determine which mushrooms are safe to eat. But you should let your taste, not your field guides, steer you toward what you do or do not *like* to eat. Give different mushrooms a try and decide for yourself.

Of course, I don't mean to imply that all mushrooms are great to eat or that you will enjoy eating *any* listed as edible. As a chef, though, I try to approach preparing and eating new mushrooms the same way I approach preparing and eating new vegetables. If I dislike a new mushroom the first time I try it (or even the second or third), I am likely to blame the way I prepared it or combined it with other ingredients. I will often try again repeatedly until I succeed or decide I'm out of ideas on how to make that species more palatable.

SOME OF MY FAVORITE MUSHROOMS TO COOK WITH

Though only a few common mushrooms show up on most store shelves, mushrooms are as varied as vegetables. Nature provides countless varieties in just about any shape, size, color, texture, aroma, and flavor you can imagine, each of which requires different methods for handling, cleaning, storing, preserving, and of course, cooking. The following is far from a complete list of every mushroom you might find; instead, it reflects some of my favorite mushrooms to cook with, many of which you'll see popping up again and again throughout these recipes.

TRYING NEW-TO-YOU MUSHROOMS

Many popular edibles, from button mushrooms to porcini, chicken-of-the-woods to morels, cause adverse or allergic reactions in some people. To be sure your body is OK with a new-to-you mushroom, it's best to eat only a few bites the first time.

The first time I try new mushrooms, I simply sauté them in a neutral oil and season with salt so that I can evaluate their taste and texture on their own. I will often try a bite of a new mushroom when cooked through but before it has browned, and another after browning. Browning mushrooms changes their taste, quite often for the better, though I actually prefer some mushrooms after just a simmer, and not browned at all—the giant sawgill (*Neolentinus ponderosus*) comes to mind. Once you have a basic idea of the flavor profile and texture of a mushroom, and know that your body can tolerate it, you can start experimenting with it in different dishes and using various cooking techniques.

It sometimes takes a few tries to get it right when cooking a new-to-you species. Remember, different mushrooms' flavors and textures work great in some applications, and less well in others. As you experiment with a new mushroom, think about the types of recipes in which you could best use it.

Scientific versus Common Names

Throughout this book, you'll see me refer to mushrooms both by their common names (e.g., porcini or king boletes) and their scientific names (e.g., *Boletus edulis*). Common names usually pose no problem when it comes to identifying mushrooms common in your local area, but for mushrooms not as regularly encountered, these names are often ambiguous or misleading if they exist at all. A mushroom known as a hen-of-the-woods in one place may be called a maitake or even a sheep's head elsewhere.

Given these issues, I strongly advise anyone serious about learning to identify wild mushrooms to learn their scientific (Latin) names. Besides clearing up ambiguity, the scientific names often provide more useful information about the species than the common names. Learning scientific names can help you understand the relationship between different mushrooms even when you aren't familiar with the species.

Cultivated Mushrooms

First, let's get familiar with the most widely available cultivated mushrooms. (If you don't see what you are looking for in this first section, you will likely find it in the section about wild mushrooms that follows.)

Beech, Shimeji, Clamshell (*Hypsizygus tessulatus*) – Brown and white varieties are both widely available, have a similar firm, crisp texture and almost nutty flavor, and can be used interchangeably. They are popular in China, Korea, and Japan. They are good sautéed on their own, and can slide seamlessly into a wide variety of recipes.
Best cooking methods: wet sautéing, pressing and searing, simmering
Best preservation methods: pickling, candying

Cordyceps (*Cordyceps militaris*) – These small, slender, orange mushrooms have become popular primarily for their purported medicinal properties, but they are both good to eat and easy to work with. They have an earthy flavor and crisp texture and don't take long to cook thanks to their small size.
Best cooking method: simple sautéing

Enoki (*Flammulina filiformis*) – These skinny white mushrooms with tiny caps have a crisp texture and pleasant, mild flavor. I like to cook them only briefly to preserve their texture. As such, I recommend adding them to stir-fries, sautés, or hot soups just before serving. The residual heat is usually enough to cook them through. Wild enoki (*Flammulina* spp.) look rather different, and are more robust than their cultivated counterparts. They can be cooked with a dry sauté or simmered in broth.
Best cooking method: warming with residual heat, dry sautéing (wild)

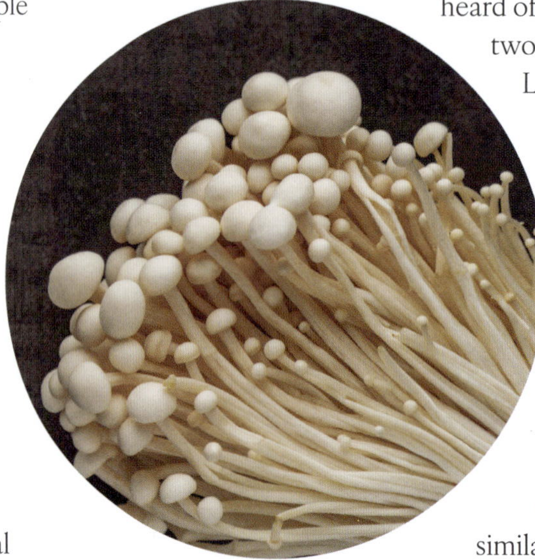

Cultivated enoki

King Trumpet, King Oyster, Trumpet Royale, Gambone (*Pleurotus eryngii*) – These oyster mushroom relatives have a chewy, meaty texture and rich, almost nutty, flavor. Many people cut the large stems into 1-inch (2.5 cm) cylinders, boil for a couple minutes, and then drain, dry, and sear them off as a vegetarian scallop substitute. Nebrodini (*Pleurotus nebrodensis*) are a closely related species that can be treated the same way.
Best cooking methods: wet sautéing, pressing and searing, boiling then sautéing

Maitake, Hen-of-the-Woods, Sheep's Head (*Grifola frondosa*) – These mushrooms have a crisp, chewy texture meaty flavor, and aroma that work well in a wide variety of applications.

The wild ones can get quite large—I have heard of fifty-plus-pound (twenty-two-plus kilogram) behemoths. Left whole and stored in the fridge, maitake keep very well for at least a week. Break off and clean pieces as needed. The easiest way to clean wild hens is to separate them into "leaves" and then rinse under cold water while scraping with a knife.

Cultivated maitake are similar to wild, though generally a lot smaller and less meaty than

Cultivated maitake

their wild counterparts. They also tend to be grown in sterile environments and do not require cleaning aside from trimming the base.
Best cooking methods: dry sautéing, wet sautéing, pressing and searing, simmering, pan roasting, oven roasting, deep frying
Best preservation methods: sautéing and freezing, boiling and freezing, dehydrating

Nameko (*Pholiota nameko*) – These are more popular in Japan than in the US, but can often be found at Asian markets. They have a crisp texture and a somewhat slimy coating, along with a rather mild flavor. The Japanese prize them precisely for their slimy texture and use them frequently in soups. They work well in stir-fries, as well. Pioppini (*Cyclocybe aegerita*) can be treated similarly to nameko and are quite popular around the Mediterranean, occasionally appearing in the US.
Best cooking methods: simmering, pressing and searing, simple sautéing
Best preservation methods: pickling, candying

Oysters (*Pleurotus* spp.) – Their pleasant texture and mild flavor make them extremely versatile. They also dehydrate well. The stems, when present, tend to be much chewier than the caps, which can provide a nice textural contrast. I use a wet sauté for cultivated oysters and a dry sauté for wild, which tend to contain a lot more moisture than their cultivated counterparts. Otherwise, I treat the cultivated and wild versions exactly the same.
Best cooking methods: dry sautéing, wet sautéing, pressing and searing, pan roasting, oven roasting
Best preservation methods: sautéing and freezing, dehydrating, pickling

Portabella (*Agaricus bisporus*) – Portabella, also spelled portobello, are simply crimini that have been allowed to mature and thus have a much stronger, meatier flavor and aroma along with a softer texture. Portabella stems have a crumbly texture and are sometimes discarded. Some people like to scrape away the gills before cooking because they can turn a dish brown, but you also lose a lot of flavor by doing so. I prefer to leave the gills in place.
Best cooking methods: dry sautéing, grilling

Shiitake (*Lentinula edodes*) – Shiitake have an excellent chewy texture and a pleasant meaty flavor when mature. Younger shiitake have a milder flavor. Some people find the stems to be unpleasantly chewy, but I personally enjoy them. Dried shiitake, which have a stronger flavor and chewier texture than fresh, can be added directly to soups, stews, or stocks, or rehydrated and then

Nameko

added to stir-fries or sautés. The soaking liquid from rehydrating shiitakes is quite flavorful, so make sure you use it in whatever you are cooking.
Best cooking methods: wet sautéing, simmering, frying (thinly sliced)
Best preservation methods: dehydrating, candying

Straw Mushrooms (*Volvariella volvacea*) – These Asian natives typically come canned. The canned mushrooms are not as flavorful as fresh, but I've never been able to find fresh straw mushrooms in the US, and I still enjoy what they add to certain Chinese and southeast Asian dishes, stir-fries, and soups. The canned mushrooms are precooked; to use them, drain well, rinse, and then drain again.
Best cooking method: NA

White Button, Cremini, Crimini (*Agaricus bisporus*) – These are the most widely grown and sold mushrooms in North America, and they are actually all the same species. White button mushrooms are very mild in flavor and usually have a somewhat firm texture. They often thrive in recipes that need more bulk than flavor from the mushroom. Crimini are a darker, slightly more flavorful cultivar of button mushrooms.
Best cooking methods: wet sautéing, boiling, boiling then sautéing, oven roasting, pan roasting
Best preservation methods: dehydrating, candying

Wine Caps (*Stropharia rugosoannulata*) – These large mushrooms are a favorite of home cultivators, though I never see them in stores. I have always gotten a grassy flavor from them, and I prefer pairing them with stronger flavors. I use them in soups and stir-fries.
Best cooking method: dry sautéing
Best preservation methods: sautéing and freezing

Wood Ear, Cloud Ear, Tree Ear (*Auricularia* spp.) – These are quite popular in Chinese, Japanese, Korean, and other Asian cuisines. They can be found dried, and often fresh, in almost any Asian market, and they also grow wild throughout much of North America. Their flavor is quite mild, but they have an almost cartilaginous texture that makes them popular in soups and salads (after cooking). You can use fresh and dried wood ears interchangeably, after briefly boiling (in the case of fresh) or soaking and then boiling (in the case of dried). Wild wood ears often have a little clinging woody debris that you can trim off with a knife.
Best cooking methods: boiling, simmering, simple sautéing
Best preservation methods: dehydrating, candying

Dried wood ear

Wild Mushrooms

This section explores some of the most commonly eaten wild mushrooms, including many of my personal favorites. Get to know new types at your own pace, and remember that there is no hurry. You have your whole life to keep trying new varieties.

Agaricus – In addition to the ubiquitous button mushroom and portabella (see pages 11–12), this genus includes hundreds of wild species in North America alone, including great and mediocre edibles and some mildly poisonous species. They are tricky for beginners to identify properly, but fortunately, with a little practice and a keen sense of smell, you can easily divide *Agaricus* into groups, which is good enough to determine edibility.

One edible group of *Agaricus* has a sweet almond extract aroma. The most famous almondy *Agaricus* is the prince mushroom (*A. augustus*). I love to use members of the "almondy" *Agaricus* group in sweet applications, either dried or candied, but they also do well in savory dishes and simply sautéed. Pristine buttons can be shaved into salads. Some people have allergic reactions to *Agaricus*, so be cautious when eating new species for the first time (especially from one of the groups that you have not previously tried).

Best cooking methods: wet sautéing, dry sautéing, boiling, boiling then sautéing, oven roasting, grilling

Best preservation methods: dehydrating, candying

Amanita – This is not a good genus to eat for anyone but very skilled and experienced collectors, as it includes some deadly poisonous species. That said, the western US has many large, robust *Amanitas* worth discovering for the table. While there are still plenty of edible *Amanitas* east of the Rockies, most of them are fairly small and delicate. Eastern collectors also find a much larger diversity of *Amanitas* in general, sometimes making identification more challenging.

The most commonly eaten *Amanitas* in Europe and North America come from two sections in the genus. Section *Vaginatae* includes the grisettes and the springtime Amanita (*A. velosa*). These typically have mild, almost sweet flavors and delicate to crisp textures. Section *Caesareae* includes the famous Caesar's Amanita (*A. caesarea*), the eastern Caesar's Amanita (*A. jacksonii*), the southwest Caesar's Amanita (*A. cochiseana*), and the coccora (*A. calyptroderma*). These tend to have a stronger flavor, often described as fishy or even metallic, and many species produce large, robust mushrooms with a firm, crisp texture.

For all *Amanitas*, the best textured (and best for eating) are more robust, fatter-stemmed fruiting bodies that are not fully mature. The stems generally have a meatier texture than the caps. As the caps mature, most have more gills than "meat," though when young, the caps can be more substantial.

Best cooking methods: dry sautéing, boiling, boiling then sautéing

Best preservation methods: dehydrating, boiling and freezing, sautéing and freezing

Amanita constricta, a common grisette

Beefsteak (*Fistulina* spp.) – These odd bracket fungi are rarely cooked like other mushrooms. They are best sliced thin and used in raw or marinated

preparations, or for mushroom jerky. They typically have a mild, slightly sour flavor, and a beautiful cross-section that looks almost like rare meat.
Best cooking method: left raw
Best preservation method: dehydrating into jerky

Black Trumpets (*Craterellus cornucopioides, C. calicornucopioides, C. fallax,* etc.) – These versatile mushrooms have a crisp yet chewy texture, an aroma that varies from mildly fruity to almost blue cheese–like (depending on species), and a deep earthy flavor that pairs well with just about any protein or vegetable. They are also great on their own, with nothing but a simple sauté and a touch of salt. If stored in an open container in the fridge, trumpets will keep very well for a couple of weeks, slowly drying out. Trumpets work surprisingly well in sweet applications, providing chocolate-like notes. Rehydrated dried trumpets are comparable to their fresh counterparts in texture, flavor, and aroma.

Because of their open funnel shape and slow growth on the forest floor, trumpets get very dirty. To harvest, cut each mushroom above the dirtiest part of the stem. Each mushroom needs to be split open and brushed out, and adhering dirt and debris should be rinsed off with cold water while you gently massage away the dirt with your fingers. Alternatively, the split mushrooms can be placed, en masse, into a large tub of cold water (or plugged sink) and gently agitated to dislodge debris and dirt. Floating debris can be strained off the top, the mushrooms removed, and the dirt wiped from the bottom. Usually, it takes at least three changes of water before the water and mushrooms are clean. After straining, store the mushrooms stacked only a few deep in a colander or open container in the fridge.
Best cooking method: dry sautéing
Best preservation methods: dehydrating, candying

Yellow Foots (*Craterellus tubaeformis, C. ignicolor,* etc.) – These somewhat dainty looking mushrooms have a pleasant, almost cartilaginous texture and a mild, earthy flavor. They are good both fresh and dried, with a neutral enough flavor to play nicely with almost any ingredients. Their thin flesh cooks very quickly. When rehydrated from dried, they produce a delicious soaking liquid that can be used as a mild tea or broth. If collected by clipping or cutting above the level of the ground, yellow foots can often be picked clean, requiring little, if any, cleaning at home.

Yellow foots, at least on the West Coast, often can get attacked by a blackish bacterial infection that turns them to a slimy, inedible mess. One yellow foot beginning to turn bad can quickly infect and ruin pounds of beautiful mushrooms, so be careful not to put any bad ones in your basket.
Best cooking methods: dry sautéing, simmering
Best preservation methods: dehydrating, candying

Blewits (*Collybia,* previously *Clitocybe nuda* and *Lepista nuda,* and closely related species) – The quality of blewits varies because, at least out west, there are several species masquerading as one. In general, blewits tend to have a pleasant, mildly chewy texture, and a specifically mushroomy flavor. I usually use them in highly flavorful soups and stews such as curries.
Best cooking method: dry sautéing
Best preservation methods: sautéing and freezing, candying

Yellow foot

Brick Caps (*Hypholoma capnoides*) – These have surprisingly robust texture and flavor. They often grow in large groups, making it easy to collect enough for a few meals. They are not a good beginner edible, however, as proper identification and potential lookalikes can be tricky.
Best cooking method: dry sautéing
Best preservation methods: sautéing and freezing, boiling and freezing

Cauliflower

Cauliflower Mushroom (*Sparassis* spp.) – This mushroom looks like a bundle of egg noodles and can get rather large. Five-pound (2 kg) specimens are common, but occasionally, much larger cauliflowers are collected. They have a fantastic texture and flavor simply sautéed in butter with a bit of salt, but they can stand up to other big flavors, and their crisp texture will handle a variety of cooking techniques. Try them simmered in soups, stewed in curries, or boiled as a noodle replacement.

Clean cauliflower mushrooms as soon as you get them home, as various insects and other small animals like to live inside. To clean, break them into manageable pieces and then soak them in a bath of cold, well-salted water for 5 to 10 minutes to chase out any inhabitants, agitating the mushrooms to dislodge dirt. If they seem very buggy, give them a second soak in salt water with a rinse between. After the salt-water soak, soak them in unsalted cold water for another 5 to 10 minutes to get the salt out. Afterward, use a paring knife to trim or scrape off any remaining dirt under gently running water. Let the pieces dry in a colander or on towels in the fridge. After cleaning, cauliflower mushrooms keep perfectly for a week or more in the fridge, and they also dehydrate well.

Some growers have begun cultivating cauliflower mushrooms. The cultivated versions come completely clean and ready to use, with the same mild texture and flavor that make the wild ones so popular.
Best cooking methods: wet sautéing, boiling, simmering, oven roasting
Best preservation methods: boiling and freezing, dehydrating, pickling

Chanterelles (*Cantharellus* spp.) – All of the many chanterelle species in North America have a pleasant meaty texture, good earthy flavor, and to varying degrees, a somewhat fruity aroma, often reminiscent of apricots. Their flavors work well with butter and in creamy preparations like the classic cream of chanterelle soup, and the fruity undertones help them seamlessly fit into sweeter applications alongside fruit. When sautéing, do not brown them too much, or they will lose much of their delicate flavor. Larger, meatier chanterelles have an unpleasant leathery texture when dried and rehydrated, so it's rarely done unless they are to be powdered. Smaller, daintier species can be dried.

The smaller species can often be picked quite cleanly. If collected carefully, minimal further cleaning is required. When dirty, they can be extremely tedious to clean. Some of the larger species are more likely to require serious cleaning at home. Larger dirty chanterelles are often most easily cleaned first by spraying with a hose before doing detailed cleaning with a knife or brush.
Best cooking method: dry sautéing
Best preservation methods: sautéing and freezing, pickling, candying, dehydrating (for small, fragrant species)

Hedgehogs (*Hydnum* spp.) – See page 193 for a detailed discussion.
Best cooking methods: dry sautéing, wet sautéing, simmering
Best preservation methods: sautéing and freezing, pickling

Hawk's Wing (*Sarcodon* spp.) – Hawk's wings have an excellent meaty texture, but their flavor varies a lot depending on where they're found. On the West Coast, they are often quite bitter and sometimes unpalatable, while in the Rockies, where they can be quite plentiful, their flavor is usually better. Older specimens can develop stronger, funky flavors, so I stick to younger fruiting bodies when collecting for the table. Because of their dense, spongy texture, they require moist cooking techniques to make sure they cook thoroughly. I find that most people like them after a simple wet sauté; browning them too much can bring out bitterness. I like to use dried hawk's wings similarly to how I use shiitake in soups and stews. Dehydrating also intensifies their aroma.
Best cooking method: wet sautéing
Best preservation method: dehydrating

Meadow Waxy Caps (*Cuphophyllus* spp.) – There are several common, often small and dainty, species in this genus. The mild-flavored ones are somewhat reminiscent of chanterelles in both texture and flavor, though lacking the latter's fruity notes. They are delicious edibles when found in good condition and in sufficient numbers to make collecting worthwhile.
Best cooking method: dry sautéing
Best preservation method: sautéing and freezing

Pig Ears, Lavender, Violet, or Purple Chanterelles (*Gomphus clavatus*) – Opinions on this common, meaty mushroom vary widely. Despite their common names—a clever marketing tactic—these mushrooms are not closely related to chanterelles. They have a mild flavor and can take on other flavors fairly well. In my experience, their texture is variable, ranging from pleasantly chewy-crisp to disappointing mushiness. Insects like them, so try to collect only pristine fruiting bodies and cook them as soon as possible.
Best cooking method: dry sautéing
Best preservation methods: sautéing and freezing, pickling

Corals (*Ramaria* spp.) – Most firm, fleshy *Ramaria* are edible, with caution, for most people, as long as they do not taste bitter or otherwise unpalatable. The safety of *Ramaria* with a more gelatinous fruiting body is dubious. A few species have historically been listed as somewhat toxic for some people, and in general, all *Ramaria* can have laxative effects if eaten in large amounts. Despite the warnings, they are popular when eaten in moderation in some circles, and they show up on my table regularly. Proceed with caution when first trying *Ramaria*, and never eat large amounts in a short time. Because they must be cooked thoroughly, I like to use them in stews.
Best cooking methods: wet sautéing, pan roasting
Best preservation methods: sautéing and freezing, boiling and freezing, pickling

Crown-Tipped Corals (*Artomyces pyxidatus, A. piperatus*) – These corals grow throughout much of the Northern Hemisphere, always growing out of wood. They have a mild, earthy, almost nutty flavor, and are good simply sautéed. They can be eaten alone or added to just about any favorite recipe.
Best cooking methods: dry sautéing, pan roasting
Best preservation methods: sautéing and freezing, boiling and freezing, pickling

Corals

Lion's Mane, Comb Tooth, Bear's Head, Coral Tooth, Bearded Tooth, Monkey's Head (*Hericium* spp.) – All of these related species are excellent edibles. They are wonderful torn or cut into bite-size pieces and cooked simply in butter until lightly browned. Their flavor and texture are often compared to fresh crab meat, and a favorite use for the cooked mushrooms is to make vegetarian crab cakes. Older fruiting bodies can turn yellowish and sometimes develop an unpleasant sour flavor. Discard these.

Field-clean wild *Hericium* as well as possible, and keep separate from other dirty mushrooms, because any dirt that gets between their furry "teeth" will make them much more difficult to clean. To clean, dip in cold water and agitate. Under gently running cold water, use the tip of a paring knife to dislodge or trim off stubborn pieces of dirt or bark. Gently squeeze out excess water like you would a wet rag, and lightly shake off before leaving to dry on towels in a single layer.

Best cooking methods: dry sautéing, wet sautéing, pressing and searing, pan roasting, oven roasting

Best preservation methods: sautéing and freezing, pickling

Matsutake

Fairy Ring Mushrooms (*Marasmius oreades*) – These can usually be picked clean, and despite their small size, they pack a surprisingly meaty flavor and chewy texture. Generally, only the caps are eaten, and the tough, wiry stems are discarded. When it comes to fresh and rehydrated dried fairy rings, there is little difference in the flavor or texture.

Best cooking methods: dry sautéing, wet sautéing, simmering

Best preservation method: dehydrating

Giant Sawgill (*Neolentinus ponderosus*) – Giant sawgills have a firm, dense, chewy texture, a mild flavor, and, as their name implies, can grow to enormous sizes. They can often be picked clean. I love using them in soups and broths. Because of their dense and chewy texture, simmer them for 5 minutes or more before eating.

Best cooking methods: wet sautéing, boiling, boiling and sautéing, simmering

Best preservation methods: sautéing and freezing, boiling and freezing

Matsutake (*Tricholoma matsutake, T. murrillianum, T. magnivelare, T. mesoamericanum*) – Matsutake have a fantastically dense texture and a penetrating, spicy cinnamon aroma and flavor with strong musky elements. I find matsutake to be one of the most versatile mushrooms. They make fantastic pickles, can be shaved raw in salads and broths, are great grilled with nothing but a pinch of salt, and harmonize beautifully with just about any seafood. When steamed or simmered, their aroma is let loose and flavors everything they cook alongside. About the only way I never seem to enjoy the flavor of matsutake is after a simple sauté in olive oil or butter, as this method emphasizes unpleasant components of their aroma and flavor. Soy sauce or tamari help tame the musky elements of their flavor. Matsutake do not dry well, as dehydrating them significantly reduces their aroma.

Best cooking methods: dry sautéing, simmering, left raw, grilling

Best preservation methods: wet sautéing and freezing in their liquid, freezing raw, pickling

Man on Horseback (*Tricholoma equestre, T. flavovirens*, etc.) – Though this mushroom has long been popular all over the Northern Hemisphere, there was a well-documented, though not well-understood, case in which several people in France died after extremely heavy consumption over the course of several days. Consequently, Spain and France have

made it illegal to sell this mushroom commercially, and many sources now list it as a toxic species. However, many people, including many of my friends in the US, still collect and eat it. No serious issues have ever been reported in North America, but it's best to eat them only occasionally, and in moderate amounts. Man on horseback has a mildly earthy, almost sweet flavor and a firm, meaty texture, and the yellowish color also looks nice in dishes.
Best cooking methods: dry sautéing, wet sautéing
Best preservation method: sautéing and freezing

Fried Chicken Mushrooms (*Lyophyllum* spp.) – There are several common and not well-defined species in this group. They often grow in large clusters, making it easy to collect lots. *Lyophyllum* have a crisp texture and meaty flavor, and are prized by many. They should always be cooked thoroughly before eating, and they can cause digestive problems for some people, so be cautious when first trying them.
Best cooking methods: dry sautéing, wet sautéing
Best preservation methods: sautéing and freezing, boiling and freezing

Honey Mushrooms (*Armillaria* spp.) – Typically extremely abundant when they fruit, honey mushrooms are quite versatile. Certain species can cook up fairly slimy, which, while a turn off for some people, makes them popular with others. Some species have very fibrous, tough stems, which should be peeled before cooking. Honeys make most people sick if undercooked, so always begin with a parboil or wet sauté to be sure they are cooked thoroughly.
Best cooking methods: wet sautéing, boiling and sautéing, boiling
Best preservation methods: sautéing and freezing, boiling and freezing, boiling then pickling

Honey Mushrooms

Golden Robes (*Floccularia* spp.) – Common in the west and in the Rocky Mountains but often overlooked, these beautiful mushrooms are vibrant yellow-gold and often shaggy. They have a pleasant, firm texture and meaty flavor when sautéed. When not buggy or too weather-beaten, they are always worth collecting.
Best cooking methods: dry sautéing, wet sautéing
Best preservation method: sautéing and freezing

Wrinkled Rozites, Granny's Nightcap (*Cortinarius caperatus*) – Among the few *Cortinarius* species commonly eaten or even recommended as an edible, these mushrooms have a pleasant, chewy texture and a mild but complex, somewhat nutty flavor, but I find some have a strong aftertaste that can be off-putting. On the other hand, that same aftertaste and good texture help them stand out in positive ways when added to dishes with big meaty flavors, like the Braised Beef Tongue on page 231. Their texture holds up nicely in stews.
Best cooking method: dry sautéing
Best preservation methods: sautéing and freezing, boiling and freezing

Ponderous Cort (*Phlegmacium ponderosum, Cortinarius ponderosus*) – These mushrooms are common on much of the West Coast and can get absolutely enormous, often growing in expansive patches. They have a pleasant, meaty flavor and an excellent, crisp, firm texture that holds up well in stews. They often get buggy, so it's best to collect younger buttons, which in keeping with the name, will still be the most

massive mushrooms in your basket. Make sure you get your identification right. The size alone is a good indicator, but several *Cortinarius* are dangerously toxic.
Best cooking method: wet sautéing
Best preservation methods: sautéing and freezing, boiling and freezing

Huitlacoche (*Mycosarcoma maydis*, previously *Ustilago maydis*) – Huitlacoche needs to be cooked thoroughly, as undercooked, it will make most people sick. To remove from the cob, simply shuck the corn as usual, remove and discard the corn silk, then slice off the kernels with a knife. I often sauté them simply with onions and chiles before adding to other dishes. Frozen huitlacoche is almost as good as fresh, but the canned products are not nearly as good, in my experience.
Best cooking methods: dry sautéing, wet sautéing
Best preservation method: freezing raw

Inky Caps (*Coprinopsis atramentaria*) – Resembling shaggy manes with a smoother cap, inky caps contain a compound, coprine, that can cause serious negative reactions if alcohol is consumed within a couple days before or after they are eaten. If you serve them to anyone else, be very careful that they are aware of the alcohol interaction.
Best cooking method: dry sautéing
Best preservation method: sautéing and freezing

Shaggy Manes (*Coprinus comatus*) – These well-known, widespread mushrooms have a pleasant flavor similar to that of button mushrooms, and a texture that tends to not stay very crisp when cooked. Unlike their close relative, the *Coprinopsis atramentaria*, they do *not* contain the compound coprine, which causes bad reactions when combined with alcohol, so there is no danger of having a drink when eating them. I love using their dark ink to color dishes. (See page 185 for more about cooking with their ink.)
Best cooking method: dry sautéing
Best preservation method: sautéing and freezing

Mica Caps (*Coprinellus micaceus*) – These extremely ephemeral mushrooms can be quite common in suburban environs. They disintegrate when cooked, though their flavor is good (comparable to that of shaggy manes). Though they are small, they typically grow in large numbers, making it easy to collect a lot of them. Like shaggy manes, you can allow them to deliquesce (naturally break down into a liquid) and then use their ink to color dishes (see page 185 for more). They do *not* contain the compound coprine, so no special care is required if you consume alcohol.
Best cooking method: dry sautéing
Best preservation method: sautéing and freezing

Shaggy Parasols (*Chlorophyllum* spp.) – These common, meaty mushrooms have a great taste, like a refined portabella, and texture similar to some of the mild-flavored *Agaricus* species. I use them in largely the same applications. They need to be thoroughly cooked to be safe to eat.

Its omnipresent green-spored parasol cousin (*C. molybdites*) is the most common cause of mushroom poisoning in the United States, so make sure you have your ID correct. Some people have bad reactions to these mushrooms, so start cautiously, and don't serve them to large groups.
Best cooking method: wet sautéing
Best preservation methods: dehydrating, sautéing and freezing, boiling and freezing

Huitlacoche

Parasol Mushroom (*Macrolepiota procera, M. macilenta, M. pallida*) – This is a beautiful and excellent edible that can get very large—15-inch (38 cm) cap diameters are common. The stems, while often very large, are also often too tough to eat. They can be used for stocks, dried and powdered, or discarded.
Best cooking methods: dry sautéing, wet sautéing, pan roasting, oven roasting, grilling
Best preservation methods: dehydrating, sautéing and freezing

Deceivers (*Laccaria* spp.) – The various species of *Laccaria* are all believed to be edible, and tend to have a fairly pleasant chewy texture, especially the stem. However, some people find the stem to be too chewy and fibrous to eat—especially with larger species such as *L. ochropurpurea*. When young, their flavor is pretty mild, but when mature, they can take on a much stronger taste. They all can be picked clean and require little further cleaning at home.
Best cooking methods: dry sautéing, wet sautéing, simmering
Best preservation methods: dehydrating, sautéing and freezing, boiling and freezing, candying

Chicken-of-the-Woods (*Laetiporus* spp.) – The quality of the many species found around North America varies from OK to excellent. As the name implies, these bracket fungi have a chicken-like texture, with a mild flavor that makes them a pretty good substitute in many recipes for poached, boiled, or fried chicken. At least one species (*L. gilbertsonii*) can be a bit sour in flavor, which many people don't like. All are best eaten as soon after collecting as possible, as their texture degrades as they begin to dry out. Stick to collecting the younger parts of the fruiting body, which are typically the softer parts toward the edges. Older chickens can have an unpleasant texture, and often off-flavors as well.

Chickens make some people sick, especially if undercooked. Be sure always to cook them thoroughly. Start with only a small amount the first time you try them.
Best cooking methods: wet sautéing, boiling then sautéing, boiling then deep frying
Best preservation methods: sautéing and freezing, boiling and freezing, boiling then pickling

Turkey Tails

Resinous Polypore, Salisbury Steak of the Woods (*Ischnoderma resinosum*) – This easily overlooked, common, soft, often sweet-smelling polypore packs a lot of flavor. The soft outer edges can be sliced up and sautéed, preferably until browned and slightly crispy. The tougher inner sections can be boiled to make a flavorful stock.
Best cooking methods: wet sautéing, simmering
Best preservation method: dehydrating

Turkey Tails (*Trametes versicolor*) – Extremely common and plentiful most seasons, these mushrooms are too woody and chewy to eat, but simmered slowly in water, they make a wonderful tea, with a mild mushroom flavor and hints of black tea. Turkey tails can also be added to broths and stocks to add depth of flavor. They work just as well fresh or dried.

To clean, simply cut off any clinging pieces of bark or wood, then give them a quick rinse in cold water.
Best cooking method: simmering to make tea and broths
Best preservation method: dehydrating

Pheasant Back, Dryad's Saddle (*Cerioporus squamosus*) – Because this beautiful, often large, mushroom grows on wood above ground

level, it can usually be picked quite clean. It is best when young enough that the bottom surface looks smooth. The younger, more tender parts near the edges are quite versatile and can be cooked in a variety of ways. The tougher parts can be dehydrated to improve their flavor and then used to flavor stocks. When cooking fresh pheasant backs, the more freshly picked the better. Their texture gets dryer and tougher as they are stored.
Best cooking methods: wet sautéing, boiling, simmering
Best preservation methods: dehydrating, sautéing and freezing, boiling and freezing, pickling

Sheep Polypore, Blue Knight, Goat's Foot, Fused Polypore (*Albatrellus confluens, Albatrellus ovinus, Albatrellopsis flettii, Scutiger pes-caprae*, and related species) – These mushrooms generally have a chewy, meaty texture, and flavor varies from species to species. This group is fairly versatile, yet underappreciated in many circles. Some are excellent edibles. Because of their dense texture, I always use a wet sauté or boil them before sautéing. This can help lessen the bitterness of some species, which can also be brought out by too much browning. Some people like to gently pound out the mushrooms to make tender, thinner "patties" before sautéing or frying.
Best cooking methods: wet sautéing, boiling and sautéing
Best preservation methods: boiling and freezing, sautéing and freezing

Morels (*Morchella* spp.) – Though very widely eaten, morels cause digestive issues for many people, and will make almost anyone sick if not thoroughly cooked, so they should be approached cautiously at first. I usually use a special cooking process (page 128) that I believe best highlights their flavor and unique texture.

Morels

Morels grow slowly and often collect a lot of dust and dirt. I always clean my morels as follows. First, split them in half (omit this step if you are going to stuff them), then soak in cold water (adding a generous amount of salt to the water if there's any sign of insect life) for a couple minutes. Agitate the water several times, strain floating debris off the top, then scoop the morels out and discard the soaking water and any grit. Repeat the soaking and agitating process until the water remains fairly clean. Dry them laid out on towels in a single layer.
Best cooking methods: special method on page 128, wet sautéing, stuffing and baking
Best preservation methods: dehydrating, boiling then pickling

Early Morels, Thimble Caps (*Verpa* spp.) – *Verpa* are closely related to morels. All data says that they are as safe to eat as morels, but can cause reactions in a small percentage of people. Treat them as if they were morels. Like morels, they need to be thoroughly cooked to be rendered safe to eat.
Best cooking methods: special method on page 128, wet sautéing
Best preservation method: dehydrating

Big Red, Snowbank False Morel, Bull Nose, Walnut Morel, Lorchels (*Gyromitra caroliniana, G. korfii, G. montana, G. gigas, G. brunnea*) – This group of meaty-textured and flavorful mushrooms is a favorite of several friends, including a few who like them better than true morels. Like true morels, they need to be cooked thoroughly for safe consumption, so use a wet sauté. The stems are full of little cavities that collect dirt and can be almost impossible to clean, so the stems are often discarded and only the caps eaten. In a different section of the genus, the *Gyromitra esculenta* group, the so-called brain mushroom or beefsteak false morel, have been popular edibles for many generations in various parts of the world, despite widespread notoriety for being deadly when not properly prepared! There are *many* documented cases of people dying from eating these mushrooms, and several other *Gyromitra* are known to contain the same toxins in large enough quantities to also be potentially fatal. While there are methods to prepare these safely for the table, I generally advise against eating them. Beware of experimenting with other *Gyromitra* species outside of the specific ones listed here, as many are dangerously toxic (potentially deadly), without special preparation.

Best cooking methods: wet sautéing, boiling then sautéing

Best preservation methods: boiling and freezing, sautéing and freezing, dehydrating

Elfin Saddles (*Helvella* spp.) – This common genus is often confused with *Gyromitra* and wrongly called "false morels." Most *Helvella* are edible when thoroughly cooked, but some have unknown edibility. Consult your local field guide to be certain about your species. The fluted elfin saddles (*H. lacunosa*, *H. dryophila*, *H. vespertina*, etc.) are quite popular with some people, many of whom prefer them dried.

Various critters often shelter inside their hollow stems, so cut them in half and clean carefully in water before cooking. Like morels, they require thorough cooking to be safe.

Best cooking method: wet sautéing

Best preservation methods: sautéing and freezing, boiling and freezing, dehydrating

Porcini, King Boletes, Ceps, Penny Buns (*Boletus* spp.) – The genus *Boletus* includes quite a few common species, varying regionally, that account for some of the most revered mushrooms throughout the Northern Hemisphere. Young, dense buttons have a mild flavor and are great simply shaved raw or marinated with good extra virgin olive oil. Their flavor gets stronger (and many collectors say better) as they mature. The pores from mature mushrooms, in particular, have a deep, rich flavor. To keep the pores from sticking to the pan and burning, separate them from the caps of mature mushrooms, and add back in at the end of sautéing, when the mushrooms are lightly browned. The scraps and pores from mature mushrooms can also be simmered to make excellent broth. All dehydrate very well, and drying tends to strengthen and deepen their flavor and aroma. Very mature, larger mushrooms are often collected specifically for drying. Some people like to separate the pores specifically for drying and powdering.

Butter Boletes

Best cooking methods: dry sautéing, wet sautéing, pressing and searing, shaved raw (young buttons), simmering, oven roasting, pan roasting, grilling

Best preservation methods: dehydrating, sautéing and freezing, boiling and freezing, freezing raw (young buttons)

Butter Boletes (*Butyriboletus* spp.) – Highly prized by many for their dense, crunchy texture, especially when young, butters have a subtle, mild flavor and do well with a variety of cooking methods. Their texture holds up even when stewed or simmered for a long time. Unfortunately, they tend to get buggy very quickly, so cook them as soon as possible after collecting.

Best cooking methods: dry sautéing, grilling

Best preservation methods: sautéing and freezing, boiling and freezing, freezing raw (buttons), dehydrating, pickling, candying

Bicolor Bolete, Two-Colored Bolete (*Baorangia bicolor*) – This popular mushroom is common all over the eastern half of the US. It has a firm texture, especially in button form, and an earthy, mildly nutty flavor. *Lanmaoa* spp. are often mistaken for bicolor boletes. These are equally edible for most people and can be treated the same.
Best cooking methods: dry sautéing, wet sautéing
Best preservation methods: dehydrating, sautéing and freezing

Admirable Bolete (*Aureoboletus mirabilis*) – This large, gorgeous, two-toned mushroom is quite common around hemlock trees in the Pacific Northwest. It can be treated similarly to other large boletes like porcini. It has a pleasant flavor with citrusy notes. The stems tend to be much firmer than the caps, especially in mature specimens.
Best cooking methods: dry sautéing, wet sautéing
Best preservation methods: dehydrating, sautéing and freezing

Chestnut Bolete (*Gyroporus castaneus* and other *Gyroporus* spp.) – These small boletes have a firm texture and nutty, almost sweet flavor. They need nothing more to shine than some browning from a simple sauté.
Best cooking methods: dry sautéing, wet sautéing
Best preservation methods: dehydrating, sautéing and freezing

Scaber Stalks, Birch Boletes, Aspen Boletes, Manzanita Boletes (*Leccinum* spp.) – A majority of species of *Leccinum* are edible for most people with thorough cooking. A significant number of people, though, have bad reactions to some species within this genus. For this reason, do not serve any *Leccinum* to large groups or to unwitting diners. To ensure thorough cooking, always cook *Leccinum* using a wet sauté. Mature mushrooms tend to have very soft, squishy caps with a lot more pores than meat. For these, focus more on cooking the stems, which tend to stay firm. Most species dry well. I tend to use these mushrooms in similar applications to other more sought-after boletes.
Best cooking method: wet sautéing
Best preservation methods: dehydrating, sautéing and freezing, freezing raw (buttons)

Slippery Jacks (*Suillus* spp.) – These mushrooms get their common name from their slimy exteriors. There is quite a bit of variability between the many different *Suillus* species, but all taste somewhere between OK and very good. Most have mild to robust earthy flavors, and some also have hints of pine or lemon. In general, the smaller, denser buttons are good sautéed fresh. More mature specimens, though flavorful, tend to have a soft, mushy texture, especially after cooking, which makes them much better suited for drying or using in applications in which they will be puréed. Dried *Suillus* make good substitutes for dried porcini and are great for flavoring broths. My Eastern European friends were all taught to peel *Suillus* to prevent digestive upsets. Peel your *Suillus* if you have a sensitive stomach.
Best cooking methods: wet sautéing, dry sautéing
Best preservation methods: dehydrating, sautéing and freezing, boiling and freezing, pickling (young buttons)

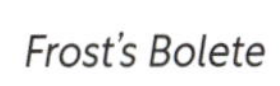
Frost's Bolete

Zeller's Bolete (*Xerocomellus atropurpureus, X. zelleri*) – *Xerocomellus* tend to have a pleasant flavor, sometimes with mild lemony notes. Their texture, especially in more mature specimens, tends to get soft and wimpy when cooked, so I prefer to use them mixed with other, more robustly textured mushrooms.

Best cooking method: dry sautéing
Best preservation method: dehydrating

Frost's Bolete (*Exsudoporus frostii*) – Besides being one of the most strikingly beautiful mushrooms on the planet, with its ruby red cap and pores and intensely reticulate stipe, frost's bolete is a very good edible, with a firm texture and a pleasant, lemony undertone. Be sure to cook it thoroughly.
Best cooking methods: dry sautéing, wet sautéing
Best preservation methods: dehydrating, sautéing and freezing, boiling and freezing, candying

Pine Spikes (*Chroogomphus* spp.) – Pine spike species have a variable texture and mostly mild flavor. Some are good enough to warrant building a dish around, while others are better suited as filler in dishes with stronger flavors. Some can also add color to a dish, such as *C. vinicolor*, which has beautiful purple-red flesh when cooked.
Best cooking method: dry sautéing
Best preservation methods: sautéing and freezing, dehydrating

Slime Spikes, Slimy Spike Caps, Hideous Gomphidius (*Gomphidius* spp.) – These mushrooms are not prized as edibles by anyone I know, but because they are often most plentiful when few other edibles are available, they are worth exploring. The young, dense fruiting bodies, especially buttons, are pleasantly earthy and firm. Mature ones generally have an undesirable mushy texture, but their flavor is still good after lightly browning. *Gomphidius* are similar in both texture and flavor to the *Suillus*, to which they are related.
Best cooking methods: wet sautéing, dry sautéing

Stalked Puffball

Best preservation methods: dehydrating, sautéing and freezing

Puffballs (*Calvatia, Calbovista*, and *Lycoperdon* spp.) – Generally speaking, puffballs suitable for eating should have a solid creamy-to-white appearance all the way through. If not, do not eat. For species that have a thick, tough outer "skin," peel it away and discard before cooking. Most puffballs have a mild, somewhat bland flavor and soft texture. The combination has always reminded me of tofu, and I often use boiled puffballs as a tofu substitute. They also work well as filler in dishes with other, stronger flavored mushrooms, as they usually take on other flavors quite well. Parboiling often reduces any off-flavors found in certain species of puffballs.

When very young, some *Amanitas* can look very much like puffballs. If it is an *Amanita*, when cut in half, you will always be able to see the outline of a mushroom in the cross section, which you will never see in a puffball.
Best cooking methods: boiling and sautéing, wet sautéing, boiling
Best preservation methods: boiling and freezing, dehydrating

Lobster Mushrooms (*Hypomyces lactifluorum*) – Lobster mushrooms appear when a certain fungus parasitizes other mushrooms, often *Russula brevipes* in Western North America and *Russula* and *Lactarius* elsewhere. They often have a seafood aroma and an otherwise mild flavor. They also tend to have a firm, crisp texture, and can be used in the same ways as their meaty, robust *Russula* and *Lactarius* hosts. I find western lobsters to have a bit of a weird aftertaste that I also get from their *R. brevipes* hosts, so I typically use them alongside other strong flavors. I do not get that flavor

from eastern lobsters. Lobsters really shine with wet cooking methods, such as in stews.
Best cooking methods: wet sautéing, boiling and sautéing
Best preservation methods: sautéing and freezing, boiling and freezing, dehydrating, pickling

Bleeding Milk Caps

***Russula* spp.** – *Russula* are a confusing group of mushrooms to identify down to species but there are a few subgroups (shrimps, green caps, and quilted caps) that are easy to recognize and generally good to eat. Fortunately, once you know a mushroom is a *Russula*, it's easy to decide whether it's worth eating. Chew on a very small piece of the raw cap and then spit it out. If it has a mild flavor, it is generally considered edible. If it has a spicy, hot (acrid) flavor, American field guides typically list it as inedible, although spicy species are eaten in parts of northern and eastern Europe, where all *Russula* are typically boiled, and the water discarded, before further cooking. Always be cautious when eating new species that aren't commonly eaten in your area, and avoid eating any that stain strongly red or black, or red *then* black when cut or bruised. *Russulas* really shine with wet cooking methods, such as in stews.
Best cooking methods: wet sautéing, boiling and sautéing
Best preservation methods: boiling and freezing, sautéing and freezing, salting, pickling

Candy Caps (*Lactarius rubidus* and *L. rufulus*) – When dried, their strongly sweet, maple syrup aroma lends them well to desserts, but they thrive in a variety of savory applications as well. A little bit of candy cap goes a long way for most recipes, and using too many can add an unpleasant bitterness. Sautéed fresh, candy caps have an earthy flavor on top of their sweet aroma, which pairs wonderfully with pork and game meats. Dried candy caps should be rehydrated before cooking to reactivate their aroma.
Best cooking method: dry sautéing
Best preservation methods: dehydrating (see page 35), candying

Saffron Milk Caps, Green Stainer Milk Caps, Bleeding Milk Caps (*Lactarius deliciosus, L. rubrilacteus L. aestivus*) – See page 66 for a detailed discussion of these very versatile, excellent, edible mushrooms. They really shine with wet cooking methods, such as in stews.
Best cooking methods: wet sautéing, oven roasting, pan roasting
Best preservation methods: boiling and freezing, sautéing and freezing, salting, pickling

Other Milk Caps (*Lactifluus* spp., previously *Lactarius* spp.) – Much like with the closely related *Russula*, people are taught to determine the edibility of new milk caps with a chew and spit test. There are a plethora of common meaty, mild-flavored milk caps in the eastern US, including *Lactifluus volemus, L. corrugis*, and *L. hygrophoroides*. They can be treated much the same as the saffron milk caps; see above and page 66 for a detailed discussion. Wet cooking methods, such as in stews, bring out the best in milk caps' texture.
Best cooking methods: wet sautéing, oven roasting, pan roasting
Best preservation methods: boiling and freezing, sautéing and freezing, salting, pickling

Saint George's Mushrooms, Moixernons (*Calocybe gambosa*) – This early season mushroom is very popular throughout Europe, where it grows commonly in grassy areas. It sometimes makes it to markets in the US in the late spring and early summer. Its robust flavor and texture do well when simply sautéed,

or paired with any springtime vegetables.
Best cooking methods: wet sautéing, dry sautéing
Best preservation methods: dehydrating, pickling

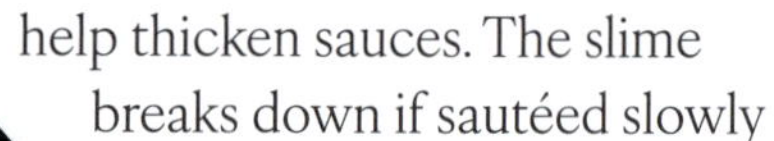

Shrimp-of-the-Woods

Shrimp-of-the-Woods, Aborted Entoloma (*Entoloma abortivum*) – These weird little mushrooms look almost like a squished puffball with a malformed mushroom inside. They are found all over eastern North America and have a crisp texture and pleasant flavor suitable for many applications. As the name implies, some people find them reminiscent of shrimp and cook them in similar preparations.
Best cooking methods: wet sautéing, dry sautéing
Best preservation methods: sautéing and freezing, boiling and freezing

Stubble Rosegill, Big Sheath (*Volvopluteus gloiocephalus*) – These common relatives of the Asian "straw mushrooms" have a distinctive grassy aroma and flavor. I like balancing them with strongly aromatic ingredients such as lemongrass, hot chiles, and ginger.
Best cooking methods: dry sautéing, simmering
Best preservation methods: sautéing and freezing, boiling and freezing, pickling

Waxy Caps (*Hygrophorus* spp.) – This section specifically refers only to the relatively meaty, mycorrhizal members of the current genus *Hygrophorus*. It's believed that all proper members of this genus are edible. All of the waxy caps were once grouped into this genus, and many that have since been split off into new genera (e.g., *Hygrocybe*, *Gliophorus*, etc.) are of unknown edibility.

The slimy members of the genus can be intimidating, but for some people, the slimy texture is the draw, and some even use it to help thicken sauces. The slime breaks down if sautéed slowly on low heat. The *Hygrophorus* that aren't slimy, such as *H. sordidus* and *H. subalpinus*, don't require special treatment in cooking, though they also tend to respond well to a slow sauté over low heat. In general, most of the common mushrooms in this genus are mild flavored, with texture varying from rather soft and insipid to dense and crisp. Some species can have unpleasant flavors, so you will have to get to know which of your local species are worth collecting.
Best cooking methods: dry sautéing, simmering
Best cooking methods: sautéing and freezing, boiling and freezing, pickling

Jelly Babies (*Leotia lubrica*) – Their mild flavor and gelatinous texture work well for candying, especially with added flavors. They have been shown to contain very small amounts of gyromitrin , the same toxin found (in much higher concentrations) in *Gyromitra esculenta*. Because of this, give them a parboil for at least 5 minutes and discard the water before any other use, and don't eat a large amount of them, especially over the course of several days.
Best cooking methods: boiling, boiling then sautéing
Best preservation method: boiling then candying

Cat's Tongue, Jelly Hogs (*Pseudohydnum gelatinosum*) – Cat's tongues have very little flavor, but a fun, chewy texture that makes them a good blank slate for other ingredients. They can be candied in syrups or juices, then either eaten as is or dehydrated and used as a mushroom "gummy snack." When flavored, they work well as a salad garnish, or, if heavily sweetened, as a dessert garnish.
Best preservation method: candying

All About Truffles

Highly prized for millennia for their intense aromas, truffles are still some of the most expensive and sought-after food products in the world. Because their intoxicating scent is quite volatile and fleeting, they are most often used raw, shaved or grated directly onto a dish at the table. The dish's heat projects the truffle's aroma directly into the noses of happy diners. Truffles are most typically used to garnish simple preparations of pasta, risotto, and eggs.

Alba and Périgord truffles typically have the most intense aromas and are usually the most expensive. Bianchetti truffles are also strong, with an almost garlic-like aroma. Summer and Burgundy truffles tend to be a little milder. The Oregon black truffle smells fruity.

Store raw truffles wrapped loosely in a paper towel in a sealed container in the fridge until ready to use. Replace the paper towel each day to prevent spoilage. Place butter, eggs, and/or cheeses in the container with the truffles, and the truffles will infuse them with their scent. You can then shave the truffles onto your chosen dish, and still enjoy hints of them when you eat the other infused products.

Another classic trick is to slice a ripe cheese, such as Brie, in half horizontally to create a sort of sandwich. Place a thin layer of truffles on the bottom half, then replace the top. Let the cheese sit in your fridge for a couple days, and you will have an intensely truffled cheese. Similarly, blending a little bit of truffle into a mousse will infuse the mousse with its aroma.

Most truffle oils contain no truffles at all (or very little, at best), and derive their aroma from artificial chemicals. While true truffles tend to be subtle in food, truffle oils are usually extremely strong, and can be overpowering if not used carefully. I almost never use truffle oil, but I know some chefs who swear by it for certain applications. When using truffle oil, know that a little bit goes a long way. For maximum impact, stir it into the dish or garnish with a few drops after you remove the dish from the heat.

How To Cook Like a Chef

The key to cooking like a chef is to trust your instincts, so I encourage you to view every recipe in this book as a starting point. These recipes have been tested, and they work well, but they are not gospel. Use the recipes as inspiration, following them as needed and twisting them as desired to suit your tastes and moods.

For most recipes in this book, the quantities of the ingredients called for, including the mushrooms, are quite flexible. If you have more or less of certain mushrooms, adjust accordingly. Pay more attention to the proportions of different components than to measuring ingredients precisely. (The exception is the dessert chapter, especially the baked items, where careful measurement is essential.)

PLEASE SUBSTITUTE!

I like to cook with whatever mushroom species that offer themselves up when I'm wandering the market or the woods, and you should do the same. I gave a lot of thought to how to make recipes work with a wide variety of mushrooms so it's as useful as possible, regardless of which type you have on hand.

People often get hung up on exactly how to perfectly pair a particular mushroom with the right ingredients. The unique aromas, textures, and flavors of different mushrooms will obviously change the result of a dish, but many times, almost any mushroom will do. Often, the final dish will be equally tasty with the substitution, just different. Don't be afraid to experiment.

The same advice about substituting mushrooms also applies to other ingredients. My ingredient choices were driven primarily by the vegetables that were in peak season while developing the recipes. If you have a flush of porcini when artichokes are at their prime, do not be afraid to substitute the artichokes in a place where I might have called for broccoli (as in the pierogi filling on page 191). The best food will come from using the best seasonal, locally available ingredients.

SALTING TO TASTE

Most of the recipes in this book do not contain a measured amount of salt. You, the cook, need to taste frequently during cooking and adjust the seasoning as appropriate.

Mushroom Substitutions

Next to every recipe in this book, you'll notice a note called "Mushroom Substitutions." These notes are meant to help you determine which, if any, mushrooms are best substituted for the specific variety (or varieties) I call for in that recipe. Many say that you can use "almost any mushrooms," meaning that almost any other mushroom will give good results, although I would avoid very distinctly flavored or especially aromatic mushrooms like candy caps and matsutake. Of course, for some recipes that rely on the particular aromas or flavors of certain mushrooms, there may be few or no substitutions that make sense. For the vast majority of the recipes, though, you will find a whole lot of options, including easy-to-source mushrooms from your local market. Use your judgment, and refer to the list on pages 10–26 for flavor and texture notes as needed.

PICKING THE RIGHT COOKING OIL OR FAT

Many recipes in this book simply call for "oil," which indicates that you can use any cooking oil or fat you prefer. Some recipes require "neutral oil" because they work much better when the fat doesn't have a strong flavor of its own. Sunflower, canola, avocado, and grapeseed oil are widely available examples of neutral oils that I use.

CLEANING MUSHROOMS

Most cultivated mushrooms can be easily cleaned with a damp cloth or a quick rinse under cold water, and some are so clean that even that seems like overkill. Wild mushrooms, though, often require serious cleaning before cooking.

In my house, we clean most solid-textured wild mushrooms with a toothbrush and paring knife under cold, gently running water. The toothbrush can remove most clinging dirt and debris, and anything not easily removed can be peeled away with the paring knife.

Some smaller, denser mushrooms (such as smaller chanterelles) can be easily cleaned with the following method: Fill a tub with cold water. Toss the mushrooms in the water and agitate them aggressively with your hands to dislodge dirt and debris. Let the grit and dirt settle at the bottom of the tub for a few seconds, then remove the mushrooms and set them on a towel to dry.

Some mushrooms require more specialized cleaning techniques, which are discussed in those mushrooms' entries under Some of My Favorite Mushrooms to Cook With (pages 9–26). If your mushrooms are buggy, salting the cleaning water to about the salinity of seawater chases out unwanted inhabitants. Mushrooms need only a few minutes in the salt water and should be rinsed well with unsalted water after soaking so they don't begin to cure.

Note that the better you clean mushrooms in the field, the easier cleaning will be at home, so spend the extra few seconds to scrape, trim, or brush as much dirt as you can from each mushroom before it enters your basket.

Cleaning Mushrooms with Water

Forget the nonsense you've heard that you should never clean mushrooms with water. This may be fine and good when buying commercially produced mushrooms grown in sterile environments, but a great many wild mushrooms grow in wet soil or forest detritus and wind up thoroughly caked in forest debris. They need to be well cleaned if you don't enjoy the texture or taste of dirt in your food.

Water will not hurt mushrooms. Some can be cleaned with nothing but a knife, brush, and damp towel, but many wild mushrooms require baths in multiple changes of water or even a spray with a garden hose to get clean. Mushrooms that require soaking can sometimes pick up excess water in the process, but it's easy to dry them off by gently shaking them and then placing them in a single layer on trays in front of a fan for an hour or two. When they're a little less wet, spread them out in a single layer on trays, plates, or towels in the fridge for a few hours or up to a couple of days. At worst, these mushrooms may need a few extra minutes of cooking time to reduce their excess moisture.

My point is simple: Don't be afraid to clean mushrooms with water. It's by far the best way to get rid of many species of dirt, forest debris, and even crawly critters.

Essential Mushroom Cooking Techniques

There is no right technique for cooking all mushrooms any more than there is one for cooking all vegetables. Which of the following techniques is best will depend on the textures, flavors, and moisture contents of the mushrooms you're using. To find the best technique(s) to use with specific mushrooms, see those mushrooms' entries under Some of My Favorite Mushrooms to Cook With (pages 9–26).

Many mushrooms—perhaps most mushrooms—cook up great with some version of a sauté, but there are a few things to keep in mind for best results.

SIMPLE SAUTÉING

Some mushrooms, especially commercially grown varieties, don't require any special cooking techniques. In these cases, just sauté as you would any other ingredient. If you find the mushrooms unexpectedly giving off a lot of water, increase the heat to high and proceed with the dry sautéing instructions (page 31).

While simple sauteing is fairly straightforward as techniques go, there are a few basic principles to keep in mind when sautéing for best results.

First, get your pan hot. Generally, you want your pans to be hot before adding anything to them. This usually takes only about 10 to 15 seconds on the burner, though it can take a little longer if you have big, heavy cast iron pans. Ideally, wet mushrooms will sizzle, hiss, and sputter when they go into a hot pan, and any oil will be hot and shimmering, but not smoking, after a couple seconds of heating.

Note: Be careful heating empty nonstick pans. You may need to add some oil, even for dry or wet sautéing, to protect their coatings from overheating, which can damage the nonstick surface and/or release unhealthy chemicals into the air. Check the manufacturer's recommendations.

Don't crowd the pan. The mushrooms should fit mostly in a single layer in the pan. If you have to pile them on top of each other, there are too many and you'll need to use a larger pan and/or cook in batches.

Use just enough oil. You don't want things swimming in oil, but make sure there is enough to coat the bottom of the pan and just barely coat the mushrooms. Some mushrooms will soak up fat while cooking. If the pan or the mushrooms look dry, add a little more oil. Otherwise, they

When Should You Add Salt?

This is actually a somewhat contentious topic in mushroom cookery. Salt draws moisture out of mushrooms' cells, but in doing so it will cause them to shrink quite a bit. So, if all you want to do is sauté the mushrooms and eat them as is, you will get plumper, juicier mushrooms if you wait to add salt until they are almost finished browning.

If you are going to purée the mushrooms into a soup or cook them for a long time (e.g., in a stew), it really doesn't matter when you season them, as they will shrink regardless. The advantage of seasoning early is that the salt will have time to penetrate more deeply and thoroughly season the mushrooms. Sometimes I value this more than plumper, larger pieces.

won't cook well or evenly. This applies both to sautéing and to pan roasting.

DRY SAUTÉING

In his book *All That the Rain Promises and More*, David Arora describes the dry sauté as a way to cook mushrooms containing a lot of moisture. You add mushrooms to a hot, dry pan to release and then cook away their excess moisture before the oil is added and the true sautéing begins.

1. Heat a heavy-bottomed pan over high heat. Add the mushrooms in a single layer and stir frequently until they start to release their moisture. Continue cooking over high heat, stirring regularly, to evaporate the moisture as quickly as possible. If the mushrooms don't give off any liquid within about 15 seconds, quickly proceed to Step 2.
2. When the liquid is almost entirely cooked off, reduce the heat to medium-low, push the mushrooms to the sides of the pan, and add oil to the cleared space in the center as the last of the moisture disappears, stirring the mushrooms until coated.
3. Continue cooking the mushrooms, stirring frequently, until they have browned as much as you desire. Salt to taste.

WET SAUTÉING

I like to use this technique for mushrooms that need thorough cooking to be rendered safe to eat, however, it's not just for thorough cooking. I will almost always use this technique to sauté any species of milk cap or *Russula*, because it transforms their textures from grainy to firm, juicy, and almost crisp. Mushrooms with a dense, spongy texture, such as hawk's wings (*Sarcodon* spp.) and *Albatrellus*, also benefit greatly from this technique, which ensures they are both moist on the inside and cooked through. I also use it for many cultivated and wild mushrooms that have begun to dry out to help remoisten them before browning.

1. Heat a heavy-bottomed pan over high heat. Add the mushrooms in a single layer along with just enough water to cover them by about ¼ inch (6 mm). As the mushrooms start to release their moisture, the liquid level in the pan may noticeably rise. Continue cooking over high heat until the water boils and reduces almost entirely, 5 to 10 minutes.
2. When the liquid is almost entirely cooked off, reduce the heat to medium-low, push the mushrooms to the sides of the pan, and add oil to the cleared space in the center as the last of the moisture disappears, stirring the mushrooms until coated.
3. Continue cooking the mushrooms, stirring frequently, until they have browned as much as you desire. Salt to taste.

Dry Sauté or Wet Sauté?

Many recipes in this book say to choose between dry or wet sautéing based on the type and moisture content of the mushrooms you're using. You should generally dry sauté mushrooms that contain more moisture, such as most wild mushrooms including chanterelles and porcini. A wet sauté is usually better for mushrooms on the drier side, like most cultivated mushrooms, including crimini and shitake. A wet sauté is also best for types that require thorough cooking to be safe to eat (like chicken-of-the-woods) or to improve their texture (like saffron milk caps). When in doubt, check Some of My Favorite Mushrooms to Cook With (pages 9–26) for recommendations.

PRESSING AND SEARING

This technique is a good way to make certain kinds of mushrooms denser and chewier, almost like meat. I love to use this technique on cultivated mushrooms that grow in clusters, like oysters or shimeji. Cooked this way, the small, clustered stems take on a texture like the individual muscle fibers in meat. It also works well with lion's mane, maitake, and whole porcini.

The technique works best if you have a second pan of roughly the same size as the one used to cook the mushrooms to weigh them down. If you

Using Mushroom Liquid in Recipes

The liquid released by mushrooms during cooking is often quite flavorful, and sometimes, rather than completely reducing it and concentrating its flavor back into the mushrooms, you can reserve it and use it for other purposes, such as the base for a broth. For example, the Matsutake with Clams, Kale, and Chorizo (page 158) calls for cooking the clams in this liquid. If you are wet sautéing mushrooms, just be sure to simmer them in the liquid for a few minutes before you drain and reserve it for another use.

don't have a pan that size, you can experiment with different trays or metal dishes.

1. Tear or cut the mushrooms or mushroom clusters into pieces roughly the size of a small fist, about 3 inches (7.5 cm) in diameter.
2. Heat a heavy-bottomed pan over medium heat. Add just enough oil to coat the bottom of the pan, then add the mushrooms in a single layer, spaced 1 to 2 inches (2.5 to 5 cm) apart. Set a clean pan on top of the mushrooms, then place a weight, such as a few large unopened cans, inside the pan to press down evenly across the tops of the mushrooms. (You can also use a heavy pan, such as a Dutch oven, to press the mushrooms without any added weights.) There should be enough weight to slowly flatten the mushrooms while they cook, but not to crush them paper thin.
3. Let the mushrooms cook undisturbed for 3 to 5 minutes, until they release their liquid. When the liquid has boiled off completely, remove the top pan and season the mushrooms with salt. Cover with the weighted pan again and let the mushrooms sear undisturbed until they are crispy and deep brown, but not burned, on the bottom, 5 to 10 minutes.
4. Flip the mushrooms, add a little more oil if needed to prevent sticking, season with salt, and then replace the weighted pan. Continue to cook undisturbed until crispy and deep brown on the other side, about 5 more minutes.

OVEN ROASTING

Many different mushrooms respond quite well to oven roasting, which slowly and evenly cooks and browns them on all sides. Larger mushrooms often cook better when cut into manageable pieces before roasting. Some large mushrooms, though, like cauliflower, hen-of-the-woods, and even large, dense porcini, can also be cooked whole and served like a roast. If your mushrooms are very wet, you'll need to dry them out a bit before you can roast them effectively. You can do this by leaving them in a single layer on a rack or on towels overnight in the fridge, or for a couple hours in front of a fan.

1. Preheat the oven. For smaller mushrooms or when more browning is desired, set the oven to 400°F (200°C). When you want the mushrooms to cook more slowly, so they cook through before they begin browning, set the oven temperature at 325°F (160°C). Line a rimmed baking sheet with parchment paper.
2. Toss the mushrooms in enough oil to lightly coat and season with salt and pepper. Place the mushrooms on the prepared baking sheet in a single layer. (If cooking larger mushrooms, use a roasting pan to keep their liquid contained.)
3. Roast, stirring or turning every 10 minutes or so if the mushrooms look like they are browning unevenly, until they are cooked through (check by cutting into a larger piece to see if the texture has changed all the way through to the middle) and browned as desired, as little as 10 minutes for smaller mushrooms or up to 45 to 60 minutes for larger, denser mushrooms

PAN ROASTING

Pan roasting is similar to oven roasting, but it is started in a pan on the stove before moving to the oven. It combines a sauté's ability to brown mushrooms with the oven's even cooking. Pan roasting works more quickly than oven roasting, and it's helpful when you want a bit more control over how the mushrooms cook and brown. This technique works best if you leave the mushrooms in larger pieces, so they don't dry out too much.

1. Preheat the oven to 400°F (200°C). Heat a heavy-bottomed oven-safe pan over high heat. Add the mushrooms in a single layer, and stir frequently until they start to release their moisture. Continue cooking over high heat, stirring regularly, to evaporate the moisture as quickly as possible. If the mushrooms don't give off any liquid within about 15 seconds, quickly proceed to Step 2.
2. When the liquid has almost entirely cooked off, reduce the heat to medium, push the mushrooms to the sides of the pan, and add oil to the cleared space in the center as the last of the moisture disappears. Sauté for about 1 minute, stirring to make sure the pan and mushrooms are coated with fat, then transfer to the oven.
3. Every 3 to 5 minutes, stir the mushrooms to make sure they brown evenly. Continue until they reach your desired level of browning, then remove from the oven and salt to taste.

BOILING

There are several reasons why mushrooms might need to be boiled. For some mushrooms (e.g., certain milk caps and *Russula*), it removes bitter or undesirable flavors. For others, like the fly agaric (*Amanita muscaria*), boiling removes water-soluble toxins, making them safe to eat. For others still, it is simply to ensure that they will get thoroughly cooked. If the mushrooms are not being boiled for detoxification, the mushroom-flavored cooking water can be saved and added to soups and sauces.

People are often quite surprised to learn that boiling does not turn most mushrooms to mush. Unlike in plants, much of mushrooms' structural strength comes from chitin, a long-chain polymer also found in crustacean shells. Chitin does not soften significantly from boiling in water, which means the mushrooms retain much of their structure. In many cases, mushrooms' texture will actually become firmer after boiling.

1. Bring a large pot of water to a boil over high heat. Salt the water generously, then add the mushrooms. (If you have a large amount of mushrooms to boil, boil them in batches. The boiling time does not begin until the water returns to a boil after you've added the mushrooms.)
2. Adjust the heat to keep the water at a rolling boil for the duration of the cooking time. Most mushrooms, cut into bite-size pieces, will be cooked through in 3 to 5 minutes. Special cases needing longer boiling are called out as needed in specific recipes.

GRILLING

Almost everyone has seen and tried some version of a grilled portabella, but many other mushrooms also work well on the grill. The caps from many mushrooms can be grilled whole whether you have a 2-inch (5 cm) diameter milk cap, a dinner plate–size prince mushroom (*Agaricus augustus*), or anything in between. Mushrooms like matsutake and porcini can also be cut into cross-sectional slices from ¼ to ½ inch (6 mm–1.25 cm) thick.

Most mushrooms cook best on a medium-hot grill. If the grill is too hot, they will brown and char too much before cooking through. If the heat is too low, they will slowly dry out without gaining much color. I like to baste mushrooms with a little bit of fat while they grill, taking care not to add too much and cause a flare-up. Exact grilling times will vary quite a bit depending on the size, density, and thickness of your mushrooms, as well as the heat of the grill. See individual recipes for more detailed information.

SIMMERING

Some mushrooms do well when simmered directly in soups or broths with no other required cooking. Simply add the mushrooms to the liquid and simmer for 5 to 7 minutes before serving.

DETOXIFYING THE FLY AGARIC (*Amanita muscaria*)

The iconic fly agaric (*Amanita muscaria*), with its red cap and white dots, has long had a reputation for both toxicity and psychoactive properties. However, because the toxins in fly agarics, ibotenic acid and muscimol, are water soluble, a simple boiling process can remove them and make the mushrooms safe to eat. This process was popularized by William Rubel and David Arora (see page 272 for more). I like to boil the mushroom for longer in even more water than their recommendations to err on the side of caution and ensure I extract as much of the mushrooms' toxins as possible. David himself taught me to do the second boil as an extra safety assurance.

Once the novelty of eating this taboo mushroom wears off, you'll find it has an excellent, crisp texture and mild flavor post-boil. After detoxing, they can work in just about any recipe where you might use boiled mushrooms. Sautéing after boiling to brown them brings out a nuttier flavor.

Note that this detoxification method works for only the fly agaric (*Amanita muscaria*) and some very closely related species. This method will *not* detoxify the death cap (*A. phalloides*), destroying angels, or any other poisonous mushrooms. There are no known methods to make these species safe for consumption. Before you try cooking any amanitas, be sure you are completely confident in your identification.

1. Cut the mushrooms into ¼-inch (6 mm) or thinner slices. Using at least 1 gallon (3.8 L) of water for every 1 pound (450 g) of mushrooms, bring the water to a boil in a large pot over high heat, add a generous pinch of salt, then add the mushrooms. Let the water return to a rolling boil, and cook for at least 7 minutes.
2. Drain and rinse the mushrooms thoroughly, discarding the water (it contains the toxins).
3. Using fresh water, repeat the procedure, again using at least 1 gallon (3.8 L) of water for every 1 pound (450 g) of mushrooms and boiling for at least 7 minutes before draining, rinsing, and discarding the water. The mushrooms are now ready be eaten or used in other recipes.

The iconic and beautiful Amanita muscaria.

Essential Preservation Techniques

Because of the ephemeral coming and going of mushrooms, preserving them for later is an essential skill for mushroom hunters. Mushrooms also tend to pop up when you have no time to cook them. As your skills and luck improve, you will sometimes collect more mushrooms than you want to—or are able to—use immediately. Plus, if you want to eat wild mushrooms out of season, you'll need to preserve the ones you find in season for later. This section gives a quick overview of some basic preservation techniques: dehydrating, freezing, and salting. For some mushrooms and applications, candying (covered in the Sweet Treats chapter, page 243) also works exceptionally well as a preservation technique.

STORING FRESH MUSHROOMS

Most mushrooms can be stored for a short time in paper bags or laid out on a towel in the refrigerator. If they are especially wet for any reason, you may want to place them in a colander set on a towel in the fridge. If you can't find room in the fridge, in cold weather you can leave mushrooms outdoors, shaded from the elements, and preferably in an area that keeps out animals like squirrels, deer, and bears.

Don't stack wet mushrooms too high on top of each other, or the ones on the bottom can degrade quickly. Likewise, don't store fresh mushrooms in sealed, airtight containers or wrapped in plastic. Always sort your mushrooms and remove potentially moldy or buggy ones before storing them. One dubious mushroom can ruin an entire prized harvest.

COOKING FOR SHORT-TERM PRESERVATION

Often, you will collect mushrooms that you know have a very short shelf life. You may have chanterelles that look like they will start going bad in the next day or two, almondy *Agaricus* or boletes that are likely to get buggy if they sit in your fridge for any length of time, or fresh candy caps that you worry will get moldy. In any of these situations, you can prepare the mushrooms right away using whichever method makes the most sense based on mushroom type and your intended application (see pages 10–26). This can extend their life for 4 or 5 days if stored properly in the fridge after cooking. Just add the already-cooked mushrooms to a recipe when you are ready to use them.

DEHYDRATING

In addition to improving their shelf life, dehydrating mushrooms concentrates, and often improves, their aroma and flavor. Dehydrating removes almost all of the moisture that bacterial and fungal pests require to survive and reproduce, and will also kill or chase away any bugs hiding in your mushrooms. Eggs can sometimes survive low-temperature dehydrating, so you might also want to freeze your mushrooms for a couple of days after drying them to make sure that any eggs get destroyed. If the mushrooms pick up a little moisture during freezing, they can be tossed back in the dehydrator for a little while before storage.

Remember that dehydrating is not the same as cooking. Mushrooms that need to be well cooked to be safe, such as morels, still need thorough cooking even after being dehydrated.

I like to store dehydrated mushrooms in airtight glass jars to protect them from pests that can and will chew right through plastic bags. I also like to toss in a desiccant pack or two—this is especially helpful if you live in a humid climate. If thoroughly dried and then appropriately stored in a sealed, airtight container, mushrooms will keep for many years. Many people believe that their dehydrated mushrooms' flavor improves with time.

Always Use the Soaking Liquid

The liquid used to reconstitute dried mushrooms acquires a ton of flavor. Make sure you use it after straining out any grit or dirt. If you cannot or don't want to use it in the dish you are using the mushrooms in, you can reduce it and freeze it to use later. Use this concentrated liquid in place of mushroom stock in recipes.

Note that certain mushrooms do not dehydrate or rehydrate well. When dried, matsutake lose their prized aroma. Meatier chanterelle species become unpleasantly leathery when rehydrated, though they do retain a pleasant aroma and flavor, making them a good candidate for powdering after drying. Hedgehogs seem to lose flavor and acquire an unpleasant texture.

As a rule, cut meatier mushrooms like porcini, slippery jacks, and corals into small slices or pieces before dehydrating, but keep hollow mushrooms like morels and black trumpets, small shelf fungi like turkey tails, and smaller mushrooms like candy caps whole.

Dehydrate using forced air and lower temperature settings to preserve the most aroma and flavor. For especially wet mushrooms, you can start at a slightly higher temperature for a couple of hours and then reduce the heat after cooking off most of the moisture.

If you have more mushrooms than your dehydrator can handle, in dry, warm weather you can spread them on a screen to partially dry in the sun, then finish them in the dehydrator later. Screens can be purchased cheaply at any local hardware store.

Mushrooms are thoroughly dehydrated when they are crispy, like potato chips.

DEHYDRATING CANDY CAPS

I have never heard any reasonable explanation of the chemistry behind this, but the slower you dry candy caps, the stronger their maple scent. My usual method is to lay them out in a single layer on a screen or shallow tray, a few feet in front of a fan, allowing them to dry slowly at room temperature. Some people like to take them through several drying cycles by misting them with water and then letting them dry out again, but I've found this to make little to no difference. If you have dried candy caps that are weak on aroma, leave them open to the air for a day before use. The ambient moisture they pick up usually brings out more of their maple goodness.

POWDERING DRIED MUSHROOMS

I like to add dried and powdered mushrooms to spice mixes and to all sorts of dishes, from No-Bake Candy Cap Cookies (page 247) to Mushroom and Scallion Pancakes (page 130). You can use a coffee grinder, spice grinder, or mortar and pestle for the task. I use powdered porcini and candy caps with enough regularity that I like to keep containers of both on hand. I have friends who use others, especially black trumpets. Don't be afraid to play around and figure out what you like best.

REHYDRATING

You can rehydrate mushrooms simply by covering them with liquid. When soft and pliable, they are ready to use, which can take from 5 to 20 minutes depending on the size and type of mushroom and temperature of the liquid. Clean mushrooms can often be rehydrated directly in a stew or soup. Many mushrooms are dehydrated without being cleaned first, necessitating a bit of special care upon rehydrating. Because they're

A good day's candy cap harvest spread on trays to dry: The fan is in the foreground, by the camera.

time-consuming to clean and often harvested in large numbers, almost nobody cleans morels, and few clean black trumpets, before dehydrating, yet both types are almost always full of sand and dirt. I always give them an extra clean after rehydrating to keep the grit out of my food. Clean rehydrated morels and trumpets the same way as fresh (see page 29). In general, if you dehydrated the mushrooms yourself, you should have a pretty good idea of how dirty they are, and how much extra care they need before eating. If you are not sure how dirty your dehydrated mushrooms may be, err on the side of caution and give them a brief extra clean before use.

PAR-COOKING AND FREEZING

Freezing mushrooms is an effective and easy way to preserve them. Just about any mushrooms can be frozen for later use, which is especially helpful for those that do not dehydrate well. Cooking mushrooms before freezing drives out excess moisture, which can otherwise expand when frozen and rupture mushrooms' cell walls, damaging their texture. Instead, pre-cooking breaks down the cell walls in controlled, desirable ways and improves flavor.

The cooking method to use before freezing will depend on the type of mushroom, its intended application, and your taste. Most people like their chanterelles sautéed, and thus sauté them before freezing. If sautéing mushrooms before freezing, do not brown them much. As soon as the water is driven out and they begin to brown, you can remove from the heat, cool them down, and pack them for freezing.

For species that do better with a wet sauté, add a little extra water to the pan, let them boil for a few minutes, and then pack and freeze them in this liquid. This does an excellent job of preserving the flavor. This method works especially well for matsutake, which I wouldn't otherwise cook using a wet sauté. If you cut them up, cover them with a little water and simmer, then freeze in this liquid, you will wind up with a wonderful base for a matsutake broth.

The tighter you pack the mushrooms, the longer they will last in the freezer. Freezing in their own liquid helps extend their storage life, as well. If you freeze a lot of mushrooms, a vacuum sealer is a worthwhile investment.

BOILING AND FREEZING

Boiling mushrooms before freezing gives you the most flexibility for later use, and works well for just about any variety. You want to boil just long enough to cook through, then simply drain and dry them as well as possible before freezing. For thin slices, boil for 1 to 2 minutes; for big chunks or whole mushrooms you may need to boil for 5 to 7 minutes.

FREEZING WITHOUT PAR-COOKING

A handful of mushrooms can be frozen fresh without any par-cooking. Porcini, butter boletes, and scaber stalks all freeze well if you stick to dense, whole immature buttons. They can be defrosted and cooked as if from fresh. Their texture will not be quite as good as fresh, but should still be nicely crisp. Matsutake are also sometimes frozen whole, although I have mostly

Substituting Dried Mushrooms for Fresh

I have often heard that 2 to 3 ounces (60 to 85 g) of dried mushrooms are equivalent to about 1 pound (450 g) of fresh mushrooms. The actual number can vary quite a bit from one species to the next, but it's an OK starting point. Some mushrooms, like morels and black trumpets, can be used very similarly, if not identically, whether fresh or dried and rehydrated. Other mushrooms, such as most boletes, become almost completely different beasts. Dried boletes and *Suillus* have a much stronger aroma and flavor, along with a texture that does not lend itself to being simply sautéed as part of a dish. Add these dried mushrooms to dishes for flavor rather than substance. They can be used similarly to fresh mushrooms in dishes where they will be puréed.

come to prefer cooking and freezing them in liquid.

CANNING WILD MUSHROOMS

I strongly advise against canning wild mushrooms unless using recipes designed to discourage the growth of *Clostridium botulinum*, a potentially deadly pathogen that most terrestrial mushrooms are exposed to and that is difficult to kill using standard canning temperatures and pressures.

OIL PRESERVING

Preserving mushrooms in oil and storing them at room temperature presents an even higher risk of botulism than does plain old canning. Because of the dangers, I do not recommend this preservation method. If you do oil-preserve mushrooms, they should be stored in the fridge and eaten within a couple of weeks, or stored longer-term in the freezer.

SALTING

For many generations, salting has been commonly used to preserve various milk caps and *Russula* throughout Scandinavia, Poland, and Russia. Unfortunately, pretty much all of the available American sources treat salting mushrooms more as a novelty than as a useful technique. I admit that I avoided salting mushrooms for years because their only use seemed to be as a salty chaser for a stiff drink. However, once I figured out what to do with them, salted mushrooms became one of my most prized staples. They keep seemingly forever, and they can be used in a number of surprising ways. Traditional recipes typically ferment the mushrooms, but my preferred method, which is described on page 52, does not use fermentation. I have found that salted mushrooms prepared in this way make a fantastic vegetarian substitute for salt cod in many different applications.

Most non-acrid (non-spicy) *Lactarius* or *Russula* can be preserved by salting, but the technique works best for more substantial, meaty species. My favorite target for salting is the ubiquitous short-stemmed *Russula* (*R. brevipes*), which is not only big and meaty, but often found in large numbers and ignored by most other mushroom hunters. On the east coast, *Lactifluus volemus* and *L. corrugis* are great choices.

American guidebooks typically list the acrid (spicy) *Lactarius* and *Russula* as toxic or inedible. Scandinavians collect and preserve several of the acrid *Lactarius* species, and I am aware of several Russian immigrants in my area who salt-preserve some of the local acrid *Lactarius* species, especially the large and plentiful golden milk cap (*L. alnicola*). I regularly use this method with great results on several species that local field guides describe as inedible, including the golden milk cap and the bearded milk cap (*L. pubescens*) that commonly grows with birch trees.

Boiling and salting will remove the spiciness, but some species can still retain an unpleasant flavor or bitterness. Because salt is cheap, and these mushrooms are often quite plentiful, it's easy to experiment.

In cultures where salting is more common, it's not unusual to mix many different *Lactarius* and *Russula* together in a single batch, but since the edibility of a lot of members of this group is not well established in much of America, proceed with caution when trying new species.

Avoid any of the *Russula* that stain strongly red or black, or red then black when bruised or cut, or in age. Some very serious poisonings, including fatalities, have been reported from an Asian *Russula* in this group, and I am not aware of anyone anywhere preserving the red or black staining *Russula* via salting (or eating via any other method).

QUICK PICKLING

Quick pickling mushrooms by steeping them in seasoned vinegar (called "marinating" by my Italian and Russian friends) is a great way to preserve species that don't dehydrate well. Mushrooms pickled in this way keep for many weeks stored in the refrigerator. I regularly eat many-month-old batches that live in my fridge. The texture begins to soften after a few weeks, but as long as no mold is present, the vinegar's acidity keeps them safe to eat. Feel free to play with different vinegars, spices, and levels of sweetness.

Helpful Equipment

You shouldn't need a lot of special equipment to execute the recipes in this book, but a few things will make your life easier.

KITCHEN SCALE

Weight is much more accurate than volume for measuring dry ingredients. Dry ingredients like flour and sugar can vary dramatically in volume depending on how tightly they are packed and even the amount of humidity in the air. Some ingredients, like nuts and grated cheese, will have a different volume depending on the size of the pieces. Similarly, it is impossible to measure most dried mushrooms accurately without a scale.

The recipes in this book include both volume and weight measurements for your convenience, but I encourage you to get comfortable weighing ingredients. You can buy a good digital kitchen scale for under twenty dollars online or at your local big box store, and the small purchase will make you a much better cook! Make sure to get a scale that can weigh in both ounces and grams and can measure to +/- 1 gram.

SPICE GRINDER, COFFEE GRINDER, OR MORTAR AND PESTLE

A spice grinder or coffee grinder is extremely handy for grinding homemade spice mixes, and also for grinding dried mushrooms into powder. Some people prefer using an old-fashioned mortar and pestle. I highly recommend having at least one of these tools handy.

DEHYDRATOR

No mushroom hunter should be without a dehydrator for preservation. There are lots of ways to dehydrate mushrooms, but none are as reliable and compact as a dehydrator. The two most important features to look for are forced air (i.e., a fan) and temperature control. The ability to accommodate extra trays as needed is convenient, but not essential.

PASTA MACHINE

Several recipes in chapter 8 (page 205) encourage you to make and roll your own pasta dough. Rolling out the dough requires you to use a pasta machine. Hand-crank and automatic machines work equally well. A pasta roller attachment for your stand mixer also works wonderfully. For most recipes, if you don't want to roll your own pasta, you can either buy premade fresh pasta sheets or substitute a suitable dried pasta.

Having fun with a pasta machine

Boletus rubriceps
Leccinum insigne
Arizona Aspen Boletes

7

Preserves, Pickles, and Condiments

Right around the time I began working on this book in 2016, Rosa's sister sent us a care package from Spain. She and her family had been vacationing in a small village in the Catalan Pyrenees, in an area well known for its mushroom hunting. The little bed-and-breakfast where they were staying sold all kinds of homemade preserves and jams made from local ingredients, including several made from local mushrooms. A few of these mushroom preserves made up the bulk of the care package we received.

I still remember the first mushroom preserve I tried from that care package—a sweet jam made from fairy ring mushrooms and leeks. I had never seen or heard of anyone using mushrooms in this way, and it sent my mind racing with a million new ideas for using my own local mushrooms. I immediately got to playing with my own jams and preserves. These days, we almost always have at least one or two of our homemade mushroom preserves in the house and regularly serve them to all of our friends—not just the myco-crew—on cheese plates, as sandwich toppings, and more.

Mushroom hunters often alternate between periods of great—sometimes overwhelming—abundance and scarcity. Making preserves, condiments, and pickles is a creative way to deal with moments of abundance while also stashing away some treats to get you through periods of scarcity. It's a good idea to keep at least a few good recipes for long-term storage in your back pocket for mushroom windfalls, so I think they're a great way to kick off the recipe section of this book.

This chapter barely scratches the surface of possible combinations for these preserves. Don't be afraid to experiment with a pound or two of whatever mushrooms you have on hand in abundance.

My fridge during mushroom season

Candy Cap Whole Grain Mustard

Makes 3 cups (675 g)

Mustard is one of the most useful items in the pantry, and most people have no idea how incredibly easy it is to make. The acidity from the vinegar and the natural antimicrobial properties of the mustard seeds give mustard a seemingly endless shelf life. It will last many months covered in the fridge. In general, the flavor mellows, and in my opinion, improves, as mustard ages. The mustard will be edible and usable right away, but it will be much better after a week, and better still, a week after that. This recipe scales very easily. The candy caps in this recipe are noticeable, but not dominant, so their flavor will be present in subsequent vinaigrettes or sauces without overpowering them. You can increase the amount if you want that maple flavor more front and center. Note that it will take two days to prepare the mustard, much of that time hands-off.

¾ cup (140 g) yellow mustard seeds

¾ cup (140 g) brown mustard seeds

0.75 ounce (21 g) candy cap powder (see page 36)

1 teaspoon salt

1 cup (240 ml) apple cider vinegar

¾ cup (180 ml) beer, preferably a non-hoppy porter or a malty beer without much bitterness

½ cup (100 g) packed light brown sugar

1. Add all the yellow and brown mustard seeds, candy cap powder, and salt to a 1-quart (1 L) container and mix well. Pour in the vinegar and ¼ cup (60 ml) beer and gently stir. Cover and leave at room temperature for 24 hours.

2. After 24 hours, stir in the brown sugar and remaining ½ cup (120 ml) beer. Using an immersion blender, purée the mustard for 3 to 5 seconds. You just want to break up some of the seeds; you don't want a smooth mustard. Add more sugar to taste. If it seems a little dry, add another tablespoon or 2 of beer. If desired, blend more. Transfer to a jar or store in a covered container in the fridge.

Tip: *The more you blend the mustard, the smoother and spicier it becomes. I blend mine very little because I prefer both the texture of whole seeds and the milder flavor. Always start by blending very briefly. You can always blend more if desired. You can experiment with different beers, or substitute dry white wine, as well as various kinds of vinegar. Adding spices instead of or in addition to the candy caps adds interesting dimensions to mustards. Whole coriander and caraway seeds are some of my favorites. Simply add as much as ½ cup (40 g) of the preferred spice to the mustard seeds in the first step.*

Mushroom Substitutions: There is no substitute for the candy caps in this recipe.

Black Trumpet Jam

Makes about 3 cups (675 g)

This recipe is based loosely on a caramelized onion and bacon jam that I used in several restaurants years ago. It's great as a burger topping, a garnish for cheeses, or a simple dip for crackers. The trumpets turn the jam a deep black color and their earthy flavor dominates, while the licorice notes of the fennel remain in the background.

1 tablespoon neutral oil

1 onion, halved and thinly sliced

1 fennel bulb, halved, cored, and thinly sliced

1 pound (450 g) fresh black trumpets, or 2 ounces (60 g) dried and rehydrated black trumpets

½ cup plus 3 tablespoons (135 g) packed light brown sugar

¼ cup (60 ml) apple cider vinegar

2 teaspoons salt

1. Heat a large, heavy-bottomed pan over medium-low heat. Add the oil, onion, and fennel and cook, stirring regularly to prevent burning, until the vegetables are well browned, 20 to 30 minutes. If the vegetables begin to stick, add a little more oil.

2. Add the black trumpets, stirring to mix in well. If using dried, reconstituted mushrooms, add their soaking liquid, too. Cook until the water released by the trumpets begins to simmer rapidly, then add the brown sugar, vinegar, and salt. Continue cooking, stirring regularly, until there are only a few tablespoons of liquid left in the pan. If using fresh mushrooms this should take only 5 to 10 minutes. If using dried mushrooms with their soaking liquid, this takes 20 to 30 minutes.

3. Remove from the heat and immediately pulse using an immersion blender or food processor until the jam is almost smooth, but still has a little texture. Transfer to a jar or let cool completely and store in a covered container in the fridge, where it can be kept for many weeks.

Tip: *If you don't like fennel, use a second onion and omit the fennel bulb. You can experiment with different vinegars. Rice vinegar, red wine vinegar, and sherry vinegar all work well, and each will provide a slightly different end result.*

Mushroom Substitutions: There is no substitute for the black trumpets in this recipe.

Chanterelle–Meyer Lemon Marmalade

Makes about 2 cups (450 g)

This irresistible preserve puts a little twist on a classic marmalade recipe, with most of the citrus replaced by chanterelles, which have an earthy flavor and fruity aroma. This marmalade won't set up as well as a traditional marmalade because it contains much less pectin, but otherwise it is similar. Use it wherever you would use a citrus marmalade. I love eating it on toast or crackers, or with my favorite cheeses. The more fragrant the chanterelles, the more their flavor will punch through in this marmalade.

2 small Meyer lemons

1 pound (450 g) chanterelles, cut into ⅛-inch (3 mm) pieces

1 cup (200 g) granulated sugar

1. Use a peeler to remove only the yellow rind from the lemons. Cut the rind into very thin matchsticks.

2. Use a sharp knife to remove all of the white pith from the outside of the lemons and discard. Working over a small bowl to catch the juice, quarter the peeled lemons, then cut the quarters into very thin slices. Discard the seeds. Save the sliced fruit and all of the juice.

3. Place the chanterelles, sugar, lemon rind, lemon pieces, lemon juice, and a pinch of salt in a medium saucepan with just enough water to cover. Bring to a boil over medium-high heat, then reduce the heat to simmer gently until the liquid is just barely starting to become syrupy, about 1 hour. Remove from the heat. Transfer to a jar or let cool completely and store in a covered container in the fridge, where it can be kept for many weeks.

Tip: *This marmalade is on the sour end of the spectrum. If you prefer a sweeter marmalade, simply add more sugar. You can use regular lemons instead of Meyer lemons, but they tend to be a bit more sharply acidic and can overpower the delicate flavor of the chanterelles.*

Mushroom Substitutions: Yellow foots make a fun, somewhat chewier and earthier marmalade.

Matsutake-Fig Preserve

Makes about 1 quart (900 g)

I absolutely love this surprising jam. The figs dominate the initial taste, but after a moment, the deep, spicy aroma and flavor of the matsutake take over. I enjoy this preserve with aged cheeses or chicken liver pâté, but I would just as soon use it for a peanut butter and jelly sandwich, or even to top ice cream. The recipe works equally well with fresh or dried figs. For dried figs, increase the amount of water to 1¼ cups (300 ml). If the figs are especially small, use a few more.

1 pound (450 g) matsutake, cut into ½-inch (1.25 cm) pieces

17 or 18 black mission figs, stems removed, then roughly chopped

1 cup (200 g) granulated sugar

½ cup (120 ml) unseasoned rice wine vinegar

1 teaspoon salt

1. Combine the matsutake, figs, sugar, vinegar, salt, and ¼ cup (60 ml) water in a small, heavy-bottomed pot. Mix well and bring to a simmer over medium heat. Adjust heat to continue to simmer gently, stirring occasionally to keep the mixture from sticking or burning on the bottom, for about 1 hour, until only a few tablespoons of liquid remain.

2. Remove from the heat and use an immersion blender or food processor to pulse the mixture until it has the consistency of a chunky jam. Transfer to a large bowl to cool. Transfer to a jar or let cool completely and store in a covered container in the fridge, where it can be kept for many weeks.

Mushroom Substitutions: There is no substitute for the matsutake in this recipe.

Chanterelle Meyer lemon marmalade (top), black trumpet jam (center), candy cap whole grain mustard (bottom left), and matsutake fig preserve (bottom right)

Mushroom Caponata

Makes about 1 quart (900 g)

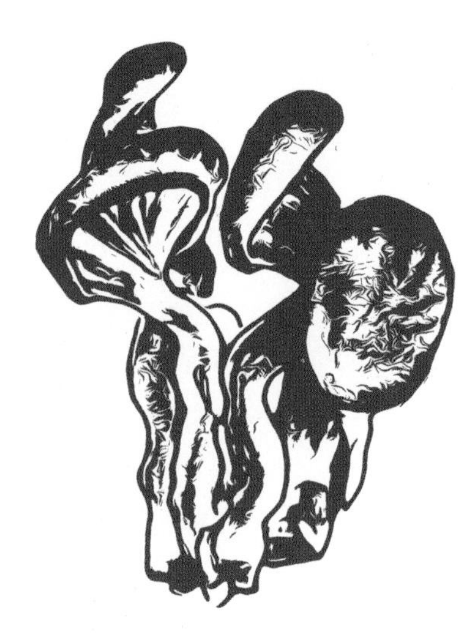

Caponata is a traditional Sicilian dish in which eggplant is the base of a hearty, chunky, sweet-and-sour relish. I have tried a million versions—even a few with dried fruit and sweet spices like cinnamon. This recipe, however, captures a lot of the flavor of a traditional caponata using oyster mushrooms instead of the eggplant, though it's a little less sweet than some recipes. Use it on top of black bean cakes, as a vegetarian entrée, or to garnish a piece of grilled fish. I also like it as a dip for good bread, or even toss it with pasta and some extra virgin olive oil for an interesting pasta salad.

¼ cup (60 ml) plus 1 tablespoon extra virgin olive oil

6 cups (650 g) oyster mushrooms, cut into ⅜-inch (1 cm) pieces

1 yellow or white onion, diced

5 garlic cloves, minced

3 cups (600 g) seeded, diced tomatoes

½ cup (120 ml) balsamic vinegar

1 tablespoon honey

½ cup (60 g) capers, drained

½ bunch fresh mint, leaves picked and chopped

1. In a large pan, dry sauté the oyster mushrooms, following the instructions on page 31, using 1 tablespoon of the oil. Continue to cook the mushrooms until well browned but not dried out. Add more oil if needed to prevent sticking.

2. Add the onion along with more oil if the pan is dry, and cook until the onion is soft, 5 to 10 minutes, then add the garlic. Sauté for 1 minute, then add the tomatoes. Season with salt and let the tomatoes cook down and release their liquid. Continue to cook, stirring often, until the liquid almost completely reduced, about 10 minutes.

3. When the mix is starting to look like a thick sauce, add the balsamic vinegar and scrape up any browned bits from the bottom of the pan. Reduce until the liquid is almost entirely gone, 1 to 2 minutes, then stir in the honey and remove from the heat.

4. Stir in the capers, the remaining oil, and the mint. Season with salt and pepper, then serve.

Tip: *I think caponata is best served at room temperature, but some people prefer it hot or cold. It can be made in advance; the flavors will get better as it sits, and it will keep for several days in the fridge.*

Mushroom Substitutions: Any soft textured, mild-flavored mushrooms will work. Avoid crisp mushrooms. Save stronger-flavored mushrooms for other applications, as they will fight with the tomato, vinegar, and capers. Think of the mushrooms as a mild base to soak up the flavor of all the other ingredients.

Chanterelle Relish with Olives and Piquillo Peppers

Makes 3 to 4 cups (675–900 g)

Wherever this relish is served, it brings a taste and feeling of the Mediterranean. It's lighter and more subtle than many of the other recipes in this chapter, and allows the fragrance of the chanterelles to shine through. Use this relish to top any type of fish or chicken or serve it as an accompaniment to rich, mild-flavored meats or cheeses.

1 pound (450 g) chanterelles, cut into ¼-inch (6 mm) pieces

7 canned piquillo peppers, drained, cut into ⅛-inch (3 mm) pieces

15 black olives, pitted and chopped

¼ cup (60 ml) sherry vinegar

¼ cup (60 ml) extra virgin olive oil

2 tablespoons chopped fresh parsley

1. Heat a heavy-bottomed pan over medium-high heat. Add the chanterelles along with a pinch of salt and dry sauté, following the instructions on page 31. (Do not add any fat to the pan or brown the mushrooms; you just want to cook them through and cook off their excess water.)

2. Once the water released by the chanterelles has almost completely evaporated, transfer the mushrooms to a bowl and stir in the peppers, olives, vinegar, and oil. Let cool completely, then stir in the parsley. The relish will keep for several days in the fridge. It is best served at room temperature, so take it out of the fridge about 1 hour before serving.

Tip: *Piquillos are pointy red peppers from Spain which you can find canned at well-stocked grocery stores. If you can't find them, substitute 1 large roasted, peeled, and seeded red bell pepper. Use good black olives for this, not the tasteless imposters that you get in cans of "black olives." Any good quality olives in styles typical of France, Spain, Italy, or Greece will work well, though each will impart its own unique character to the relish.*

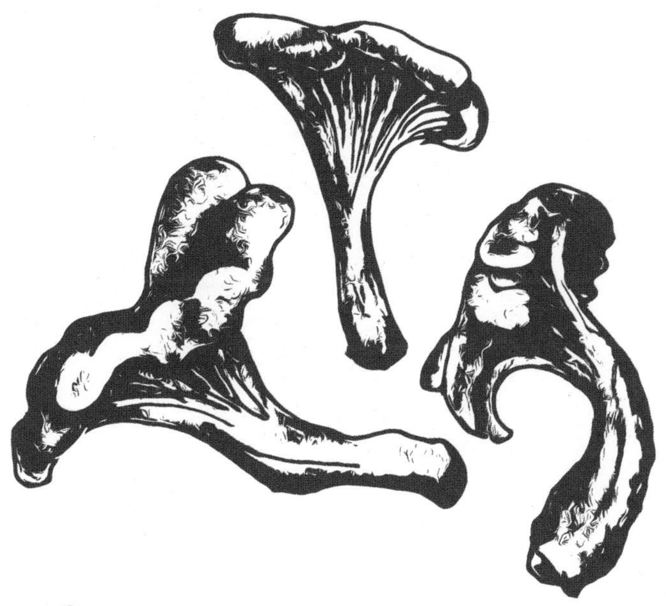

Mushroom Substitution: Yellow foots work well here, as do beech (shimeji), hedgehogs, and even oysters.

Candy Cap Mostarda

Makes about 3 cups (675 g)

I think of mostarda as Northern Italy's answer to fruit chutney—a sweet-and-sour condiment with a spicy kick provided by mustard. There are many traditional variations, and even more modern reinterpretations, but all have a fruit or combination of fruits as a base. I've seen apples, pears, figs, cherries, and grapes used, and often a combination of fresh and dried fruits. The fruits are candied, with or without spices, and generally there's a mustardy kick to the syrup. Vinegar adds an acidic bite that balances the sweetness. This recipe's take on mostarda replaces much of the dried fruit with candy cap mushrooms. It perfectly complements nearly any pâté, salami, or other cured meat product you find, as well as most cheeses. People always beg for more when it appears on my menus.

2 sweet, crisp apples such as Fuji or Gala, peeled, cored, and cut into ¼-inch (6 mm) pieces

¾ cup (150 g) granulated sugar

1 ounce (28 g) dried candy caps

¼ cup (40 g) raisins

½ cup (120 ml) apple cider vinegar

2 teaspoons mustard powder

2 tablespoons yellow mustard seeds

1 tablespoon brown mustard seeds

1. Toss the apples with the sugar and a pinch of salt in a large bowl and let stand for 1 to 2 hours, until the apples have released their liquid. Stir occasionally to ensure as much moisture as possible gets drawn out of the apples. You should wind up with a lot of sweet syrup in the bowl.

2. While you wait for the apples, soak the dried candy caps in just enough warm water to cover, and soak until soft, about 20 minutes, then remove the mushrooms, chop them into ¼-inch (6 mm) pieces, and add to a bowl with the raisins.

3. Bring the mushroom soaking water to a boil in a saucepan over high heat, then pour over the candy caps and raisins. Let stand for 20 to 30 minutes to cool completely.

4. Add the candy cap mixture to the bowl with the apples and let stand another 30 minutes to allow the flavors to meld.

5. Strain the liquid into a pan, reserving the fruit and mushroom mixture separately, and bring to a simmer over medium heat. Reduce until about ¼ cup (60 ml) remains, about 20 minutes. Whisk in the vinegar and mustard powder and bring back to a simmer. Reduce again until a bit less than ½ cup (120 ml) remains, then stir in the reserved fruit and mushrooms. Continue reducing until liquid again gets thick and syrupy, 10 to 15 minutes. Transfer to a bowl and stir in the yellow and brown mustard seeds. Mix well and let cool completely.

6. Cover and refrigerate overnight. Stir to mix well before using. Transfer to a jar or store in a covered container in the fridge, where it can be kept for a month. The mostarda's flavor will improve as it sits for the first few days.

Mushroom Substitutions: There is no substitute for the candy caps in this recipe.

Salt-Preserved Mushrooms

Makes 1½ to 2 cups per 1 pound (450 g) mushrooms

Mushrooms preserved in this manner will last at least several months, and theoretically years, with no obvious degradation. As long as the top layer remains entirely sealed in salt, there is very little chance of any unwanted mold appearing. At this high salt concentration, no microorganisms can survive. Salt-preserved mushrooms can be used in a variety of fun recipes, like the Salted Mushroom Hummus (page 120), Salted Mushroom–Butternut Squash Cakes (page 69), or Salted Mushroom–Sweet Potato Salad (page 106)

Lactarius* or *Russula

Lots of kosher salt

Mushroom Substitutions: Try any favorite milk caps or *Russula*. *Amanitas* and mild-flavored *Agaricus* also work well. Experiment with any mild, densely textured mushrooms.

1. Trim any long stems flush with the caps so the mushrooms will sit flat when layered upon each other. Reserve the stems.

2. Bring a large pot of water to a boil over high heat. Add the mushrooms and boil for 10 minutes. Do not crowd the mushrooms; if necessary, boil in batches, using fresh water for each batch. Strain and let the mushrooms cool enough to comfortably handle.

3. Add a thin layer of salt to the bottom a clean container. Place a single layer of mushrooms, without any overlapping, on top of the salt, laying the reserved stems sideways into any large gaps, then sprinkle another thin layer of salt over the mushrooms. Repeat with another single layer of mushrooms and another layer of salt. Repeat this process until the container is full or you are out of mushrooms. Cover the top layer of mushrooms with more salt, then top with a weight about the same dimensions as your container and add a last layer of salt. (The weight ensures that the mushrooms stay covered.) Cover and store in the fridge until ready to use. Mushrooms should be ready in a week, though it may take a few more days for very large, meaty mushrooms.

Tip: *When in doubt, err on the side of using more salt. With this salting method, there is no such thing as too much salt.*

To use the salted mushrooms, first rinse off any clinging salt, and then soak in fresh water, changing the water every few hours, for at least a few hours to overnight depending on the size of the pieces and how well desalted you want them. Taste a small piece to decide if they have soaked long enough. The mushrooms can be desalted up to 3 days in advance and stored in a covered container in the fridge.

Pickled Matsutake

Makes about 2 quarts (2 L)

The matsutake season in coastal California often booms for only a few weeks, and in a good year, I frequently collect far more than I know how to quickly consume. Their dense, crisp texture lends itself wonderfully to pickling, and that spicy cinnamon essence really shines through in this very simple pickling liquid. I enjoy these on the sweet side, but if you prefer them less sweet, cut down the amount of sugar in the recipe. This is as simple a pickling liquid as you will come across. The matsutake flavor negates the need for any added spices.

2 pounds (900 g) fresh matsutake, cut into ¼-inch (6 mm) slices

1 quart (1 L) unseasoned rice wine vinegar (4.3% acidity)

3 cups (600 g) granulated sugar

1 tablespoon salt

1. Place the matsutake in a clean, heat-safe container.

2. Combine the vinegar, sugar, and salt in a saucepan and bring to a boil over high heat. Remove from the heat and pour the liquid over the mushrooms. Let cool completely, uncovered, then transfer to a covered container and refrigerate at least overnight before using.

Tip: *If substituting mushrooms that need thorough cooking to be safe to eat (e.g., honey mushrooms or morels), boil the mushrooms for 5 minutes before pickling or boil the mushrooms in the pickling liquid for several minutes before allowing the liquid to cool down.*

Mushroom Substitutions: You could use this simple pickling liquid for any mushrooms or vegetables, but the lack of spices is intended to really showcase the special aroma and flavor of the matsutake.

Pickled Chanterelles

Makes about 1.5 quarts (1.4 L)

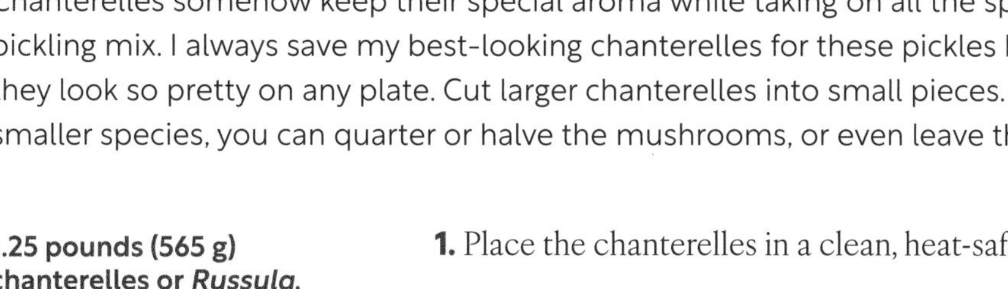

Chanterelles somehow keep their special aroma while taking on all the spices in this pickling mix. I always save my best-looking chanterelles for these pickles because they look so pretty on any plate. Cut larger chanterelles into small pieces. With smaller species, you can quarter or halve the mushrooms, or even leave them whole.

1.25 pounds (565 g) chanterelles or *Russula*, cut into ¼- to ½-inch (6 mm to 1.25 cm) slices if large, halved or quartered if small

2 bay leaves

½ teaspoon black peppercorns

½ teaspoon fennel seeds

¼ teaspoon red pepper flakes, optional

3 cups (720 ml) apple cider vinegar

½ cup (100 g) granulated sugar

1 teaspoon salt

1. Place the chanterelles in a clean, heat-safe container.

2. Place the bay leaves, peppercorns, and fennel seeds, and the red pepper flakes, if using, on a piece of cheesecloth and tie closed with twine to make a sachet. (If preferred, you can place the spices directly in the pickling liquid in Step 3.)

3. Combine the vinegar, sugar, salt, and ½ cup (120 ml) water in a saucepan. Add the sachet (or loose spices) and bring the mixture to a boil over high heat.

4. Pour the liquid, along with the sachet, over the mushrooms. Let cool completely, uncovered, then transfer to a covered container and refrigerate at least overnight before using. Remove the sachet after 2 days. (If not using a sachet, the pickles will still taste great, but you'll be unable to remove the spices. This makes the flavor a bit stronger and requires that you pick around the spices when eating your pickles.)

Tip: *If substituting mushrooms that need thorough cooking to be safe to eat (e.g., honey mushrooms or morels), boil the mushrooms for 5 minutes before pickling or boil the mushrooms in the pickling liquid for several minutes before allowing the liquid to cool down. If your mushrooms are very wet, they will give off a lot of water in the pickle, so cut back a bit on the water in the recipe.*

Mushroom Substitutions: Almost any mushrooms will work here, but I prefer dense or crisp textured mushrooms.

Pickled Coccora or Caesar's

Makes about 1.5 quarts (1.4 L)

Many people describe the taste of coccora mushrooms (*Amanita calyptroderma*) as "fishy," which led me to this riff on pickled herring. This means a sweet pickling liquid with strong notes of allspice and fresh dill. I grew up eating pickled herring as a special treat. More than a decade of living with a Swedish girlfriend further reinforced my love for this often unappreciated food. Just like pickled herring, these pickles are delicious with boiled potatoes, sour cream (or yogurt), and a little chopped red onion, but also work amazingly well as a garnish for simply prepared fish or scallops.

5 cups (600 g) coccora or Caesar's, stem cut into ½-inch (1.25 cm) slices and caps cut into 1-inch (2.5 cm) pieces

½ bunch of fresh dill

1 tablespoon plus 1½ teaspoons whole allspice berries

2 cups (480 ml) champagne vinegar or distilled white vinegar

2 cups (400 g) sugar

1 teaspoon salt

1. Place the coccora and dill in a clean, heat-safe container.

2. Place the allspice on a piece of cheesecloth and tie closed with twine to make a sachet. (If preferred, you can place the spices directly in the pickling liquid in Step 3.)

3. Combine the vinegar, sugar, salt, and 2 cups (480 ml) water in a saucepan. Add the sachet (or loose spices) and bring to a boil over high heat.

4. Pour the liquid, along with the sachet, over the mushrooms and dill. Let cool completely, uncovered, then transfer to a covered container and refrigerate at least overnight before using. Remove the sachet after 4 days.

Tip: *This recipe was developed using vinegars with roughly 4 to 4.5 percent acidity. If your vinegar has a lower acidity level, you will need to use less water. If your vinegar is more acidic, you may want to add more water. If your mushrooms are very wet, they will give off a lot of water in the pickle, so cut back a bit on the water in the recipe.*

Mushroom Substitutions: This recipe was developed to take advantage of the fishy flavor of Caesar's Amanita and the related coccora, but you can try it with almost any mushrooms.

Spicy Pickled Coccora Relish

Makes about 1¼ cups (280 g)

This recipe came about as a way to use up a massive haul of Caesar's that I had brought home from Arizona and pickled. It was late August, and the Hatch chiles and corn were at the height of their season. If you can't find Hatch chiles, or prefer something milder, poblanos work well. This relish makes an excellent topping for crab cakes, fish sausage, or a variety of grilled seafood.

1 ear sweet corn, shucked

2 Hatch or poblano chiles

1 cup (240 g) Pickled Caesar's or Coccora (page 56), liquid reserved, cut into ¼-inch (6 mm) pieces

1. Cook the corn on a hot grill for about 3 minutes per side, until lightly charred on all sides. Let cool enough to comfortably handle, at least 10 minutes, then cut the kernels off the cob.

2. Char the chiles on a very hot grill or direct flame for about 3 minutes per side, until the skin blisters and chars all over. Let cool for 15 to 20 minutes in a covered bowl to lightly steam. Peel off the skin and remove the stem and seeds under a light stream of cold water and discard. Cut the flesh into ¼-inch (6 mm) pieces.

3. Mix the pickled mushrooms, chiles, and corn together in a large bowl, adding some of the reserved pickling liquid to reach your desired consistency. Season with salt and pepper. Let sit for at least 30 minutes before serving to allow the flavors to meld.

The beautiful coccora is a common relative of Caesar's Amanita in western North America.

Pickled Suillus Buttons

Makes about 2 quarts (1.9 Kg)

One of my Russian mushrooming friends, Tatyana Vinogradov-Nurenberg, brought a jar of these to the first annual "Bolete Camp" organized by James Edmonds, near Mount Shasta. Everyone in attendance absolutely loved them, and we all wanted the recipe, which goes back several generations in her family, so I was thrilled she agreed to share it here. Use only the smallest, densest *Suillus* buttons for this recipe.

1 generous tablespoon citric acid powder, optional

2 pounds (900 g) small, firm, dense *Suillus* buttons

2 tablespoons granulated sugar

4 teaspoons salt

6 whole allspice berries

3 bay leaves

3 whole cloves

1-inch (2.5 cm) piece cinnamon stick, broken into 3 pieces

¼ cup plus 3 tablespoons (100 ml) distilled vinegar, plus more to taste

4 garlic cloves

1. Add the citric acid, if using, to a large pot of boiling water, then add the *Suillus* buttons. Cook the mushrooms for about 5 minutes, until cooked through, then drain and cool quickly in ice water or under cold running water to stop them cooking. Drain well and set aside.

2. Bring 3¼ cups (780 ml) water to a boil in a large saucepan over high heat. When boiling, add the sugar, salt, allspice, bay leaves, cloves, and cinnamon stick. Let simmer for 10 minutes to allow the water to absorb the flavors, then add the vinegar. Taste and add more vinegar a few teaspoons at a time until the acidity level tastes good to you. Remove from heat and let stand for 10 minutes.

3. Place the mushrooms in clean, heat-safe containers with the garlic, then pour in the warm pickling liquid to fully cover the mushrooms. Let cool completely, then transfer to a covered container tightly and refrigerate.

4. The pickles should marinate in the fridge for 1 week before serving, and they will keep for many weeks.

Tip: *Many* Suillus *species will turn a very dark, almost black color when boiled. The citric acid prevents this cosmetic issue without adding substantial flavor. You can omit the citric acid if the color change does not concern you. If your mushrooms are very wet, they will give off a lot of water in the pickle, so cut back a bit on the water in the recipe.*

Mushroom Substitutions: Honey mushroom buttons are another favorite here. Tatyana also recommends porcini buttons, though I personally always have other uses in mind for my porcini. I suspect this would also be great with firm, dense crimini buttons.

Mushroom Escabeche

Serves 8

Escabeche is a traditional and popular Spanish method for preserving proteins. It's basically a different kind of pickling technique. After cooking the protein (typically via searing or roasting), you cover it with a flavored vinegar and white wine sauce. Cooking the mushrooms first with a press and sear technique not only gives added flavor, but adds a wonderful meaty texture. This recipe is more or less exactly the same as how I would make an escabeche of fish or a small game bird. This escabeche of mushrooms makes a great accompaniment to simply prepared fish or poultry, or as the center of a lighter plate with boiled potatoes and your favorite vegetable.

2 pounds (900 g) oyster mushrooms

1 tablespoon neutral oil

6 or 7 garlic cloves, peeled

6 whole cloves

1 tablespoon whole black peppercorns

3 bay leaves

1 cup (240 ml) white wine

1 cup (240 ml) white wine vinegar or cider vinegar

1 teaspoon pimentón de la vera (Spanish smoked paprika)

1. Cook the oyster mushrooms in batches using the press and sear technique, following the instructions on page 31. Season with salt and cook with the oil until the mushrooms are nicely browned. Transfer the mushrooms to a casserole or baking dish when they finish cooking.

2. After the last batch of mushrooms has finished cooking, add the garlic to the empty pan over medium heat, stirring regularly to prevent burning, until it begins to brown, about 30 seconds. Add the cloves, peppercorns, and bay leaves and let cook for a few seconds more to bring out their aromas.

3. Pour in the wine, then increase the heat to high and bring to a boil. Let simmer for 30 seconds to 1 minute to cook off some of the alcohol, then pour in the vinegar and 1 cup (240 ml) water. Bring back up to a simmer, then add the pimentón. Let simmer for 10 more seconds to cook the pimentón, then immediately pour the hot liquid over the mushrooms.

4. Let the mushrooms marinate at room temperature for 1 to 2 hours, then serve, or transfer with the sauce to a covered container and store in the fridge, where the mushrooms can be kept for several weeks, as long as they remain immersed in the sauce.

Mushroom Substitutions: Any substantial, meaty mushrooms that you like to cook using the press and sear technique (page 31) will work here. Lion's mane, cultivated oysters, and beech (shimeji) are some of my favorites.

Q.C PASSED

2

The Messy Drawer

Every kitchen I have ever been in, whether a professional kitchen or one in someone's home, has one messy drawer so chock-full of random tools that it barely opens and closes. Even though it's an unseemly mess, nobody can figure out a better place to put certain things than in that drawer, so stuff keeps piling in. And it isn't useless junk—some of the best and most used tools in the kitchen live there. Any time someone can't find something, it is almost certainly buried in that drawer. Every once in a while, an ambitious effort will be made to reorganize the mess, but before long, it's always back to overflowing.

The Mushroom Hunter's Kitchen may be a book rather than a literal, physical kitchen, but it is no different. In this case, instead of random tools, I had an unseemly pile of recipes and ideas that didn't neatly fit into any other chapter in the book. After going back and forth on what to do with each individual recipe, the only suitable answer was to collect them here in this "messy drawer" of a chapter.

This chapter truly is a hodgepodge of ideas—from recipes that highlight certain special wild mushrooms, like huitlacoche and saffron milk caps, to simple but impactful sauces you can use on just about anything, to a variety of mushroom leathers—that are extremely useful, but that don't easily fit elsewhere in the book. Though they may seem a bit disconnected from one page to the next—just as at home, the messy drawer holds some of the most useful tools in my kitchen arsenal—many of my favorite recipes live inside this messy drawer.

Southwest Ceasar's Amanita, White King Boletes, Puffballs, and Larch Waxy Caps

Chile-Miso Glazed Mushrooms

Serves 6

I like to use this chile-miso glaze to perk up mushrooms that have good texture but not a ton of flavor. This recipe deliberately produces a lot of extra glaze, as I like having extra to serve with whatever vegetable or protein I am pairing the mushrooms with. I use these mushrooms to top a piece of chicken or fish, or add vegetables and serve on rice to make them a meal. The glaze also makes a great base for stir-fries. I prefer to use a darker miso here for a stronger flavor. If you like, you can make the mushrooms less sweet by reducing the sugar by as much as half.

GLAZE

3 tablespoons miso paste

2 tablespoons mirin

1 tablespoon unseasoned rice wine vinegar

1 tablespoon chile paste, like sambal oelek

1 tablespoon soy sauce

2 teaspoons light or dark brown sugar

1 teaspoon freshly grated ginger

MUSHROOMS

1 pound (450 g) crimini, white button, or shiitake mushrooms, cut into bite-size pieces

1 tablespoon neutral oil

2 tablespoons unsalted butter

Thinly sliced scallions, optional

1. To make the glaze, mix the miso, mirin, rice wine vinegar, chile paste, soy sauce, brown sugar, and ginger together in a bowl until well combined. Stir in ½ cup (120 ml) water. Set aside.

2. To make the mushrooms, wet or dry sauté the mushrooms (depending on their type and moisture level), following the instructions on page 31, using the oil. Sauté until lightly browned, but do not season with salt.

3. Pour the glaze into the pan and stir to coat the mushrooms. The glaze will quickly boil. Let the glaze slowly simmer over medium-low heat, stirring regularly as it reduces, 3 to 5 minutes.

4. When the glaze is thick enough to cling to the back of a spoon, remove the pan from the heat and add the butter. Stir the butter into the sauce, making sure all of the mushrooms are thoroughly coated. Serve hot, garnished with the scallions, if using.

Tip: *You can prepare this dish through Step 3 up to 2 days ahead. Let the mushrooms cool in their glaze and store them covered in the fridge. To serve, slowly bring the mushrooms and glaze up to temperature in a pan over medium heat, adding 1 or 2 tablespoons water as needed to thin the glaze, then proceed to Step 4.*

Mushroom Substitutions: Almost any mushrooms will work, though this is especially good with mild flavored, firm-textured mushrooms.

Mushroom Meatballs

Makes about 10 meatballs

This recipe is for my mother, who, after becoming a vegetarian thirty years ago, can finally eat meatballs again. It's also a tribute to Saverio, my stepdad, who passed on unexpectedly way too young. Saverio's mother always stuffed her meatballs with raisins, and they instantly became a favorite of mine. (You can leave the raisins out of this recipe, though, if you prefer.) Use these in an updated vegetarian version of spaghetti and meatballs or a vegetarian meatball sandwich with the quick tomato sauce from the Stuffed Blue Knight "Ravioli" (page 224) or use your family's favorite all-day-simmered tomato sauce recipe.

¼ cup (40 g) raisins

¼ cup (60 ml) Marsala

1.5 pounds (680 g) mixed fresh mushrooms, cut into ⅛-inch (3 mm) pieces

2 tablespoons unsalted butter

½ yellow or white onion, minced

1 large garlic clove, minced

1 tablespoon fresh parsley, finely chopped

½ teaspoon fresh oregano, finely chopped, or ¼ teaspoon dried oregano

¾ cup (80 g) bread crumbs

¼ cup plus 2 tablespoons (38 g) finely grated Parmesan, Pecorino Romano, or hard, aged Gouda

1 egg, beaten

1. Combine the raisins and Marsala in a small bowl and set aside.

2. Wet or dry sauté the mushrooms (depending on their type and moisture level) until they just begin to brown, following the instructions on page 31, using the butter. When browned, continue cooking over medium-low, season with salt and pepper, add the onion and garlic, and sauté until the onion is just starting to brown, 5 to 10 minutes. Remove from the heat and stir in the parsley and oregano. Adjust the salt and pepper to taste.

3. Transfer the mushroom mixture to a large bowl and stir in the bread crumbs. When cooled completely, stir in the cheese and egg. Knead the mixture with your hands for about 30 seconds to make sure everything is thoroughly and evenly mixed. Cover and refrigerate for at least 30 minutes or up to 1 day to fully hydrate the bread crumbs.

4. Drain the raisins, discarding the liquid. Preheat the oven to 350°F (180°C) and line a rimmed baking sheet with parchment paper. Scoop the mushroom mixture into 2- to 3-tablespoon portions. Press each portion into a ball in your hand. Using a finger, make an indentation into the middle of each one. Place a few of the plumped raisins into the indentation, then press to seal the mushroom mixture around the filling. Place the meatball on the prepared baking sheet, then repeat until all of the mushroom mix is used up.

5. Bake the meatballs until lightly browned, 20 to 30 minutes. Remove from the oven. At this point, the meatballs are ready to eat, but they are even better if simmered for 1 to 2 minutes in the sauce in which they are to be served.

Tip: *This vegetarian meat substitute need not be limited to traditional Italian American meatball flavors. The possibilities are endless once you know the base technique. For example, to make Greek keftedes-style meatballs, leave out the raisins, add ½ teaspoon cinnamon, and substitute 3 tablespoons chopped fresh mint and 1 tablespoon fresh dill for the parsley.*

Mushroom Substitutions: Almost any mushrooms will work here. Use a mix of two or three different mushrooms for a well-rounded texture and flavor.

In Defense of Saffron Milk Caps

Members of the *Lactarius deliciosus* group go by several names, including saffron milk caps, green stainers, and bleeding milk caps. The Catalans, who revere them above all other mushrooms, call them *rovellons*, which means "rusty ones," referring to how they first bleed red before slowly staining green. Although they are beloved in much of Europe, many American mushroom hunters are dismissive of them—an attitude I want to change.

There are two key reasons many people have an aversion to these mushrooms. One, many field guides call them mediocre (or worse) edibles—probably because, two, many people don't know how to cook them well. Thrown into a pan with some fat for a quick, high-heat sauté until well-browned, you'll likely find them to have an off-putting grainy texture and an unpleasant bitterness.

So, how should you cook them?

First, to break down that unpleasant grainy texture, it's important to cook them for a good while, preferably with moist heat. Parboiling them before sautéing works, but I prefer using a wet sauté (see page 31). Milk caps' affinity for wet cooking methods, along with their robust texture, make them work wonderfully in stews.

Second, browning saffron milk caps too much can add to their bitterness. As a rule, as soon as they begin to brown, I add the finishing touches (typically garlic and parsley) and then remove the pan from the heat, or add liquid ingredients to the pan to stop the browning process.

Most of the discussion surrounding the saffron and bleeding milk caps applies very well to a much larger group of mushrooms. I handle the shrimp *Russula* (*Russula xerampelina*), other mild *Russula*, and some of the common large, meaty milk caps from the east in the same way. These include *Lactifluus hygrophoroides*, *Lactarius volemus*, *L. corrugis*, *L. indigo*, and others.

Everyday Saffron Milk Caps (Rovellons)

Serves 6 as a side dish

I have seen more Catalan preparations for milk caps, or rovellons, than I can count. Because they have such a big, meaty flavor and a texture that holds up in various applications, they play well in almost any savory dish you can imagine, as long as you treat them right. This recipe is the most common and simplest way we cook rovellons in my house. It makes a great side dish for a wide variety of meats, fish, seafood, and pastas, or a meal when served on toast with eggs. I prefer to use the oven-roasting method only for younger fruiting bodies; mature mushrooms' texture becomes unpleasantly insubstantial.

2 pounds (900 g) saffron milk caps, cut into 1-inch (2.5 cm) pieces

1 tablespoon plus 1½ teaspoon extra virgin olive oil

2 garlic cloves, minced

2 tablespoons fresh parsley, chopped

To cook using the wet sauté method, follow the wet sauté instructions on page 31. When the pan is nearly dry, reduce the heat to medium-low and add the oil. Sauté the saffron milk caps, stirring regularly, until they just start to brown, 5 to 10 minutes. (You do not want to brown them much or they will become bitter.) Season with salt, stir in the garlic, and sauté for 1 to 2 more minutes, until the garlic is fragrant but not browned. Stir in the parsley and cook for another 30 seconds or so. Taste and adjust the salt if needed. Serve hot.

To cook using the oven-roasting method, trim all but ½ inch (1.25 cm) from the stems and toss the saffron milk caps with the oil, garlic, and parsley, then season with salt. Lay the mushrooms stem-side up in a single layer on a rimmed baking sheet lined with parchment paper. Roast at 350°F (180°C) until lightly browned, 30 to 45 minutes. Serve hot.

Mushroom Substitutions: Shrimp *Russula*, or any mild-flavored milk caps or *Russula* work well.

Salted Mushroom-Butternut Squash Cakes

Serves 4 as an entrée or 8 as an appetizer

These cakes work well as a light entrée served with garlicky sautéed greens, or in a smaller bite, as an appetizer or hors d'oeuvre. The spices in the cakes stand out and contribute a lot of flavor, so a scoop of Greek yogurt is all you really need to top them. I suggest leaving the mushrooms a bit on the salty side (you'll need to soak for a few hours, but don't soak them for too long), to keep them from getting lost among the other ingredients in the cakes.

2 cups (340 g) Salt-Preserved Mushrooms (page 52)

3 tablespoons plus 1½ teaspoons neutral oil

2 cups (280 g) butternut squash, peeled and cut into ¼-inch (6 mm) pieces

1 large onion, diced

Pinch of minced fresh rosemary leaves

1 fennel bulb, cut into ¼-inch (6 mm) pieces

1 large garlic clove, minced

½ teaspoon ground coriander

½ teaspoon cumin seeds, toasted

2 eggs, beaten

1 cup (100 g) bread crumbs

All-purpose flour, for forming the cakes

Greek yogurt or sour cream

Mushroom Substitutions: In lieu of salted mushrooms, try using boiled, drained, and cooled butter boletes, crimini, any mild *Lactarius* or *Russula*, lobsters, or your favorite *Agaricus* or *Amanita*. Season the boiled mushrooms well with salt.

1. Rinse the mushrooms to remove visible salt. Fill a container with water. Transfer the mushrooms to the container, cover, and soak for at least 3 hours or up to 6 hours, changing the water every few hours, then drain well. Cut the mushrooms into ¼-inch (6 mm) pieces.

2. Heat a large, heavy-bottomed pan over medium-high heat. Add 1 tablespoon of the oil. Add the butternut squash, season with salt and pepper, and sauté, stirring regularly to prevent sticking, for 5 to 7 minutes, until the squash is just beginning to soften. Transfer to a bowl and set aside.

3. Return the empty pan to medium heat. Add 1 tablespoon of the remaining oil, then add the onion and rosemary. Season with salt and pepper. Cook, stirring regularly, until the onion is soft and just beginning to brown, 7 to 10 minutes.

4. Add the onion mixture, mushrooms, squash, fennel, garlic, coriander, and cumin to a large bowl. Season with salt and pepper, going easy on the salt if the mushrooms are still salty. Mix in the eggs, then the bread crumbs, making sure that the ingredients are thoroughly and evenly combined. Cover and let rest in the fridge for at least 30 minutes or up to 24 hours to allow the flavors to meld and the bread crumbs to hydrate.

5. Using your hands or a ring mold, form the mixture into patties about 4 inches (10 cm) in diameter, pressing firmly to ensure they don't fall apart. If the cakes aren't holding together, add up to 3 tablespoons flour to the mixture.

6. Heat a large, heavy-bottomed pan over medium heat. Add the remaining oil and carefully place as many of the cakes in the pan as will fit, cooking in batches if necessary. Once crispy and golden brown on the bottom, about 4 or 5 minutes, use a spatula to carefully flip each cake. Cook until the other side is crispy and golden brown, another 4 or 5 minutes. Line a plate with a clean kitchen towel or paper towel, and transfer the cakes to the plate for a few seconds to drain. Serve hot with Greek yogurt or sour cream.

Tip: *The onions and squash can be cooked a day or two in advance of making the cakes, as long as they are properly stored in the fridge until needed.*

Duxelles

Makes 3 to 4 cups (675–900 g)

Everyone should know how to make duxelles because they're so versatile. They can be served as a rich crostini topping, a filling for stuffed vegetables, pasta (see the *Suillus* Agnolotti on page 179), chicken breasts, fish fillets, or even other mushrooms. Freezing a large batch in smaller portions is a great way to preserve extra mushrooms.

2 pounds (900 g) fresh mushrooms, roughly chopped

1 teaspoon oil

3 garlic cloves, finely chopped

2 shallots, minced

½ cup (120 ml) dry white or red wine, sherry, Marsala, Madeira, or non-hoppy beer

5 fresh thyme sprigs, leaves only

2 tablespoons cold unsalted butter, cut into pieces

1. Wet or dry sauté the mushrooms (depending on type and moisture content), following the instructions on page 31. Season with salt and pepper and continue to sauté until lightly browned.

2. Push the mushrooms to the sides of the pan, clearing a space in the center, increase the heat to medium, then add the oil, garlic, and shallots to that cleared space. Let the garlic and shallots sizzle for about 5 seconds, then mix in with the mushrooms. Be careful not to burn the garlic or shallots.

3. Add the wine and scrape any browned bits off the bottom of the pan. Continue cooking over medium heat until the wine is almost entirely reduced, about 2 minutes.

4. Remove from the heat, mix in the thyme leaves, and season with salt and pepper.

5. Blend the mixture using an immersion blender or food processor, adding a few pieces of cold butter at a time. For coarser duxelles, blend for only a few seconds. For a smooth consistency, blend longer. After blending, adjust the salt and pepper to taste. Transfer to a covered container and store in the fridge, where it can be kept for 5 days.

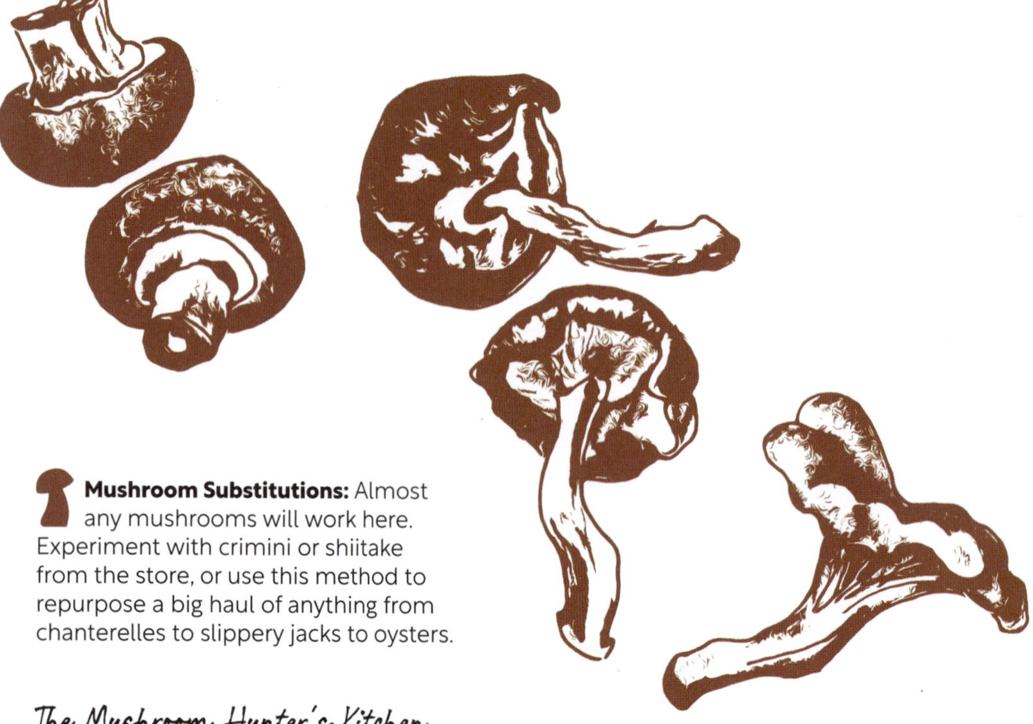

Mushroom Substitutions: Almost any mushrooms will work here. Experiment with crimini or shiitake from the store, or use this method to repurpose a big haul of anything from chanterelles to slippery jacks to oysters.

Candy Cap–Red Wine Sauce

Makes about 1 cup (240 ml)

Candy caps' maple aroma permeates this powerfully flavored red wine reduction to create a sauce worthy of a special occasion. I can't think of a better way to top a steak or pork chop. Use an inexpensive but drinkable red wine to make the sauce—a dry wine that isn't too acidic or tannic. I like to use the smallest candy caps in my stash for this recipe so that I can leave them whole when serving. If you are using larger mushrooms, you may want to cut or tear them into pieces after they soften up, then return them to the sauce.

1 teaspoon oil

3 shallots, minced

2 garlic cloves, minced

¼ teaspoon minced fresh rosemary leaves

1 bottle (750 ml) red wine

0.25 ounce (7 g) dried candy caps

¼ cup (60 g) cold unsalted butter, cut into pieces

1 tablespoon honey

1. Heat a medium saucepan over medium heat. Add the oil, then add the shallots, garlic, and rosemary. Cook for about 1 minute, until very fragrant, stirring regularly and being careful not to let it burn. As soon as the shallots and garlic begin to brown, add the wine and half of the candy caps.

2. Turn the heat up to high. When the wine comes to a boil, reduce the heat to keep the sauce at a gentle simmer until it reduces to about ¾ cup (180 ml), 30 to 45 minutes. (If you over-reduce the sauce, stir in a little bit of water to make up the difference.) Remove from the heat and add the remaining candy caps.

3. Whisk in the butter a few pieces at a time to emulsify, adding more as the previous addition melts. When all of the butter is incorporated, whisk in the honey, then season with salt. Serve hot.

Tip: *You can complete the recipe through Step 2 several days in advance, then cool and refrigerate the sauce in an airtight container. When ready to use, gently heat it in a small saucepan and continue with Step 3.*

Mushroom Substitutions: There is no substitute for the candy caps in this recipe.

Huitlacoche Purée

Makes about 1½ cups (360 ml)

One of my most memorable wild mushroom finds came on a hot summer day, late in August, deep in California's arid Central Valley. Some friends and I were heading home from a backpacking trip and had stopped to stretch our legs alongside a cornfield when someone let out a puzzled exclamation: "What the hell is that thing?" I looked up to see a cluster of beautifully grotesque, bulging, blackish-gray masses emerging from an ear of corn. I recognized it immediately as huitlacoche. Called "corn smut" by American farmers, who worry about losing crops to it, huitlacoche is one of the most prized ingredients in Mexico. Farmers there sell it for a much higher price than the corn that it "ruins." It has a subtle, dark, smoky flavor that plays exceptionally well with chiles, corn, squash, beans, and various meats and seafood. It is a favorite special-occasion ingredient of mine, and I love to use this thick, intensely rich purée as a decadent side, served underneath a protein like seared scallops or grilled fish, or to turn a simple corn soup into something special (see page 173). For a thinner sauce, add water or stock while blending until it reaches the desired consistency.

3 fresh poblano chiles

1 tablespoon neutral oil

1 yellow onion, diced

1 cup (225 g) huitlacoche "kernels," thawed if frozen

2 tablespoons cold unsalted butter, cut into pieces

1. Roast the poblanos under a broiler or grill over high heat, turning them as needed until the skin is charred on all sides, about 3 minutes per side. Transfer to a covered bowl to steam while cooling. When cool, peel the charred skin from the chiles and remove the seeds and ribs, then cut the flesh into ½-inch (1.25 cm) pieces.

2. Heat a heavy-bottomed pan over medium heat. Add the oil, then the onion. Sauté the onion until just beginning to brown, 5 to 7 minutes, stirring regularly. Add the huitlacoche, about ½ cup (120 ml) water, and season with salt. Continue to cook until completely reduced, about 5 more minutes, then add the chiles and continue to sauté for another 2 to 3 minutes to let the flavors come together.

3. Remove from the heat and purée using a blender, immersion blender, or food processor until almost smooth, then add the butter, a few pieces at a time, and blend until completely smooth. Taste, and adjust the salt as needed. Serve.

Mushroom Substitutions: There is no substitute for the huitlacoche in this recipe.

Making Mushroom Leathers

Mushroom leathers are a grown-up version of the fruit roll-ups that many of us ate when we were kids. They make for a delicious and portable savory snack—especially when you're out in the wet forest picking more mushrooms! They are extremely easy to make and allow you to play with different flavors. The recipes and techniques easily scale to any sized batches.

The basic method works equally well whether you start with fresh or dried mushrooms. In the recipes that follow, there are a few different ideas to get you started, but the possibilities are limited only by your imagination, so don't be afraid to experiment with any mushrooms you like, and to combine them with other fruits and vegetables. Since I started demonstrating this technique many years ago, countless people have brought me creative new leathers to try, and they've all been great.

Almost any mushrooms can be made into mushroom leathers. Matsutake are the only mushrooms I really can't recommend, as they typically lose their prized aroma during dehydration.

I like to lay leathers flat on a piece of parchment paper before rolling them up for storage to prevent the layers from sticking to each other. Stored in a ziplock bag, they will keep for at least a month at room temperature.

Peach-Candy Cap Leather

Makes one 12-inch (30 cm) round leather

There isn't much mushroom hunting to do in California in the hot summer months when peaches are in their sweet, juicy prime, so it's a good time to get into my stash of dried candy caps and make some fun snacks. Substitute whole raspberries for the peaches to make a tart, beautiful red leather.

0.25 ounce (7 g) dried candy caps

1 pound (450 g) ripe peaches, pitted and cut into 1-inch (2.5 cm) pieces

¼ cup plus 2 tablespoons (85 g) packed light brown sugar

¼ cup (60 ml) Grand Marnier

1. Soak the candy caps in 1 cup (240 ml) water until softened, about 20 minutes.

2. Add the peaches to a saucepan with the sugar and a pinch of salt. Place the pan over medium heat. Within about 2 minutes, the peaches will start to give up a lot of liquid. If they begin to stick to the pan before releasing their liquid, add a few tablespoons water. Let the peaches cook in their own juice until most of the liquid has evaporated, 5 to 10 minutes.

3. Strain the candy caps, reserving the soaking liquid, and add the mushrooms to the pan with the fruit. Cook for 3 minutes, stirring regularly, to activate the aroma of the mushrooms, then add the Grand Marnier and scrape any browned bits from the bottom of the pan. When the pan is almost dry, 1 to 2 minutes, add the reserved soaking liquid. Cook until the soaking liquid has reduced to only a couple tablespoons, about 10 minutes, then remove from the heat.

4. Purée the contents of the pan using a blender or immersion blender until smooth.

5. Spread the purée in a thin, even layer about ⅛ inch (3 mm) thick on your dehydrator's fruit leather tray. If you do not have a fruit leather tray, spread the purée on a sheet of parchment paper and place that in the dehydrator. Dehydrate at 130°F (55°C) until the purée has become a firm yet pliable sheet. The leather is done when it no longer feels sticky or wet and you can lift and manipulate it as a solid sheet. The time required to dehydrate the leather will vary quite a lot depending on how much moisture was left in the purée and how thinly you spread it, anywhere from 4 hours to overnight.

Mushroom Substitutions: There is no substitute for the candy caps in this recipe.

Black Trumpet Leather

Makes one 12-inch (30 cm) round leather

This was one of the first mushroom leathers I made many years ago, and it's still one of my favorites. It has a striking black color almost like fresh road tar, a wonderfully concentrated, rich, earthy taste, and strong aroma of black trumpets.

2 ounces (60 g) dried black trumpets, or 10 ounces (280 g) fresh

2 teaspoons neutral oil

2 large shallots, thinly sliced

¼ cup (60 ml) Marsala or dry white wine

1 tablespoon soy sauce

1. Soak the dried black trumpets in 2 cups (480 ml) water for 20 minutes, until softened. Remove the mushrooms and clean them thoroughly, straining and reserving the soaking liquid separately. (If using fresh mushrooms, skip to Step 2.)

2. Heat a heavy-bottomed pan over medium heat. Add the oil and shallot, and sauté, stirring regularly, until the shallots are soft and beginning to brown, about 5 minutes.

3. Add the black trumpets and cook for another 3 minutes, stirring regularly, to cook the mushrooms through. Add the Marsala and scrape any browned bits off the bottom of the pan. When the Marsala has almost completely reduced, about 2 minutes, add the reserved soaking liquid and the soy sauce. Continue to cook until completely reduced, 5 to 10 minutes. Remove from the heat, and add salt to taste.

4. Purée the contents of the pan using a blender or immersion blender until smooth.

5. Spread the purée in a thin, even layer about ⅛ inch (3 mm) thick on your dehydrator's fruit leather tray. If you do not have a fruit leather tray, spread the purée on a sheet of parchment paper and place that in the dehydrator. Dehydrate at 130°F (55°C) until the purée has become a firm yet pliable sheet. The leather is done when it no longer feels sticky or wet and you can lift and manipulate it as a solid sheet. The time required to dehydrate the leather will vary quite a lot depending on how much moisture was left in the purée and how thinly you spread it, anywhere from 4 hours to overnight.

Mushroom Substitutions: Almost any mushrooms will work here, though you won't get the cool black color from most.

Fat Jack Leather

Makes one 12-inch (30 cm) round leather

The fat jack (*Suillus caerulescens*) is one of the most common mushrooms to grow with Douglas Firs. It has a pleasant flavor, with hints of pine and lemon, that really pops in this simple application. I have made versions of this leather using whatever local Suillus species I can collect when presenting and cooking for mushroom groups around the western US. Everyone is always surprised that *Suillus* taste so good.

1 pound (450 g) fresh fat jacks, chopped into ½-inch (1.25 cm) pieces

1 tablespoon neutral oil

1 large shallot, finely chopped

¼ cup (60 ml) dry white wine

1. Dry sauté the fat jacks, following the instructions on page 31, using the oil.

2. When the mushrooms start to brown, increase the heat to medium, add the shallot, and continue cooking until it starts to get a little color, 3 to 5 minutes.

3. Add the wine and scrape up the browned bits stuck to the pan. Continue cooking until the wine has completely reduced, 2 to 3 minutes.

4. Purée the contents of the pan using a blender or immersion blender until smooth.

5. Spread the purée in a thin, even layer about ⅛ inch (3 mm) thick on your dehydrator's fruit leather tray. If you do not have a fruit leather tray, spread the purée on a sheet of parchment paper and place that in the dehydrator. Dehydrate at 130°F (55°C) until the purée has become a firm yet pliable sheet. The leather is done when it no longer feels sticky or wet and you can lift and manipulate it as a solid sheet. The time required to dehydrate the leather will vary quite a lot depending on how much moisture was left in the purée and how thinly you spread it, anywhere from 4 hours to overnight.

Mushroom Substitutions: Almost any mushrooms will work here.

Porcini Leather

Makes one 12-inch (30 cm) round leather

What's not to like about an intensely porcini-flavored snack? I often keep a roll of these around for snacking when there aren't many mushrooms to pick locally. The meaty flavor is so satisfying, and it helps me reminisce about my favorite hunts.

1 ounce (28 g) dried porcini

1 tablespoon neutral oil

1 large yellow onion, sliced

1 garlic clove, minced

¼ cup (60 ml) dry white wine

1. Soak the dried porcini in 2 cups (480 ml) water until softened, 10 to 20 minutes. Strain, reserving the liquid separately, and set aside.

2. Heat a heavy-bottomed pan over medium heat. Add the oil, then add the onion. Sauté until the onion is soft and lightly browned, 10 to 15 minutes.

3. Add the garlic and porcini and sauté for another 3 minutes to cook the garlic and heat the mushrooms through. Season with salt, then pour in the wine and scrape up any browned bits stuck to the bottom of the pan. When the wine has reduced almost completely, add the soaking liquid. Continue cooking until completely reduced, about 10 minutes.

4. Purée the contents of the pan using a blender or immersion blender until smooth.

5. Spread the purée in a thin, even layer about ⅛ inch (3 mm) thick on your dehydrator's fruit leather tray. If you do not have a fruit leather tray, spread the purée on a sheet of parchment paper and place that in the dehydrator. Dehydrate at 130°F (55°C) until the purée has become a firm yet pliable sheet. The leather is done when it no longer feels sticky or wet and you can lift and manipulate it as a solid sheet. The time required to dehydrate the leather will vary quite a lot depending on how much moisture was left in the purée and how thinly you spread it, anywhere from 4 hours to overnight.

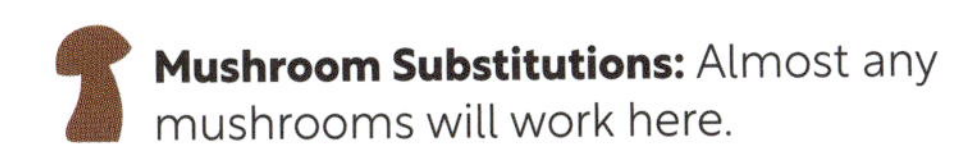

Mushroom Substitutions: Almost any mushrooms will work here.

3

Breakfast and Brunch

Springtime hunting in the Sierra Nevada

is challenging. Most mushrooms don't even emerge through the duff, so you search for suspicious "shrumps"—mushrooms pushing up little mounds in the fir or pine needles. After a while, you learn to tell the difference between rodent diggings and mushrooms without checking each one, and on a good day, you may even convince yourself that you can tell the difference between a bolete shrump and that of a less-interesting imposter. Really, though, you never know what is hiding under the duff until you push it away and can actually see the mushroom (or lack thereof). No matter how many half-decayed *Cortinarius* you uncover, hope springs eternal: The next could always be a glorious spring king!

One beautiful spring day, I was out with friends, hoping to find "spring kings" (*Boletus rex-veris*), a variety of porcini that I had yet to find in the wild. We knew the season had just begun because we had seen scattered reports of online acquaintances finding a few. After checking a few spots, my friends had each spotted one or two, but I was still carrying an empty basket. We pulled up to a new place along a dirt logging road, and as I was locking the car, I heard an excited cry: One of my friends had spotted a perfect fairy ring of spring kings popping up around a young fir tree. Our luck was changing, or so we thought. We were proved wrong after searching the area extensively for another hour netted precisely zero additional boletes. We decided to take a break and cook an outdoor lunch. After a big meal, I convinced my friends to humor me and check one more spot, as I was still batting zero.

We drove down another nearby logging road, found what looked like a decent area, and parked. After another long search, we found nothing. We got back in the car and headed toward civilization. I had started to accept that I was never going to find any spring kings of my own, and would be resigned to relying on charitable friends' donations.

Then, it happened. I saw something out of the corner of my eye and slammed on my brakes, skidding to a stop on the dirt road. I ran from the car, door left open—the vehicle may still have been running—I didn't care. I was so giddy that any passersby may have thought me drunk. I sat on my knees, frantically digging in the dirt on the side of the road, letting out incoherent, triumphant shouts in the direction of the car. I was sitting entirely encircled by at least twenty perfect spring kings. My very first patch were all beauties, including several pounds of pristine, dense, bug-free buttons.

Spring Kings

When I got home, I knew I had to do something special with this find. I decided on mushroom-and-potato latkes garnished with simple, marinated raw porcini. At work, we had just gotten in some of the first local wild salmon of the year, so I set aside some of the belly scraps to turn into salmon tartare for the forthcoming porcini feast.

The Porcini-Potato Latkes with Salmon Tartare (page 82) and the Marinated Porcini Buttons (page 109) in the next chapter, Salads and Cold Preparations, re-create the very happy brunch that we ate with the first spring kings I ever collected. All three dishes are delicious on their own, but when served together, they create a meal worthy of a special occasion. Many of the other recipes in this chapter are no less worthy of a special-occasion breakfast or brunch, though they're also well-suited for those quiet days at home.

Porcini-Potato Latkes with Salmon Tartare

Serves 4 to 6

I always loved my mom's potato latkes, which were just pressed-together shredded potato and onion with a little matzo meal to bind them. In my version, porcini add an irresistible earthy undertone; they make the latkes a little denser, but it's a worthwhile trade-off. Cooking off the mushrooms' excess water first will yield crispier and more cohesive latkes. I do not add any egg to the latke mix, as I feel it takes away from the flavor of the potatoes and mushrooms, and the moisture given off by the potatoes and onions, combined with the matzo meal, provide more than enough binding power. Use as little matzo meal as possible because it dilutes the flavor of the potatoes and mushrooms as well as making for a denser, heavier pancake. I like to eat these latkes on their own, garnished solely with sour cream, but you can take them to another level by serving them with the Marinated Porcini Buttons (page 109) and the Salmon Tartare.

PORCINI-POTATO LATKES

1 pound (450 g) fresh porcini, cut into ¼-inch (6 mm) slices

1 tablespoon neutral oil, plus extra for frying

1 pound (450 g) russet potatoes (about 2 potatoes), peeled

¼ medium yellow onion, grated or minced

1 tablespoon salt

1 teaspoon freshly ground black pepper

¼ cup (30 g) matzo meal, plus extra if needed

Butter

SALMON TARTARE

1 pound (450 g) sushi-grade salmon, cut into ¼-inch (6 mm) pieces

¼ cup (60 ml) extra virgin olive oil

1 shallot, finely diced

2 tablespoons drained and roughly chopped capers

Zest and juice of 1 Meyer or regular lemon, or more to taste

Sour cream

1. To make the porcini-potato latkes, dry sauté the porcini, following the instructions on page 31, using the oil. Brown the mushrooms lightly but don't let them get too dark, as they will be cooked again. Set aside to cool.

2. Grate the potatoes into a large mixing bowl. Mix in the onion, salt, and black pepper, and set aside. Chop the mushrooms into ¼-inch (6 mm) pieces.

continued ›

Mushroom Substitutions: If possible, use mature porcini for this recipe, but almost any mushrooms will work well. For cultivated choices, portabella are great, but reduce the amount to 0.5 pound (225 g).

3. Use your hands to squeeze out as much moisture as possible from the potato and onion mixture, and drain out the water. Mix the mushrooms into the potato and onion mixture, then add the matzo meal, stirring to coat everything evenly.

A good day for porcini—time to make some latkes!

4. Heat a large heavy-bottomed pan over medium heat. Add the oil. Using your hands, grab a handful of the shredded potato mixture, form a ball, then press it into a round, flat pancake shape. Press it tight and flat between your hands to squeeze out as much liquid as possible. You want the latke to be about ⅜ inch (10 mm) thick when you are done. Place the latke into the pan. Repeat until the pan is full, but leave at least 1 inch (2.5 cm) between the latkes. Add 1½ tablespoons butter to the space between the latkes. Do not move the latkes until they are ready to be flipped. When the bottom of the latke is crispy and golden brown, 4 to 5 minutes, carefully flip it and gently press on the top to get a nice flat surface on the bottom.

5. When the second side is crispy and golden brown, another 4 to 5 minutes, transfer to a cooling rack or plate lined with paper towels to drain, and sprinkle with a small pinch of salt. Repeat until all latkes are cooked, adding more oil and butter to the pan as needed. Keep the cooked latkes uncovered in a 200°F (90°C) oven.

6. To make the salmon tartare, add the salmon, extra virgin olive oil, shallot, capers, lemon zest, and lemon juice to a bowl and mix well to combine. Season with salt and pepper.

7. Serve the latkes hot with the sour cream and salmon tartare.

Tip: *If matzo meal isn't available, substitute all-purpose flour.*

Candy Cap Breakfast Sausage

Makes 3.5 pounds (1.6 Kg) sausage

This is my take on a classic maple syrup-flavored breakfast sausage—only in this version, candy caps replace the maple syrup. It's delicious with eggs and toast, and it makes an interesting substitute for sausages in almost any recipe. I make it regularly and have served it to many large groups of people, who always love it. Increase the sugar to 2 tablespoons plus 1½ teaspoons if you prefer a sweeter breakfast sausage. Sausage will always be better if you grind your own meat, which means you will need a meat grinder or stand mixer grinder attachment for this recipe. However, if you prefer, you can use ground meat from the store, and simply mince and then mix all of the ingredients together. To consistently make good sausage, you really need to weigh your ingredients. The volume of ingredients can vary quite a bit depending on several factors, making it difficult to consistently get a proper balance of flavors.

1.5 ounces (40 g) dried candy caps

2½ cups (600 ml) cold water

1 tablespoon plus 2 teaspoons granulated sugar

3.5 pounds (1.6 kg) pork butt, very cold, diced into ½- to 1-inch (1.25–2.5 cm) cubes

2 tablespoons kosher salt

1½ teaspoons freshly ground black pepper

4 or 5 garlic cloves, chopped

½ large bunch fresh sage leaves, chopped

1. Cover the dried candy caps with the cold water and let sit for 30 minutes until softened. Strain, reserving the soaking liquid separately, and finely chop the mushrooms.

2. Add the soaking liquid to a saucepan and bring to a simmer over medium heat. Add the sugar and let the liquid simmer gently until it is reduced to about ½ cup (120 ml), 20 to 25 minutes. Remove from the heat and let cool completely.

3. Combine the pork, salt, pepper, garlic, and reconstituted candy caps in a large bowl. Mix well and store in the fridge until ready to grind. This can be done up to 1 hour before grinding.

4. Set up the grinder with a ¼-inch (6 mm) plate. Add the sage to the meat mix, then grind the mixture into a large mixing bowl set over a larger bowl of ice.

5. Add the cooled soaking liquid to the sausage mix. Mix well with a large spoon or your gloved hands until the sausage is sticky, 2 to 3 minutes.

6. Heat a small frying pan over medium heat. Use your hands to make a small flat patty out of about 1 tablespoon of the sausage meat. (This will be your "test" patty for assessing the seasoning of the sausage.) Add a couple drops of oil to the pan, then add the patty. When the first side is browned, about 3 minutes, flip the patty to brown the other side, another 2 or 3 minutes. Let cool for 1 to 2 minutes, then taste. If necessary, adjust the seasoning of the rest of the sausage.

7. Refrigerate the rest of the meat for a few hours to allow the candy caps' aroma and flavor to permeate the sausage completely. (The uncooked sausage will last about 5 days in the fridge or 5 weeks in the freezer.)

8. When ready to cook, form the sausage into 3- to 4-tablespoon patties and cook the sausage according to Step 6. Serve hot.

Mushroom Substitution:
There are no substitutes for the candy caps in this recipe, because what makes the sausage special is their maple aroma.

Savory Mushroom Crepes

Makes 6 large or 10 to 12 small crepes

Crepes provide a flexible vehicle for using all kinds of mushrooms. Savory crepes can not only be filled with mushrooms and topped with mushroom sauces, but as in this case, mushrooms can also flavor the batter. Mushroom crepes present so many possibilities that I decided to include both this savory version and a mildly sweet version (page 94). You can use any filling you like here; if it's not mushroom season, these are great with almost any vegetable filling you can imagine.

SAUCE

0.5 ounce (14 g) mixed dried mushrooms such as yellow foots, lobsters, or porcini

1 bunch fresh parsley, roughly chopped

Juice of ½ lemon

1 cup (150 g) fresh mushrooms, cut into ½-inch (1.25 cm) pieces

1 tablespoon neutral oil

1 shallot, halved and thinly sliced

2 garlic cloves, minced

¼ cup (60 ml) white wine

¼ cup (60 ml) heavy cream, plus more if needed

Fresh herbs, such as parsley, dill, or tarragon

CREPES

1 cup (125 g) all-purpose flour

¾ cup (180 ml) milk

2 large eggs

1 tablespoon porcini powder

1 teaspoon salt

¼ teaspoon freshly ground black pepper

1 tablespoon unsalted butter, melted

FILLING

1 pound (450 g) chanterelles, cut into ½-inch (1.25 cm) pieces

2 tablespoons unsalted butter

2 leeks, white parts only, halved, rinsed thoroughly, and cut into ½-inch (1.25 cm) slices

1 bunch kale, de-stemmed and torn into large pieces

¼ cup plus 2 tablespoons (90 ml) white wine

1. To make the sauce, cover the dried mushrooms with 1 cup (240 ml) water and set aside to soak for at least 10 minutes to soften.

2. To make the crepes, combine the flour, milk, ½ cup (120 ml) water, eggs, porcini powder, salt, and pepper in a blender. Blend until smooth, then, while the blender is running, stream in the melted butter, and blend for another 2 or 3 seconds to thoroughly combine. Strain the batter to remove any lumps. The consistency should be similar to heavy cream.

3. Heat a small nonstick pan over medium heat. When pan is hot, lift it off the burner and pour about 3 tablespoons of batter into the pan, quickly tilting to coat the bottom with a thin layer. (If the crepe batter is setting before you can get it evenly spread in the pan, you can either thin it with a tablespoon of water, reduce the heat, or both.) Place the pan back on the heat until the crepe looks dry and firm on top, 1 to 2 minutes. Carefully flip the crepe and cook for about 20 seconds on the other side. Transfer to a plate. Repeat with the remaining batter, stacking the cooked crepes with paper towels or parchment paper between each layer. Cover with plastic wrap to keep them from drying out if storing for more than a few minutes.

4. To make the filling, dry sauté the chanterelles, following the instructions on page 31, using 1 tablespoon of the butter, until lightly browned. Season lightly with salt, then transfer to a bowl and set aside.

5. In the same pan, over medium heat, add the remaining butter and the leeks. Season with salt, and sauté, stirring regularly, until the leeks are softened but not browned, 3 to 5 minutes. Stir in the kale and cook until just beginning to wilt, 1 to 2 minutes. Mix in the cooked mushrooms

Mushroom Substitution: Almost any mushrooms will work here.

and wine, and scrape up any browned bits from the bottom of the pan. When only 1 tablespoon of liquid remains, 1 to 2 minutes, remove from the heat, taste, and adjust the seasoning if necessary.

6. Spread a large spoonful of filling down the center of a crepe and roll up like a scroll, placing seam-side down in an oven tray. Repeat to fill all of the crepes. Keep them warm in a 200°F (90°C) oven while finishing the sauce.

7. To continue making the sauce, blend the parsley and lemon juice using a blender or immersion blender, adding just enough water to engage the blades. It should be finely chopped but not perfectly smooth, 10 to 15 seconds.

8. Dry or wet sauté the fresh mushrooms (depending on their type and moisture level), following the instructions on page 31, using the oil. While the mushrooms cook, drain the rehydrated mushrooms, reserving the liquid, and chop them roughly. When the fresh mushrooms are lightly browned, increase the heat to medium, and add the shallot and garlic. Continue cooking for about 30 seconds, stirring often so they don't burn. Add the rehydrated mushrooms and cook for another 2 minutes to let the flavors meld. Add the wine, scraping up any browned bits from the bottom of the pan, and cook until reduced to only 1 tablespoon, 2 to 3 minutes. Add the reserved soaking liquid and continue cooking until it is reduced to about ¼ cup (60 ml), about 5 minutes, then stir in the cream. Simmer for a moment. Remove from the heat and stir in the parsley puree. Taste, and adjust the salt if needed. If the sauce is too thick, you can stir in a couple more tablespoons of cream.

9. Serve immediately, spooning the sauce over the warm crepes. Garnish with fresh herbs.

Chanterelle, Bacon, and Potato Hash

Serves 2 to 4

Breakfast potatoes were one of the first things I ever learned to cook, and they're still among my favorite dishes to make for loved ones. This recipe is deceptively simple. It is important not to overcrowd the potatoes in the pan, as they will get mushy instead of crispy if stacked up high. The mushrooms add both a deep, earthy flavor, and a pleasant, chewy texture to balance and elevate the potatoes. If you like, you can make this vegan by skipping the bacon and cooking with your preferred vegetable oil.

3 slices of thick-cut bacon, cut into ½-inch (1.25 cm) pieces

1 pound (450 g) chanterelles, smaller mushrooms quartered or halved, larger mushrooms cut into ½-inch (1.25 cm) pieces

½ onion, diced

1 pound (450 g) Yukon Gold potatoes, cut into ½-inch (1.25 cm) pieces

Mushroom Substitution: Almost any mushrooms will work here.

1. Cook the bacon in a large nonstick pan over medium-low heat, stirring regularly, until the pieces are crispy, about 10 minutes. Line a plate with a clean kitchen towel or paper towel. Transfer the pieces to the plate to drain. Pour all of the bacon fat from the pan into a small bowl and set aside.

2. Dry sauté the chanterelles, following the instructions on page 31, using some of the reserved bacon fat. Season with salt and continue to sauté until the mushrooms are very lightly browned, then transfer to a bowl and set aside.

3. With the pan still over medium-low heat, add 1 tablespoon of the reserved bacon fat to the pan, then add the onion, season with a pinch of salt, and sauté until softened, 3 to 5 minutes.

4. Add the potatoes to the pan. Sauté until they are tender and just starting to brown, 15 to 30 minutes, stirring regularly to keep them from sticking to the pan. Turn the heat up to medium-high and continue cooking until the potatoes begin to get crispy, 5 to 10 minutes, stirring frequently. Season well with salt and pepper.

5. Add the chanterelles back to the pan and continue to sauté until hot, about 1 minute. Stir in the bacon, remove from the heat, season with salt and pepper, and serve.

Tip: *To prevent the potatoes from sticking, I highly recommend using a good nonstick pan or a very well-seasoned cast iron pan. Potatoes stick badly to stainless steel unless you use high heat, a lot of fat, and keep them moving constantly.*

Candy Cap Granola

Makes about 6 cups (650 g)

The maple essence of candy caps turns this standard granola into something magical. I like to eat it with yogurt for a light meal or transform it into an easy snack on the run (page 91). You can adjust the proportions and types of nuts, seeds, and dried fruit to your taste. Shredded, unsweetened coconut also makes a great addition. The only real rules are that the oats should make up at least half of the total volume, and the dried fruit should be mixed in only after the rest of the ingredients have come out of the oven. The granola keeps well for several weeks stored at room temperature in an airtight container, but it never lasts that long in my house. This recipe scales well. I often make double or triple batches.

1 cup (200 g) packed light or dark brown sugar

0.25 ounce (7 g) dried candy caps

3 cups (270 g) rolled oats (not instant oats)

½ cup (55 g) slivered almonds

½ cup (60 g) walnut pieces

½ cup (65 g) sunflower seeds

½ cup (60 g) pumpkin seeds

⅓ cup (80 ml) neutral oil

½ cup (65 g) dried cranberries

1. Preheat the oven to 300°F (150°C). Line a rimmed baking sheet with parchment paper.

2. Combine 1 cup (240 ml) water with the brown sugar and dried candy caps in a small saucepan. Bring to a boil over medium-high heat, then immediately reduce the heat to low and simmer gently while covered to help avoid over-reducing the syrup, for about 5 minutes. Remove from the heat and let stand, still covered, for 10 to 15 minutes to cool slightly, then blend until smooth using a blender or immersion blender.

3. Combine the oats, almonds, walnuts, sunflower seeds, and pumpkin seeds in a large mixing bowl. Pour in the candy cap syrup and the oil and stir until all of the ingredients are evenly coated.

4. Pour the mixture onto the prepared baking sheet and spread it into a layer about ¼ inch (6 mm) thick. Transfer to the oven and bake for 60 to 90 minutes, until evenly and lightly browned, stirring every 10 to 15 minutes to ensure even baking.

5. Remove from the oven and let cool completely, then mix in the dried fruit.

Mushroom Substitutions: There is no substitute for the candy caps in this recipe.

Candy Cap Granola Bars

Makes 16 to 20 bars

Turning the Candy Cap Granola (page 89) into more portable granola bars is simple, and the bars are every bit as irresistible as the regular granola. I like to add a bit of candy cap powder to emphasize their aroma in the bars. If making the granola specifically to turn into bars, chop the nuts into smaller pieces before starting. The smaller pieces bind together more easily as bars.

¾ cup (135 g) quinoa, uncooked

1 teaspoon candy cap powder

14 ounces (400 g) pitted dates (about 28 dates), chopped

1 recipe Candy Cap Granola (page 89)

1. Bring 2 cups (480 ml) water to a boil in a small saucepan over high heat. Add the quinoa, candy cap powder, and a pinch of salt, cover, and reduce the heat to low to simmer gently until all of the water is absorbed, about 15 minutes. (The quinoa should look mushy and overcooked; this will help bind the granola bars.) Remove from the heat and let cool completely, at least 30 minutes.

2. Pulse the dates in a food processor until they become almost paste-like. Set aside, then pulse the cooled quinoa mixture in the empty food processor until thick, smooth, and sticky.

3. Combine the processed quinoa and dates in a mixing bowl, then add the granola. Use your hands to incorporate the granola into the quinoa-date mixture, squeezing and kneading until it starts to come together (this will be a bit sticky and messy). Once thoroughly mixed, transfer the mixture to a cutting board and roll it into a ¾-inch-thick (2 cm) rectangle. Use a heavy, sharp knife to cut it into 16 to 20 pieces. Any stray granola can be pressed back into the bars before dehydrating.

4. Arrange the granola bars on a dehydrator tray and dehydrate for 6 to 8 hours at 145°F (60°C) or bake for 3 to 4 hours in a 200°F (90°C) oven. Serve immediately, or store, covered or wrapped, at room temperature for up to 2 weeks.

Mushroom Substitutions: There is no substitute for the candy caps in this recipe.

Oyster Mushroom Chilaquiles

Serves 4 to 6

There are at least as many versions of chilaquiles as there are cooks who make this classic Mexican breakfast dish. All involve cooking fried tortillas (traditionally stale, leftover ones) in a salsa with any number of other proteins or vegetables. I love both the texture and flavor mushrooms add to this dish, and they also make the chilaquiles more satisfying and filling. Serve topped with over-easy eggs for a crowd-pleasing breakfast dish. The recipe that follows is a quick, easy, flavorful salsa that marries well with most mushrooms. You can also use the enchilada sauce from the Lobster Mushroom Enchiladas (page 217) with good results.

SALSA

1.5 pounds (680 g) Roma tomatoes, chopped

1 small red onion, chopped

½ bunch fresh cilantro

2 serrano chiles, chopped

1 teaspoon salt

1 pinch ground cumin

CHILAQUILES

1 pound (450 g) oyster mushrooms, larger mushrooms cut or torn into 1-inch (2.5 cm) pieces, smaller mushrooms left whole

2 tablespoons neutral oil

1 large yellow or white onion, halved and cut into ⅛-inch (3 mm) slices

1 pinch ground cumin

8 cups (200 g) fried corn tortillas, broken into large pieces, or store-bought tortilla chips

GARNISH

Fresh cilantro leaves

Sunny-side-up or over-easy eggs

Queso fresco, optional

Sour cream, optional

1. To make the salsa, place the tomatoes, onion, cilantro, chiles, salt, and cumin in a blender and blend until thoroughly combined. Taste and adjust the seasoning as needed.

2. To make the chilaquiles, wet or dry sauté the oyster mushrooms (depending on their freshness and moisture level) in a large, heavy-bottomed pan, following the instructions on page 31, using 1 tablespoon of the oil. Cook until browned, being careful not to burn the mushrooms. Season with salt. Transfer the mushrooms to a bowl and set aside.

3. Adjust the heat to medium, add the remaining oil, and the onion and cumin. Season with salt and pepper. Cook until the onion just begins to brown slightly, 5 to 7 minutes.

4. If the salsa has begun to separate, stir it to recombine. Add the oyster mushrooms back to the pan, then add the salsa. Cook for 3 to 5 minutes, until there are no puddles of extra water released by the tomatoes left simmering in the sauce, then taste and adjust the salt as needed. Add the fried tortillas and stir gently to thoroughly coat with the salsa, being careful to avoid breaking the tortillas as much as possible. As soon as the chips are softened and coated in sauce, remove the pan from the heat.

5. To garnish and serve, sprinkle with the cilantro leaves, top with the eggs, and serve immediately with the cheese and sour cream, if using, allowing diners to top their own plates as desired.

Tip: *You can fry fresh corn tortillas or use store-bought corn tortilla chips. If you buy chips, use the most heavy-duty chips you can find, as you want them to hold together when cooked with the sauce. Also, make sure that they do not have any added flavorings beyond salt.*

Mushroom Substitutions: Almost any mushrooms will work here.

Candy Cap-Cheese Blintzes with Strawberry-Chanterelle Sauce

Makes 10 blintzes

Growing up, we ate blintzes—either savory potato or sweet cheese blintzes like these—as special treats, so I wanted to twist a childhood favorite into a mushroomy treat. This recipe leaves the crepe unsweetened and the filling only very lightly so, as the sauce has plenty of sweetness to go around. The candy-cap flavor is present but not overpowering, and you can certainly increase the amount of candy cap in the crepes or filling, if desired. The strawberries meld with the earthy, fruity essence of the candied chanterelles making a playful and surprising topping.

CREPES

4 or 5 dried candy caps

¾ cup (180 ml) whole milk

1 cup (125 g) all-purpose flour

2 large eggs

½ teaspoon salt

1 tablespoon unsalted butter, melted

FILLING

½ teaspoon candy cap powder

2 cups (450 g) cottage cheese, drained for several hours

2 egg yolks, optional

1 tablespoon powdered sugar

SAUCE

1 cup (240 g) candied chanterelles in large pieces, with their syrup (see page 243)

4 ounces (115 g) strawberries, cut into ¼-inch (6 mm) slices

2 tablespoons unsalted butter, plus more as needed for cooking blintzes

1. To make the crepes, soak the dried candy caps in the milk and ½ cup (120 ml) water. Set aside until soft, 10 to 15 minutes.

2. To make the filling, mix the powdered candy caps into the cottage cheese. Set aside.

3. To make the sauce, mix together the candied chanterelles and their syrup and the strawberries in a small saucepan. Warm over low heat, stirring occasionally, until the sauce is warmed through, 5 to 7 minutes, then set aside.

4. To continue making the crepes, combine the soaked candy cap mixture, flour, eggs, and salt in a blender. Blend until smooth, then, while the blender is running, stream in the melted butter, and blend for another 2 or 3 seconds to thoroughly combine. Strain the batter through a fine-mesh strainer to remove any lumps.

5. Heat a small nonstick pan on a medium flame. When pan is hot, lift it off the burner and pour about 3 tablespoons of batter into the pan, quickly tilting to coat the bottom with a thin layer. When the batter stops flowing, place the pan back on the heat until the crepe appears dry and firm on the top, 2 to 3 minutes. Cook only on one side, then stack on a plate. Repeat with the remaining batter, stacking the cooked crepes with paper towels or parchment paper between each layer. Cover with plastic wrap to keep them from drying out if storing for more than a few minutes.

6. To continue making the filling, combine the cottage cheese with the egg yolks, if using, and powdered sugar and mix well.

7. Lay 1 crepe cooked side up on your work surface and place a generous spoonful of filling in the center. Fold the sides over the filling and roll the crepe up like a burrito, leaving it seam-side down. Repeat to fill all of the crepes.

8. Heat a heavy-bottomed pan over medium heat. Add the butter. When the butter is sizzling, add the blintzes seam-side down, leaving at least 1 inch (2.5 cm) between them. When browned and crispy on the bottom, about 3 minutes, flip each blintz and brown the other side. Cook in batches, adding more butter to the pan as needed. Serve the blintzes hot, topped with the strawberry-chanterelle sauce.

Mushroom Substitution: Try candied yellow foots or waxy caps (*Hygrophorus* spp.) instead of the chanterelles. Dried almondy *Agaricus* could replace the candy caps.

Matsutake Congee

Serves 8

People enjoy countless versions of rice porridge throughout Asia, and each culture has its own names for their versions. "Congee" is the name I hear most commonly where I live in California. I adapted this recipe from one taught to me by a Hong Kong–born chef friend of mine, Raymond So. He loves serving it, minus the matsutake, with various types of seafood; I have served my Japanese-influenced, mushroomy version at formal events, garnished with simply cooked shrimp, abalone, and scallops. It's a brilliant way to showcase the unique aroma and flavor of matsutake, but it's also an excellent vehicle for any mix of your favorite mushrooms, wild or cultivated. Congee and similar porridges are often served as breakfast, but you can enjoy it at any meal.

¾ cup (180 g) jasmine rice

6 cups (1.5 L) chicken, mushroom (page 36), vegetable, or shellfish stock

One 2-inch (5 cm) piece of kombu

Generous pinch of bonito flakes

0.5 pound (225 g) matsutake, torn or cut into ½-inch (1.25 cm) pieces

1 bunch scallions, thinly sliced

Zest of 1 lime

2 to 3 tablespoons roasted, salted peanuts

1 small matsutake button, thinly sliced, optional

Simply cooked shrimp, abalone, or scallops, optional

1. Place the rice in a fine-mesh strainer and rinse in cold water until the water runs clear. Then cover with a generous amount of cold water. Let soak for 30 minutes, then drain well.

2. Make the broth while the rice soaks. Add the stock and kombu to a large saucepan and bring to a boil over medium-high heat. Reduce the heat to medium-low and simmer for 10 minutes, then turn off the heat and add the bonito flakes. Let sit for 1 minute, then strain all of the solids out of the broth.

3. Add the strained broth back into the pan along with the rice, matsutake, and a pinch of salt. Bring to a simmer over medium-high heat, stirring often. Reduce the heat to medium-low and simmer gently, stirring regularly, until the congee reaches the thickness of a loose oatmeal, 20 to 30 minutes. Adjust the salt, and if the congee is too thick, stir in more broth or water.

4. Optionally, purée the congee to your desired consistency using a blender or immersion blender. (Some people insist that it is essential to purée congee a bit, or a lot, while others find even the suggestion of blending offensive. I personally prefer it buzzed briefly.)

5. Serve the congee hot with the scallions, lime zest, peanuts, shaved matsutake, and shrimp, abalone, or scallops, if using, on the side, allowing diners to garnish their own bowls as desired.

Mushroom Substitution: The matsutake give this dish a special aroma and depth of flavor, but almost any mushrooms will work here.

Rosemary Buttermilk Biscuits with Mixed Mushroom Gravy

Serves 9

A flaky, hot, fresh-from-the-oven biscuit smothered in a proper gravy is one of life's simple pleasures. Over the years, my preference has shifted from a gravy with a classic sausage base to this vegetarian mushroom gravy, both for this version's lighter feel and for the depth of flavor I get from using a mix of mushrooms. These biscuits are an update on the traditional buttermilk variety. The key to light, fluffy biscuits is working quickly while keeping the ingredients cold. The rosemary permeates them as they bake and goes beautifully with the mushroom gravy. The recipe also scales up very well to make larger batches.

BISCUITS

2¾ cups plus 1 tablespoon (350 g) all-purpose flour, plus extra for rolling

1 tablespoon baking powder

1 teaspoon baking soda

1½ teaspoons salt

1 teaspoon sugar

½ teaspoon minced fresh rosemary

½ cup (115 g) plus 2 tablespoons cold unsalted butter, cut into small pieces

1 cup (240 ml) cold buttermilk

GRAVY

0.5 ounce (14 g) dried mushrooms

3 cups (720 ml) milk

1 pound (450 g) mixed fresh mushrooms, cut into ¼-inch (6 mm) pieces

1 tablespoon neutral oil

2½ tablespoons unsalted butter

½ yellow onion, diced

1 garlic clove, minced

Pinch of red pepper flakes

½ teaspoon chopped fresh parsley

½ cup (120 ml) Marsala or dry sherry

½ cup (65 g) all-purpose flour

½ bunch fresh sage, minced

GARNISH

1 tablespoon chopped fresh sage

Zest of 1 lemon

Freshly ground black pepper

Mushroom Substitution: Almost any fresh mushrooms will work here. I like to use a mix of at least two or three different types for a variety of textures and flavors. I usually lean toward strongly aromatic dried mushrooms like porcini or *Suillus*.

1. Preheat the oven to 375°F (190°C) and line a rimmed baking sheet with parchment paper.

2. To make the biscuits, add the flour, baking powder, baking soda, salt, sugar, and rosemary to a large bowl and whisk together. Work the butter into the flour using a pastry cutter or by pinching together the butter and flour with your fingers. When the butter is coated in flour, in pieces a bit smaller than peas, slowly pour in the buttermilk while mixing with a large spoon.

3. Turn the dough onto a lightly floured surface and knead and fold it just until it comes together. If the dough is too wet, dust with a little extra flour.

4. Roll the dough into a ¾- to 1-inch-thick (2–2.5 cm) rectangle, then fold in half. Repeat the rolling and folding twice, each time rolling to ¾ to 1 inch (2–2.5 cm) thick. The third time, cut the biscuits into your desired shape with a knife or cookie cutter. Set on the prepared baking sheet and let rest for 20 minutes.

5. Transfer to the oven and bake until lightly browned on top, 15 to 20 minutes.

6. To make the gravy, add the dried mushrooms and milk to a bowl and soak until soft, about 10 minutes, then remove the mushrooms and chop into ¼-inch (6 mm) pieces. Reserve the milk, straining out any grit.

7. Wet or dry sauté the fresh mushrooms (depending on their type and moisture level), following the instructions on page 31, using the oil, plus ½ tablespoon of the butter. When the mushrooms begin to brown, add the reconstituted dried mushrooms. Continue to sauté until the mushrooms are evenly browned.

8. Increase the heat to medium, then add the onion, garlic, and red pepper flakes and season with salt and pepper. Sauté until the onion is soft, about 5 minutes, then add the parsley. Cook for 30 seconds, then stir in the Marsala, scraping up any browned bits from the bottom of the pan.

9. When 1 tablespoon of liquid is left in the pan, after 1 to 2 minutes, stir in the remaining butter. Once the butter has melted, stir in the flour. Cook for 1 to 2 minutes, stirring continuously, to lightly toast the flour. Stir in the reserved milk a little bit at a time, beating the lumps out of the mix between each addition, until the gravy becomes smooth and thick. Let the gravy come to a simmer, then add the sage and adjust the salt and pepper as needed. Reduce the heat to medium low and let simmer for 2 or 3 minutes, stirring regularly so the bottom does not burn, to cook the raw taste out of the flour, and thicken the gravy. If the gravy is too thin, let it simmer an extra 1 to 2 minutes. If it is too thick, add more milk or water.

10. To garnish and serve, slice a biscuit in half and spoon the gravy on top. Top with a pinch of chopped sage, a bit of lemon zest, and some freshly ground black pepper.

4

Salads and Cold Preparations

Most of the dishes in this book stem from memorable adventures with friends—the Candy Cap and Roasted Beet Salad (page 118) comes to mind, the reward of a day spent picking candy caps with my friend Wendy So.

One of my most memorable adventures happened on the Mendocino coast after a weekend of working a local mushroom club event. On our way out from the event, my friend Thea and I had decided to caravan to pick black trumpets. We stopped at a gas station, Thea and her partner Lon in their blue SUV at the pump behind me, and reconfirmed the plan: They were to follow me and Rosa to the trumpet spot we both knew.

As I made my way to the road, I saw a blue SUV coming up to the roundabout past me, with a woman waving to me from the passenger seat. I guessed Thea and Lon had decided to lead. No big deal. I started following them.

They sped into the woods—faster than I had expected, which was fine with me. But as we approached the last few curves before our agreed-upon turnout, they showed no signs of slowing down. I told Rosa that I was nervous they were going to miss it. Sure enough, a few moments later, they blew right past the turnout.

With no cell reception, and no way to check in, I figured that Thea must've come up with a better idea. She knew those woods, those roads, and other nearby mushroom spots at least as well as me, so I just tried to keep up. Their speed kept increasing along the curvy mountain road. I could barely maintain the pace. Every time I caught up, it seemed like they would speed up. I laughed to Rosa and said, "Man, they're in a hurry."

This went on for two miles past the agreed-upon spot. Then another mile. Then a few miles more. Every few curves, we flew past another potential trumpet patch I knew. I was getting annoyed. We'd already sped past countless areas where I would've happily stopped, and still the speed kept increasing. What's more, all the while, the car *behind* was right on top of me, flying around each wooded turn just as fast as Lon and me. I decided I would turn off with or without my friends. Seeing my opening, I put the pedal to the floor to get up close to their bumper and started aggressively honking, flashing my turn signal to make sure they knew I was turning into the logging road up ahead. Thankfully, they got the hint, slowed down, and made the turn in front of me.

I parked and hopped out of the car, ready to confront them with a litany of questions centered on the theme of "what the hell?"

The passenger-side window rolled down—to reveal a woman who was most definitely not Thea and a driver who was definitely not Lon. They looked more than a little concerned.

After a few nervous seconds of uncomfortable, silent staring, I broke out in laughter. Then I offered a deep heartfelt apology and explained how I'd come to chase them down this mountain road for the past fifteen miles. It turned out they'd come from the same mushroom event we had, and had recognized me in the car—hence the waving from the roundabout.

As we all laughed, I realized the car that had been riding my bumper the whole way—a blue Volvo—had made the turn as well. It was Lon and Thea, of course, both appearing perplexed and annoyed. Looking back and forth between their car and the blue Subaru I'd been following, I had to allow them a few well-earned moments to roll their eyes and laugh at me.

I redeemed myself, slightly, when I explained that I knew a great spot for trumpets further up this dirt road. After inviting our still-shocked new friends to join us on the hunt, both cars followed me (at a more relaxed pace this time) down the dirt road to the area I knew.

It turned into exactly the kind of day we had hoped, and we spent hours floating from patch to patch of black trumpets and hedgehogs. Rosa, Thea, Lon, and I were all still laughing about the car chase later that day over dinner and beers. They still remind me of it at every opportunity. And every time I make the Mushroom Tartare (page 111), which I first made using the mushrooms we collected that day, I still have to laugh.

Thea, happy with her haul of black trumpets

Roasted Vegetable and Mushroom Salad with Black Trumpet Vinaigrette

Serves 3 to 4 as a main or 6 as a side

This hearty salad makes a light, satisfying meal on a hot summer day. I love all the different textures, and how the sweetness of the roasted vegetables plays off the earthy depth of the mushrooms. The recipe makes enough vinaigrette for a couple batches of the salad, and it will keep for at least a week in a covered container in the fridge, though it may separate a bit after lengthy refrigeration. Let it warm up to room temperature for 30 minutes to an hour before giving it a quick whisk to bring it back to life.

BLACK TRUMPET VINAIGRETTE

0.3 ounce (10 g) dried black trumpets or 5 ounces (140 g) fresh

1 cup (240 ml) warm water

2 teaspoons neutral oil

¼ cup (60 ml) Banyuls vinegar or sherry vinegar

½ cup (120 ml) extra virgin olive oil

SALAD

1 large eggplant, cut into ½-inch (1.25 cm) pieces

¼ cup (60 ml) extra virgin olive oil

1 large head of cauliflower, cut into florets

4 cups (450 g) maitake (hen-of-the-woods) mushrooms, broken into 1-inch (2.5 cm) pieces

3 cups (115 g) loosely packed rinsed arugula

1. To make the vinaigrette, add the dried black trumpets and warm water to a bowl and soak until softened, 15 to 20 minutes. Strain, reserving the liquid separately, then clean the mushrooms, if necessary. If using fresh black trumpets, skip to Step 2.

2. Heat a heavy-bottomed pan over medium-high heat. Add the neutral oil and black trumpets. Add a pinch of salt and stir regularly until the mushrooms are lightly browned, about 3 minutes. Add the soaking liquid and cook until reduced to about ¼ cup (60 ml), 4 to 5 minutes. Add the vinegar and purée the mixture using a blender or immersion blender until smooth. While blending, slowly drizzle in the olive oil to emulsify. Taste and add salt if needed. If at any point the vinaigrette becomes too thick to blend properly, you can add a little cold water to loosen it.

3. To make the salad, preheat the oven to 375°F (190°C). Line three rimmed baking sheets with parchment paper. Toss the eggplant with salt, pepper, and 2 tablespoons of the extra virgin olive oil. Spread out in a single layer on one of the prepared baking sheets and, once the oven is hot, roast until soft all the way through and just starting brown, 15 to 25 minutes. Remove from the oven and let cool completely.

4. Toss the cauliflower with salt, pepper, and 1 tablespoon of the extra virgin olive oil. Spread in a single layer on the second prepared baking sheet and roast until lightly browned, 20 to 30 minutes. Remove from the oven and let cool completely. (If there is space in the oven, the cauliflower can be roasted at the same time as the eggplant; just start checking the eggplant for doneness a few minutes before the cauliflower.)

5. After removing the eggplant and cauliflower from the oven, increase the temperature to 400°F (200°C). Toss the maitake with the remaining extra virgin olive oil, salt, and pepper, then spread out on the third prepared sheet to oven roast, following the instructions on page 32. Remove from the oven and let cool completely.

Mushroom Substitution: Almost any mushrooms will work in the salad. You can substitute yellow foots for the black trumpets in the vinaigrette, which will lighten both the flavor and the color.

6. Toss the mushrooms, cauliflower, and eggplant together in a large mixing bowl, adding enough of the vinaigrette to coat, and mix thoroughly to coat evenly. Let marinate in the fridge for up to 2 hours.

7. Add the arugula, a pinch of salt, and another 1 to 2 tablespoons of vinaigrette to the bowl. (You want only enough vinaigrette to barely coat all of the greens, so it's better to underestimate what you need on the first addition. You can always mix in a little more.) Serve.

Tip: *Banyuls vinegar is unique, made from the classic French fortified wine of the same name. Its flavor is almost halfway between that of sherry vinegar and red wine vinegar. It is worth adding to your pantry, but if you can't find it, substitute sherry vinegar.*

Warm Coral Mushroom, Potato, and Kale Salad

Serves 2 as a main or 4 to 6 as a starter or side

Though the species in the *Ramaria* genus often look like coral, as their common names suggest, they also tend to resemble cauliflower far more than the *Sparassis* species typically known as "cauliflower mushrooms." I not only break corals into florets like cauliflower, but often cook them similarly and use them in dishes in place of cauliflower as well. I like this warm wilted salad as a meal on its own, but it also works as a nice side for a meaty main dish. You could even bulk it up by adding some actual roasted cauliflower, which would add a mild sweetness.

SALAD

1 pound (450 g) fingerling potatoes, halved lengthwise

2 tablespoons extra virgin olive oil

1 pound (450 g) coral mushrooms, broken into 1 to 1½-inch (2.5–4 cm) pieces

1 tablespoon neutral oil

1 large bunch of kale, stemmed and roughly chopped

1 garlic clove, crushed

½ cup (85 g) good-quality green olives, such as Picholine, pitted

MEYER LEMON VINAIGRETTE

Zest and juice of 2 Meyer lemons

1 tablespoon whole grain mustard

¼ cup (60 ml) extra virgin olive oil

1. To make the salad, preheat the oven to 350°F (180°C). Toss the potatoes with salt, pepper, and 1 tablespoon of the extra virgin olive oil. Lay them in a single layer on a rimmed baking sheet and, once the oven is hot, roast until the potatoes are starting to brown and are easily pierced with a fork, 30 to 45 minutes depending on the size of the potatoes.

2. Increase the oven temperature to 400°F (200°C). Pan roast the corals, following the instructions on page 32, with the neutral oil. Cook until lightly and evenly browned, taste, and adjust the salt as needed.

3. To make the Meyer lemon vinaigrette, whisk the lemon zest, juice, and mustard together in a bowl. Add a generous pinch of salt and a grind of fresh black pepper, then slowly add the extra virgin olive oil while whisking to emulsify. Taste and adjust the salt and pepper as needed.

4. To continue making the salad, add the remaining extra virgin olive oil and the garlic to a pan set over medium heat. When the garlic starts to sizzle, about 30 seconds, add the kale and stir to coat with the oil. Season with salt and continue to stir until the kale is barely wilted, about 3 minutes. Remove and discard the garlic.

5. Add the kale, corals, and potatoes to a large mixing bowl. Add the vinaigrette, a pinch of salt, and a couple grinds of pepper. Mix to coat all ingredients thoroughly. Just before serving, garnish individual portions with the olives.

Tip: *If you can't find Meyer lemons, you can substitute 2 regular lemons plus ½ teaspoon of honey.*

Mushroom Substitutions: Any firm-fleshed, mild-flavored corals (*Ramaria* spp.) will work well here. The red-tipped coral *Ramaria botrytis* and the yellow-tipped *R. rasilispora* are two great choices. Almost any good-textured and mild, earthy, or meaty-flavored mushrooms can be substituted successfully.

Wood Ear Mushroom Salad

Serves 2 as a main, or 4 to 6 as a starter or side

In the summer of 2022, wood ears were everywhere in the Rocky Mountains. I came up with this salad to share the unusually large bounty at that year's Telluride mushroom festival. Everybody loved the salad as much as I did, and I quickly began making it for friends using store-bought wood ears. It has a great mix of crisp, contrasting textures, pretty colors, and bright flavors from the vinaigrette and vegetables. You can serve it on its own as a salad course, or, for a light, healthy meal, serve it under a simply cooked piece of fish. You can do all the knife work and make the vinaigrette ahead. Store the vegetables covered in the fridge until needed, but do not mix in the vinaigrette until you are ready to serve.

SALAD

4 cups (340 g) fresh wood ear mushrooms, or 2 ounces (60 g) dried

2 carrots, peeled and sliced into thin 2-inch-long (5 cm) matchsticks

1 English cucumber, sliced into thin 2-inch-long (5 cm) matchsticks

1 bunch scallions, green parts only, thinly sliced on the bias

1 tablespoon sesame seeds, toasted

VINAIGRETTE

¼ cup (60 ml) unseasoned rice vinegar

2 tablespoons sugar

2 tablespoons tamari or soy sauce

One 1-inch (2.5 cm) piece of ginger, peeled

1 teaspoon toasted sesame oil

1. To make the salad, bring a large pot of water to a boil over high heat. Add the wood ears and a generous pinch of salt. Boil for 3 minutes, until cooked through. Drain and immediately rinse the mushrooms under cool water to chill them, then cut into thin strips.

2. To make the vinaigrette, stir the vinegar and sugar together in a small bowl, then add the tamari. Adjust the sugar, vinegar, or tamari to taste. Grate the ginger into the vinaigrette mix and stir in the toasted sesame oil.

3. To continue making the salad, mix the carrots, cucumbers, scallions, and mushrooms together in a large bowl. Toss with the vinaigrette, top with the sesame seeds, and serve.

Tip: *If using dried wood ears, soak them in warm water for 10 minutes before boiling. Reconstituted wood ears will require 6 to 8 minutes boiling to sufficiently soften.*

Mushroom Substitutions: You could make a luxurious version of this salad using yellow foots or black trumpets instead of the wood ears.

Salted Mushroom-Sweet Potato Salad

Serves 4 as a side or 8 as an appetizer

The first time I made this salad, Rosa and I were fighting for the last scraps before licking our plates clean. I've since served it a few times at dinner parties where it was similarly well received. The contrast of soft and crunchy, delicate and chewy textures make this salad as interesting as it is flavorful. Leaving the mushrooms a bit on the salty side here adds a flavor punch that is lost if the mushrooms are soaked overnight. Use little or no salt when dressing the salad to balance their saltiness. Serve with seared sea scallops or mild white fish to make a beautiful light dinner that will impress anyone. A little extra vinaigrette is all the sauce your seafood will need.

SALAD

1 cup (170 g) rinsed Salt-Preserved Mushrooms (page 52)

2 small sweet potatoes

1 large sweet apple such as Jonagold or Honeycrisp, cored and cut into ½-inch (1.25 cm) pieces

7 radishes, sliced into thin rounds

2 hard-boiled eggs, peeled and quartered

2 tablespoons fresh oregano leaves

PIQUILLO VINAIGRETTE

2 canned piquillo peppers, plus 2 tablespoons of their liquid, or 1 small roasted, seeded, and peeled red bell pepper

2 tablespoons sherry vinegar

¼ cup (60 ml) extra virgin olive oil

1. To make the salad, rinse the mushrooms to remove visible salt, then cover them in water and soak for 3 hours. Drain well, then cut into ¼-inch (6 mm) strips.

2. Add the sweet potatoes to a saucepan, cover with cold water, and add a generous pinch of salt. Bring to a boil over medium-high heat, then reduce the heat to keep at a simmer until the sweet potatoes can be easily pierced with a skewer or small knife, about 10 minutes. Drain and set aside to cool completely, then peel and cut into ½-inch (1.25 cm) pieces. Refrigerate for at least 30 minutes.

3. To make the piquillo vinaigrette, using a blender or immersion blender, blend the peppers and their liquid with the vinegar and a pinch of salt and pepper. Once smooth, slowly add the extra virgin olive oil while still blending until emulsified. Adjust the seasoning to taste. Refrigerate until ready to use.

4. To continue making the salad, combine the mushrooms, sweet potatoes, apple, radishes, eggs, and half of the oregano leaves in a bowl. Season with salt and pepper, then add the vinaigrette. Gently mix to coat everything evenly. Serve cold, garnished with the remaining oregano leaves.

Tip: *Piquillos are pointy red peppers from Spain which you can find canned at well-stocked grocery stores. If you can't find them, substitute 1 large roasted, peeled, and seeded red bell pepper.*

Mushroom Substitutions: In lieu of salted mushrooms, try using boiled, drained, and cooled white button mushrooms, any mild *Lactarius* or *Russula*, lobsters, or your favorite *Agaricus* or *Amanita*. Season the boiled mushrooms well with salt before assembling the salad.

Salad of Sweet Poached Jelly Babies, Celery, Celery Root, and Almonds

Serves 4 as a hearty appetizer

I often find jelly babies (*Leotia lubrica*) at the same times and in the same places as black trumpets during the Northern California winter season. They do not have much of a flavor on their own, but they do have an interesting gelatinous texture that makes them a good candidate for candying. When Rosa saw her first jelly babies, she kept saying that they looked like "grapes on a stick," so I figured, "Why not make them taste like grapes?" Thus came about this take on a grape and celery root salad I've loved making for years, featuring candied jelly babies in place of grapes.

SWEET POACHED JELLY BABIES

1 cup (225 g) jelly baby mushrooms

1 cup (240 ml) green or white grape juice

SALAD

1 large celery root, peeled and cut into thin matchsticks

3 celery stalks, cut ⅛-inch-thick (3 mm) on the bias

A couple handfuls of rinsed baby arugula

1 recipe Meyer Lemon Vinaigrette (page 104)

½ cup (50 g) chopped or sliced almonds, toasted

1. To make the sweet poached jelly babies, bring a pot of water to a boil over high heat, add the jelly babies, and boil for 5 minutes to cook thoroughly. Drain and discard the water, and rinse the mushrooms. Sweet poach the jelly babies in the grape juice, following the instructions on page 242.

2. To make the salad, combine the celery root, celery, arugula, and candied jelly babies in a large bowl, season with salt and pepper, and toss with the vinaigrette, then top with the almonds and serve.

Tip: *Jelly babies have sometimes been listed as toxic, though there are no documented poisonings. They should not be consumed in large amounts, especially repeatedly, and you should always cook them thoroughly before consuming. Boiling them and discarding the water before further cooking will help decrease the concentration of their toxins and the likelihood of experiencing any issues.*

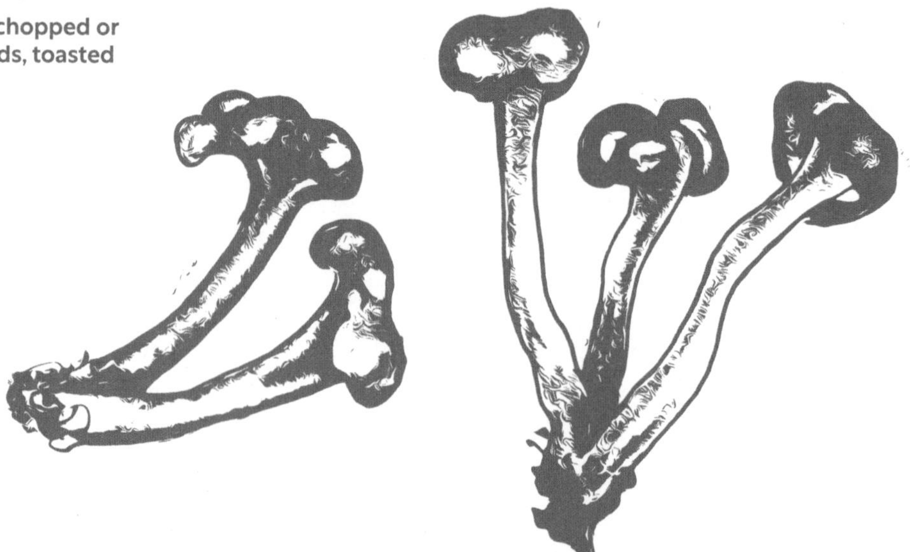

Mushroom Substitutions: You can substitute candied beech mushrooms (shimeji), waxy caps (*Hygrophorus* spp.), cat's tongue (*Pseudohydnum gelatinosum*), or witch's butter (*Tremella aurantia*) for the jelly babies. If using any of these mushrooms, skip the boiling in Step 1.

Marinated Porcini Buttons

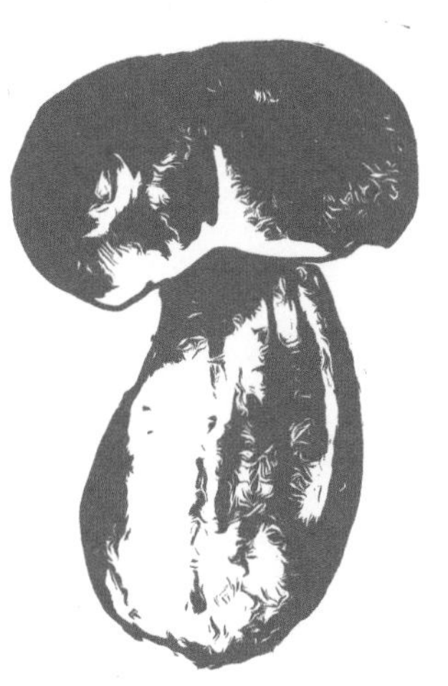

Serves 6 to 8 as an appetizer

This dish was inspired by one I ate at one of legendary mycologist David Arora's mushroom classes. John Pisto, a well-known Monterey chef, had left an enormous bowl of porcini marinating, intended for use in a salad, but someone discovered them, word spread, and they all quickly disappeared before mealtime. Lesson learned: Hide them until you are ready to serve! This classic Italian use of porcini is perfect as a snack or appetizer, mixed into a simple green salad, or as a garnish for nearly any savory dish you can imagine. Use only young, fresh, dense, bug-free mushrooms for this recipe. They present beautifully when sliced—each piece a thin cross-section of the entire stem and cap. The marinated mushrooms will keep for a couple of days in the fridge—if you can keep them a secret for that long.

0.5 pound (225 g) pristine porcini buttons, thinly sliced

¼ cup (60 ml) extra virgin olive oil

Zest and juice of 1 Meyer lemon or 1 regular lemon

2 garlic cloves, minced

Pinch of red pepper flakes, optional

Mix together the porcini, extra virgin olive oil, lemon zest and juice, and garlic, the red pepper flakes, if using, and salt to taste in a large bowl. Let sit at room temperature for at least 30 minutes or up to 1 day before serving.

Mushroom Substitutions: There is no substitute for fresh young porcini in this recipe.

Porcini and Arugula Salad

Serves 4 as an appetizer

This very simple salad is all about the marinated porcini. The kohlrabi provides some contrasting piquant flavor and radish-y crunch, but it stays in the background to allow the porcini to shine.

1 recipe Marinated Porcini Buttons (page 109)

3 cups (115 g) loosely packed rinsed baby arugula

1 large kohlrabi bulb, peeled and shredded on the large holes of a box grater

Set aside a few of the best-looking porcini slices for garnish. Mix together the remaining marinated porcini with the arugula and kohlrabi and season with salt and pepper in a large bowl, making sure that neither the porcini nor the kohlrabi clump up. Serve, garnished with the reserved mushrooms.

Tip: *If you can't find kohlrabi at your local market, substitute 1 bunch of your favorite radish.*

A lone porcino, standing proud

Mushroom Substitutions:
There is no substitute for the marinated porcini in this recipe.

Mushroom Tartare

Serves 4 to 6 as an appetizer

Based on a classic beef tartare, this recipe replaces the raw beef with mushrooms cooked two ways. Where I live in Northern California, black trumpets and hedgehogs often grow together and are hunted at the same time. They have contrasting textures, flavors, and colors that beautifully complement one another. It makes a pretty appetizer, but I also like to eat it as a light meal with some seasonal vegetables on the side.

4 cups (170 g) fresh black trumpets

4 cups (285 g) fresh bellybutton hedgehogs

1 tablespoon neutral oil

½ teaspoon whole grain mustard

Juice and zest of 1 lemon

1 large shallot, minced

2 tablespoons chopped fresh parsley

1 tablespoon capers, drained and chopped

¼ cup (60 ml) extra virgin olive oil

Egg yolks, optional

Oil-packed, salted anchovy fillets, optional

Toasted country bread

1. Bring a pot of water to a boil over high heat. Add a generous pinch of salt, then add the black trumpets. Boil for 3 to 4 minutes to cook through, then drain well and let cool completely. Chop into ⅛- to ¼-inch (3–6 mm) pieces.

2. Dry sauté the hedgehogs, following the instructions on page 31, using the neutral oil. Cook them only until they first begin to brown, then season lightly with salt and remove from the heat. When cool enough to handle, cut into ⅛- to ¼-inch (3–6 mm) pieces.

3. Mix the mustard into the lemon juice, then pour into a large bowl with all the mushrooms, the shallot, parsley, capers, and lemon zest. Season with salt and pepper and mix well. Slowly pour in the extra virgin olive oil while stirring, making sure everything gets thoroughly coated. Taste, and if necessary, adjust the seasoning.

4. To serve, scoop the tartare into ring molds or ramekins, pressing down enough to form a loose patty that will hold its shape once unmolded, then place on a serving plate and remove the mold. Top each portion with an egg yolk and/or anchovy fillets, if using, and serve with the toasted bread.

Mushroom Substitutions: Almost any mushrooms will work here, but try to use at least two different types for contrasting flavor and texture. If you want your mushroom tartare to have the sticky texture of the classic dish, substitute a slimy mushroom such as nameko (*Pholiota nameko*) or a waxy cap (*Hygrophorus*) for the black trumpets. Lion's manes impart an interesting crabmeat-like texture.

Matsutake and Apple Salad with Lardons and Bacon Vinaigrette

Serves 4 as an appetizer

Apples are in season in Northern California from late fall until well into winter, perfectly timed to pair with matsutake, which usually come up in force around December. This hearty, satisfying seasonal salad lets both of these ingredients shine at their simple best. The musky cinnamon aroma of the matsutake works well with both the sweet and tart apples, the watercress gives a peppery bite, and the bacon provides smoky, earthy depth to tie things together.

SALAD

0.5 pound (225 g) slab bacon, skin removed, cut into ½-inch (1.25 cm) pieces

½ Honeycrisp apple or other sweet, crisp apple, cored, and cut into ⅛-inch (3 mm) slices

½ Granny Smith apple or other tart, crisp apple, peeled, cored, and cut into ¼-inch (6 mm) slices

1 small fennel bulb, halved, cored, and cut into ⅛-inch (3 mm) slices

1 bunch of rinsed watercress or arugula, roughly torn into pieces

1 large or 2 medium dense matsutake buttons, thinly sliced

BACON VINAIGRETTE

2 tablespoons apple cider vinegar

1 tablespoon dark brown sugar

1 teaspoon Dijon mustard

1 teaspoon soy sauce

1. To make the salad, heat a heavy-bottomed pan over medium heat. Add the bacon to the pan in a single layer. Reduce the heat to medium-low and cook the lardons to render their fat, stirring regularly, so they brown evenly on all sides. Line a plate with a clean kitchen towel or paper towel. When browned, transfer the lardons to the plate to drain, reserving the rendered fat separately. You should have at least ¼ cup (60 ml) of bacon fat; if you don't have enough, make up the difference with extra virgin olive oil.

2. To make the bacon vinaigrette, let the bacon fat cool just until it's still warm and liquidy, but not hot, or it won't emulsify well. Whisk together the vinegar, brown sugar, mustard, soy sauce, and a pinch of salt in a bowl until smooth and homogeneous. Slowly pour in the reserved bacon fat, whisking steadily to emulsify. Taste, and if desired, add salt, sugar, or a splash of vinegar to balance the flavors.

3. To continue making the salad, add the lardons, apples, and fennel to a large bowl, pour in the vinaigrette, and toss to combine. Add the watercress, matsutake, and a pinch of salt and very gently mix. Serve immediately.

Tip: *Slab bacon merely is bacon that hasn't been sliced yet. If you can't get slab bacon from your local butcher or market, just use the thickest cut bacon you can find. It's best to make the vinaigrette just before serving the salad because it's not a very stable emulsion. The bacon fat can coagulate if it cools too much, breaking the vinaigrette, but keeping the vinaigrette too warm will also break the emulsion.*

Mushroom Substitutions: There is no substitute for the matsutake here.

Prince Mushroom, Kale, and Buckwheat Salad

Serves 4 to 6

One morning, while working a breakfast shift, I added cranberries and almond extract to a batch of buckwheat pancakes. They were a hit, but the whole morning, every time I got the batter out to cook more, the almondy smell made me think of the prince mushrooms (*Agaricus augustus*) that I had been finding in prodigious quantities in the prior weeks. Those pancakes led me to make this simple yet brightly colored and complexly flavored salad that can be a complete meal on its own or with a cup of soup. The buckwheat plays very well with the savory, meaty mushrooms, while the cranberries complement the strong, sweet almond aroma. Besides their bright flash of color, the mustard flowers also add some spicy sharpness to the salad.

½ cup (85 g) toasted buckwheat groats (kasha)

1 bunch lacinato (dinosaur) kale, thick stems removed, cut or torn into small pieces

3 small, pristine fresh prince mushroom buttons, thinly sliced

¼ cup (33 g) dried cranberries

2 tablespoons almond, walnut, or extra virgin olive oil

½ cup (60 g) loosely packed mustard flowers or sliced radish

Lemon wedges

1. Bring 2 to 3 quarts (2–3 L) water to a boil in a large pot over high heat. Season generously with salt, then add the buckwheat. Simmer just until the buckwheat starts to soften, 5 to 10 minutes, beginning to check after about 4 minutes (buckwheat cooks very quickly, but is best slightly al dente), then drain immediately.

2. Add the buckwheat to a large bowl with the kale, mushrooms, and cranberries. Add a pinch of salt, a few grinds of black pepper, and the almond oil. Mix well and garnish with the mustard flowers. Serve with the lemon wedges so diners can add a bit of acidity as desired.

Tip: *If you don't have mustard flowers, sliced radish will provide a similar spicy punch.*

Mushroom Substitutions: Any almondy *Agaricus* will work well here.

Mixed Mushroom Terrine

Serves 8 as an appetizer

A slice of this terrine, garnished with the Candy Cap Mostarda (page 51) and served with a light, bright, crisp salad, is worthy of any dinner party. It features an array of contrasting crispy and soft textures and earthy, nutty, and sweet flavors from the mushrooms, nuts, and fruit. In my house, it also makes for a very popular snack or light lunch with some good mustard, crackers, and a side salad. This recipe fills a 3-cup (720 ml) mold or loaf pan. Individual portions freeze well for later use.

TERRINE SPICE BLEND

¼ teaspoon fennel seeds

¼ teaspoon whole coriander seeds

¼ teaspoon white or black peppercorns

3 whole cloves

¼ teaspoon cayenne pepper

¼ teaspoon freshly grated nutmeg

TERRINE

1 pound (450 g) fresh mushrooms for terrine base, cut into ½-inch (1.25 cm) pieces

2 tablespoons neutral oil

¼ cup (60 ml) Marsala or dry sherry

½ tablespoon unsalted butter

0.5 pound (225 g) crisp-textured fresh mushrooms, cut into ½-inch (1.25 cm) pieces

½ teaspoon salt

½ teaspoon freshly ground black pepper

¼ cup plus 2 tablespoons (50 g) hazelnuts, ground to a coarse powder

¼ cups (30 g) walnuts, ground to a coarse powder

1 teaspoon chia seeds, optional

¾ cup (180 ml) cream

3 eggs

⅓ cup (150 g) fresh or frozen huckleberries, wild blueberries, lingonberries, or rehydrated raisins, thawed if frozen

1. To make the terrine spice blend, toast the fennel seeds, coriander seeds, peppercorns, and cloves in a small, dry pan over medium heat, stirring often to prevent burning. When lightly toasted and very fragrant, 30 to 60 seconds, remove from then pan, and let cool completely. Once cool, grind finely using a small spice grinder or a mortar and pestle. Mix in the cayenne and nutmeg.

2. To make the terrine, wet or dry sauté the terrine base mushrooms (depending on their type and moisture level), following the instructions on page 31, using 1 tablespoon of the neutral oil. Cook until lightly and evenly browned, then add the Marsala and scrape up any browned bits. Turn off the heat and stir in the butter until melted and well incorporated. Season with salt and set aside to cool.

3. Wet or dry sauté (depending on their type and moisture level) the crisp-textured mushrooms, following the instructions on page 31, using the remaining neutral oil. Cook until lightly and evenly browned, then season with salt and set aside to cool.

Mushroom Substitutions: Almost any mushroom or mix of mushrooms will work in the terrine base, but choose ones that you really enjoy with stronger flavors, such as chanterelles, hedgehogs, or portabella. The mushrooms used for garnishing should be crisp textured, like butter boletes, *Russula*, *Lactarius*, or even crimini or button mushrooms.

continued ›

4. Once cooled, add all of the terrine base mushrooms to the bowl of a food processor with the terrine spice, the ½ teaspoon salt and ½ teaspoon black pepper, and process until mostly smooth. Add the hazelnuts, walnuts, and chia seeds and process just long enough to incorporate . Taste and adjust the salt and pepper if needed. Add the eggs and process until evenly incorporated. Finally, with the processor running, slowly pour in the cream, making sure the mixture is well emulsified. The mixture should be somewhat smooth, but a few chunks are OK.

5. Preheat the oven to 300°F (150°C). Line the bottom and at least two sides of a terrine mold or loaf pan with parchment paper, leaving enough extra parchment on each side to fold over the top of the terrine.

6. Add about half of the crisp-textured mushrooms to the terrine mixture and pulse to break them up, but not purée. Transfer to a large mixing bowl and mix in the rest of the crisp-textured mushrooms and the huckleberries. Add salt and/or pepper to taste.

7. Fill the mold with the mushroom mixture and fold over the extra parchment. Place a weight on top of the terrine. If you don't have a lid designed for this purpose, you can make a foil packet filled with dried beans, folding the packet to be the size of the mold or loaf pan. Bring a kettle of water to a boil.

8. Set the terrine into a roasting pan or baking dish with high sides and place in the oven. Pour in enough hot water to create a water bath that reaches about halfway up the side of the terrine pan. Bake for 1 to 2 hours, until the terrine is set and a toothpick inserted in the middle comes out clean.

9. Remove the terrine from the water bath, set the mold or loaf pan on a cooling rack, and let cool completely in the pan. Do not remove the weight from the top. Once cooled, refrigerate for at least 4 hours or preferably 12 to 24 hours before unmolding.

10. To unmold the terrine, remove the weight, then run a knife around any edges that weren't well-lined with parchment. Carefully invert the mold over a cutting board or serving platter and lift it away. Remove the parchment, slice, and serve. I prefer to serve the terrine slightly colder than room temperature.

Tip: *The parchment paper is essential to get the terrine out of the pan in one piece after cooking. It need not cover all sides of the pan, but you will want to cover at least the entire bottom and the two longer sides with the same sheet. Traditional meat-based versions often use bacon, ham, or other cured meats as a pan liner.*

Candy Cap and Roasted Beet Salad

Serves 4 to 6

I first made this recipe after a memorable day collecting candy caps with my good friend Wendy. Fresh candy caps have an earthy, umami flavor to go with their sweet aroma. When your drying trays are full, the fresh ones really shine in applications like this. Use any beets that look good. Red, gold, or beautifully striped Chioggia beets all work equally well. I love using the Candy Cap Whole Grain Mustard (page 43) to make the vinaigrette for this salad.

SALAD

1 pound (450 g) beets

1 to 2 tablespoons extra virgin olive oil

1 garlic clove, crushed

1 pound (450 g) fresh candy caps

1 tablespoon neutral oil

3 cups (115 g) loosely packed rinsed arugula

SHERRY VINAIGRETTE

1 shallot, minced

2 tablespoons sherry vinegar

1 tablespoon whole grain mustard

½ teaspoon honey

¼ cup (60 ml) extra virgin olive oil

1. To make the salad, preheat the oven to 350°F (180°C). Place the beets in the center of a large piece of aluminum foil, drizzle with the olive oil, and sprinkle with a generous pinch of salt and pepper. Add the garlic and fold the foil around the beets to create a sealed packet. Place the foil packet on a baking sheet and transfer to the oven once it is hot. Roast for 30 to 90 minutes, depending on the size of the beets, until the skin can be easily peeled. Use a towel to check to avoid burning yourself. Once cooled enough to handle, peel and cut the beets into 1-inch (2.5 cm) pieces. (The beets can be roasted in advance and stored in the fridge for up to 4 days.)

2. To make the sherry vinaigrette, whisk together the shallot, vinegar, mustard, and honey. Slowly add the olive oil and whisk until emulsified. Season with salt.

3. To continue making the salad, dry sauté the candy caps, following the instructions on page 31, using the neutral oil. Season with salt.

4. While still warm, toss the mushrooms with the beets, arugula, a pinch of salt, and the vinaigrette. Mix thoroughly and serve.

Mushroom Substitutions: Almost any mushrooms will make for a delicious salad, but only candy caps will give it the intended maple flavor.

Chicken Liver and Porcini Mousse

Makes about 2 cups (450 g)

Many mushrooms have an intense and slightly gamy umami flavor, not too far from that of chicken livers. The similarities can make the two ingredients good partners, but they can also cause the mushrooms to disappear a little bit in the mix. I prefer dried mushrooms here because they tend to have a stronger flavor and aroma than fresh, which helps them stand out. This recipe also uses a pretty large proportion of mushrooms to livers, and leaves half of the mushrooms in large, chunky pieces to help them remain noticeable. Try this smooth, rich, spreadable pâté with Candy Cap Mostarda (page 51) or Matsutake-Fig Preserve (page 46) to cut through the intense richness. The mousse will keep for about a week stored in a covered container in the fridge.

1.5 pounds (675 g) chicken livers

2 shallots, thinly sliced

¼ cup plus 2 tablespoons (90 ml) dry sherry

3 garlic cloves, roughly chopped

Pinch of fresh thyme leaves

0.5 ounce (14 g) dried porcini

1½ cups (360 ml) warm water

1 teaspoon porcini powder

1 tablespoon neutral oil

2 tablespoons cold unsalted butter, cut into small pieces

1 to 2 tablespoons fresh grated truffles, preferably Périgord, optional

1. Use a sharp knife to cut away any large veins, pieces of fat, and connective tissue from the chicken livers. Toss the livers with the shallots, 3 tablespoons of the sherry, garlic, thyme, and a couple grinds of fresh black pepper in a large bowl. Cover and leave in the fridge to marinate for at least 4 hours or up to 24 hours.

2. When ready to make the mousse, cover the dried porcini with the warm water. Set aside until needed, but for at least 10 minutes to soften the mushrooms. When ready to cook the other ingredients, strain and reserve the liquid separately.

3. Separate the livers from the shallots and garlic. Add the porcini powder to the livers and season with salt and pepper.

4. Heat a heavy-bottomed pan over medium-low heat. Add the neutral oil, then add the shallots and garlic and sauté, stirring often, until they are soft but not browned, 2 to 3 minutes. Turn up the heat to medium-high and add the livers and soaked porcini. Cook, stirring, until the livers are barely cooked through, about 5 minutes. Add the remaining sherry and scrape up any browned bits. When the liquid has reduced completely, 2 to 3 minutes, transfer the contents of the pan to a bowl and set aside to cool.

5. Add the reserved mushroom soaking liquid to the empty pan. Simmer over medium heat to reduce the liquid until only 1 to 2 tablespoons remain, 10 to 15 minutes. Pour it over the cooked liver mix.

6. Once the mix has cooled enough to handle, remove the porcini, cut them into ⅛-inch (3 mm) pieces, and set aside.

7. Add the chicken liver mixture to a food processor or blender with a tamper and process until very smooth, periodically scraping down the sides of the bowl or using the tamper to push everything toward the blades. Add the butter a few pieces at a time and process until fully incorporated. Adjust the seasoning to taste. Transfer to a serving dish and stir in the reserved porcini and truffles, if using.

Mushroom Substitutions: Almost any dried mushrooms will work here.

Salted Mushroom Hummus

Makes about ¾ cup (160 g)

This hummus has fooled a lot of my friends over the years. Most people I have served it to believed it to be a "standard" hummus made from chickpeas until told otherwise. A properly prepared hummus will balance the lemon and tahini, while the garlic provides a spicy punch, and the olive oil smooths things out; you can adjust the amounts of all to your taste. I deliberately use mild mushrooms that contribute more bulk than flavor. You can experiment with more flavorful mushrooms. Be sure to taste the hummus before seasoning it; depending on how well you desalted the mushrooms, you might not need to add any salt.

1 cup (170 g) Salt-Preserved Mushrooms (page 52)

1 tablespoon plus 1½ teaspoons tahini

Juice of ½ lemon

2 large garlic cloves, crushed

¼ cup (60 ml) extra virgin olive oil

1. Rinse the mushrooms to remove visible salt, then cover them in water and soak for at least 8 hours, changing the water every few hours, then drain well.

2. Process the mushrooms, tahini, lemon juice, and garlic using a small food processor or immersion blender until smooth.

3. Once smooth, continue processing while slowly pouring in the extra virgin olive oil until the oil is evenly incorporated. Add salt to taste. Serve immediately, or store in the fridge for up to 4 days.

Mushroom Substitutions: In lieu of salted mushrooms, try using boiled, drained, and cooled white button mushrooms, any mild *Lactarius* or *Russula*, lobsters, or your favorite *Agaricus* or *Amanita*.

Mushroomy Muhammara

Makes about 3½ cups (780 g)

Originally from Syria, muhammara is a dip made up of roasted peppers, walnuts, pomegranate molasses, and spices. It is not as well known in the West as dips like hummus or baba ghanoush, but I really think it should be. Typically, muhammara does not contain mushrooms, but they add a wonderful earthy depth that blends in seamlessly with the traditional ingredients. I sometimes make a meal of just this dip with good pita and some crudités to scoop it up. Sumac is a Middle Eastern spice that adds a fruity tang. Aleppo pepper is a mild type of chile flake. Pomegranate molasses can be found at Middle Eastern or other specialty markets; there is no substitute for it in this dish.

1 cup (120 g) walnuts

1 pound (450 g) crimini mushrooms, halved

1 tablespoon neutral oil

3 red bell peppers

2 tablespoons pomegranate molasses

1 to 2 teaspoons Aleppo pepper or red pepper flakes

1 teaspoon ground sumac

¼ cup (60 ml) extra virgin olive oil

Pita

1. Heat the oven to 325°F (160°C). Spread the walnuts on a rimmed baking sheet and bake, stirring every few minutes to ensure they brown evenly without burning, until lightly toasted, about 10 minutes.

2. Toss the mushrooms in the neutral oil and a generous pinch of salt, spread in a single layer on a rimmed baking sheet, and oven roast at 375°F (190°C), following the instructions on page 32. When cooked, set aside with any liquid released during roasting.

3. Char the whole peppers under a broiler or grill over high heat, rotating them as they blister and char, until the skin is charred all over, 3 to 5 minutes. Transfer to a bowl and cover with plastic wrap to steam while they cool down. Once cool enough to handle, remove the skin and seeds, reserving the flesh. Holding the peppers under gently running cold water often makes peeling the skin easier.

4. Add the walnuts, mushrooms, peppers, pomegranate molasses, Aleppo pepper, and sumac to a food processor and process until well combined. Adjust the salt and other spices to taste. With the food processor running, slowly pour in the olive oil, and continue processing until thoroughly incorporated. Serve with pita for dipping.

Tip: *Muhammara usually contains bread crumbs, but I find them unnecessary; I like my muhammara a little coarse and not perfectly emulsified. If you want yours to be smooth and very well emulsified, you can add a couple tablespoons of bread crumbs while blending. They will help bind the oil with the other ingredients.*

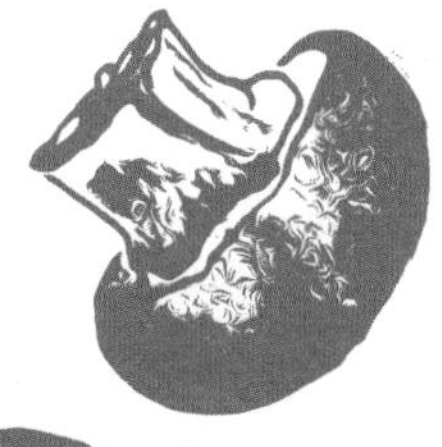

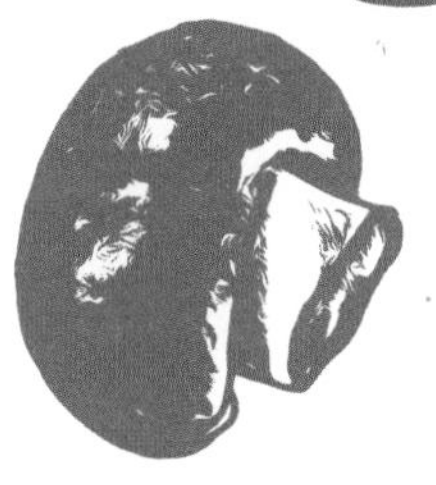

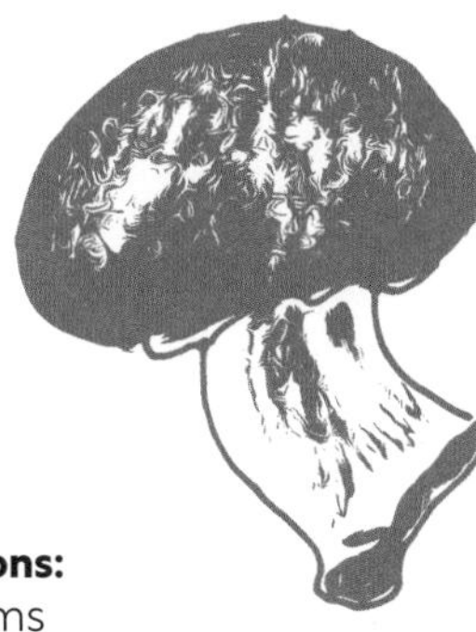

Mushroom Substitutions: Almost any mushrooms will work here.

Mushroom Ceviche

Serves 4

When I was just a green line cook, I learned a ton from a Peruvian colleague, Ciano, who had been in the business for decades. One of the things he taught me was the "right way" to make ceviche, something he and I agree the Peruvians do better and more simply than anyone else. This mushroom ceviche recipe follows the technique Ciano taught me, except I boil the mushrooms first. (In classic ceviche, the acid "cooks" the seafood without any need for heat, but since mushrooms get their structure from chitin (see page 33), boiling them will improve their texture and their ability to absorb the marinade.) Pay attention to the details—the order and timing of adding each ingredient is the key to a dish that wows.

1 pound (450 g) coccora, cut into ¼-inch (6 mm) slices

1 sweet potato, peeled and cut into ½-inch (1.25 cm) pieces

¼ small red onion, thinly sliced

Juice of 5 limes or 7 key limes

1 serrano chile, including its ribs and seeds, finely chopped

5 or 6 fresh cilantro sprigs (about 25 leaves)

1. Bring a large pot of water to a boil over high heat and salt generously. Add the coccora and boil for 5 minutes to cook through, then drain and dry them well. Store covered in the fridge until ready to use, up to 3 days.

2. Place the sweet potato in a saucepan, cover with cold water, and add a generous pinch of salt. Bring to a boil over high heat, then reduce to medium-low to simmer. Simmer for 3 to 5 minutes, until the sweet potatoes are tender, then drain, let cool completely, and store in the fridge until ready to use. Do not overcook. The pieces should hold their shape and not fall apart when handled.

3. Place the onion in a small container and cover with ice water (this removes some of the harshness from their flavor and keeps them nice and crisp). Store in the fridge until ready to use.

4. About 30 minutes before serving, mix the mushrooms with the lime juice, chile, and a generous pinch of salt. Store in the fridge until ready to serve.

5. When ready to serve, stack the cilantro leaves neatly in piles of 4 or 5 leaves and slice as thinly as possible. You want paper-thin ribbons. Drain the red onion well, then add to the mushroom mixture with the cilantro. Adjust the seasoning to taste.

6. To serve, divide the sweet potato pieces between individual plates and neatly spoon the mushroom ceviche and any extra marinating liquid on top.

Tip: *Peruvians lovingly call the marinating liquid "leche de tigre" (tiger's milk), and diners pick up their dishes to drink down all of the spicy, sour leche when the ceviche is gone. I highly recommend doing the same.*

Mushroom Substitutions: Oysters, beech (shimeji), pioppini (*Cyclocybe aegerita*), nameko, lobsters, and mild *Russula*, especially shrimp, all work wonderfully here. Baby shiitake and even lion's mane also work well, along with any firm-textured, edible *Amanita*, such as Caesar's or detoxified fly agaric (*A. muscaria*; see page 34).

5

Appetizers and Sides

In Western North America, morels often come up in huge numbers in areas that burned in a forest fire the previous year, making drives down old logging roads a big part of morel hunting. In the best conditions, these narrow, curvy, steep dirt roads are full of big divots, potholes, and trenches that take some creativity to navigate safely. In less-than-ideal conditions, driving these roads becomes a white-knuckle adventure.

Rosa and I once drove out to a remote mountain area where there had been a massive fire in the summer. The edge of the main burn began about twenty miles off the freeway—the last ten of which were down dirt roads. Driving slowly up one of these roads, we found a spot that looked like exactly the kind of habitat morels like, as it was still wet and it had clearly been a cooler part of the burn, with live trees and green vegetation. Some exploring revealed three beautiful blonde morels—but that was all. Even though these were a different type than the burn morels we were looking for, we figured we must be getting close, so we headed farther up the road.

Patches of snow started appearing as we climbed higher. We drove through a couple of small patches without incident before coming to an intimidating expanse of snow-covered road. To go farther, we would first have to drive across a hundred feet of snow, uphill to a small crest, from where the last seventy-five feet gently sloped down. There were tire tracks across the snow, but also a couple of clear spots where wheels had spun and a vehicle had gotten stuck. We could either press on in my Honda, and risk getting stuck or sliding out of control in the hope of finding more morels on the other side, or turn back and drive the twenty-plus slow miles back to the freeway with only three morels to show for our efforts. The choice seemed obvious. So, we got back in the car, crossed our fingers, and I stepped on the gas. We were almost at the top of the snow field when the car began losing traction and momentum. Uh-oh.

My wheels were spinning uselessly as we stopped right before the crest, in the same exact place as some prior car. My back wheel was embedded in a muddy pit in the snow. We tried putting branches under the wheel, tried rocking the car, but every attempt made our predicament worse. We had lots of food and water, and plenty of stuff to keep us warm—but unless help came along, we would have to make camp and wait a day or two for the warm weather to melt the snow enough to free us.

Just as we began resigning ourselves to that reality, two hikers came by, one with a large shovel. They looked at my Honda stuck in the snow, then at me standing there in shorts and sandals, then at the stoic Rosa. I don't believe their assessments of me were particularly flattering, but they helped us get unstuck. Eventually, Rosa managed to pop the car into gear while the rest of us pushed, and got up on top of the snow again. She put it in park and left me to deal with the last leg of the drive.

With no way to turn around, I went forward, fighting to keep the car pointed in the right direction, as I slid down the slope. I didn't dare to slow down this time, fearing sliding out of control into a tree or boulder less than getting stuck again. Thankfully, after a few agonizing seconds, I felt the relief of wheels biting into hard dirt.

After parking safely on solid, dry ground, I got out and laughed, cheered, laughed some more, and breathed an enormous sigh of relief. I stood there looking at the mud coating the entire front of my body, blood dripping from my knee, and my now scabbed-over knuckles, and vowed to never again go gallivanting around in the wilderness in sandals and shorts. (Rosa thinks there is another lesson I missed here.)

And despite all the trouble we'd gone to, we found no more mushrooms that trip. We got back late that evening after a twelve-hour-day, exhausted, with a haul of three measly morels—and were never so relieved and happy to be home after a hunt.

There's usually a lot less risk than in this story, but my morel hunting always comes with a side of adventure. I think it makes the morels taste better. While many of the recipes in this chapter came out of other silly escapades, you need only risk some dirty dishes to try them out.

Driving down a snowy logging road while out hunting morels

Morels and Favas

Serves 4

To mushroom hunters, nothing says spring has arrived more than the sprouting of morels, and nothing at the farmers market says spring more clearly than the first appearance of fava beans. I enjoy no springtime dish as much as simply cooked morels with favas. My chef instructor taught me this technique for cooking morels way back in culinary school, and to this day, I almost always cook them like this, whether I add any vegetables to them or not. If you don't want to use favas, skip Steps 3 and 4 and serve the morels by themselves. You can also substitute one or more of almost any spring vegetable. Peas, asparagus, artichokes, broccoli, spring onions, fiddleheads, and ramps all play well with the morels here. Even roasted green chiles and corn are great.

¼ cup (60 g) unsalted butter plus 1 tablespoon reserved for finishing, optional

1 pound (450 g) fresh morels, left whole or cut to pieces

½ cup (75 g) shelled, blanched, and peeled fava beans

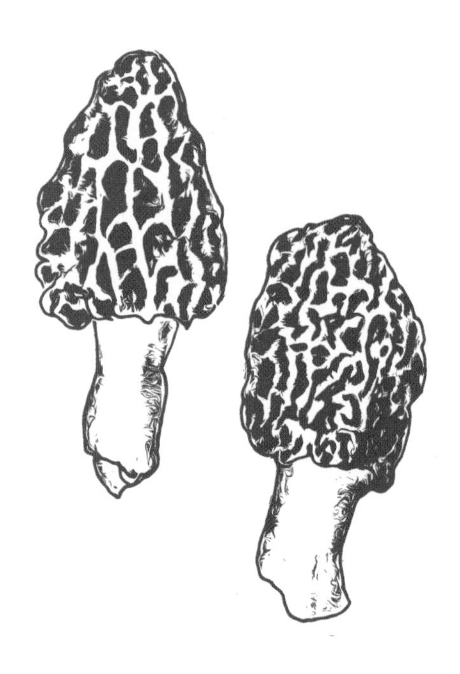

Mushroom Substitutions: Thimble caps (*Verpa* spp.) work equally well.

1. Heat a heavy-bottomed pan over medium heat. Add ¼ cup (60 g) of the butter and about 3 tablespoons water, continually swirling the pan gently to emulsify the water with the butter as it melts. Once it looks like a smooth butter sauce, add the morels to the pan. Stir or swirl the pan regularly to keep the morels cooking and the sauce emulsified. The mixture should be very liquid, with the mushrooms swimming in a loose sauce. If it seems like the pan is drying out, add a couple more tablespoons of water and stir or swirl to mix with the butter and mushrooms. (You can not overcook the mushrooms as long as there is a little water in the pan. Always feel free to add a bit more water and keep them cooking longer.)

2. After at least 10 minutes of cooking, cover and simmer for 4 minutes, swirling or stirring occasionally, to ensure the morels are cooked through. Continue stirring or swirling regularly for 1 more minute, then season with salt to taste.

3. Stir in the fava beans and add another 1 or 2 tablespoons water, if the pan is getting dry, to give the vegetables just enough time to warm or cook through, as needed.

4. The emulsion will likely have broken during simmering; to re-emulsify the sauce, add the reserved 1 tablespoon of butter, if using, after removing the pan from the heat. Stir or swirl the pan until the butter is melted and incorporated. This should bring the emulsion back. Serve immediately.

Tip: *Undercooked or uncooked morels will make most people sick. If you aren't sure if the mushrooms are cooked enough, err on the side of cooking them a couple minutes more. As long as there is liquid in the pan, you can't overcook them. I generally serve morels saucy, just like this. If you want an even saucier product, such as for dressing pasta, you can stir in a bit of cream until emulsified. Adjust the seasoning as needed and serve hot.*

Spinach and Mushroom Gratin

Serves 6 to 8

I first ate this gratin at the quaint and charming Hotel Victor in the tiny medieval village of Rialp, in the Catalan Pyrenees, where Rosa was born. I instantly fell in love with it, and consequently had to work out a recipe for use at home. At the hotel, the dish featured *Hygrophorus marzuolus* (*marçot* or *marçol* mushrooms, in Catalan). I really love it as a hearty side dish, but it also makes a great lunch or light dinner. I like to prepare this in a *cazuela*, a traditional shallow ceramic pan used in Spain and much of Latin America for both cooking and serving, but you can just as easily start this in a large pan and then transfer to your favorite baking dish to bake and serve.

1 pound (450 g) chanterelles

1 tablespoon neutral oil

3 tablespoons unsalted butter

1 yellow onion, diced

1 garlic clove, minced

2 tablespoons all-purpose flour

2 cups (480 ml) whole milk

Freshly grated nutmeg

¼ cup (25 g) finely grated Parmesan, or other flavorful, hard, aged cheese

2 pounds (900 g) frozen spinach, thawed

1. Wet or dry sauté the chanterelles (depending on their freshness and moisture level), following the instructions on page 31, using the neutral oil. Cook until the mushrooms are lightly browned, then season with salt and set aside.

2. Heat a cazuela or large, heavy-bottomed pan over medium-low heat. Add the butter, then, when melted, add the onion, garlic, and a pinch of salt. Cook, stirring regularly, until the onion is very soft and translucent but not browned, about 7 minutes.

3. Preheat the oven to 375°F (190°C). Stir the flour into the onions and garlic and cook, stirring continuously, for about 2 minutes, to lightly toast the flour. Whisk in the milk a little bit at a time, making sure to incorporate it fully and stir out any lumps between each addition. Add black pepper and nutmeg to taste, and adjust the heat to medium to bring up to a simmer for 1 to 2 minutes, until thickened. If the sauce is thicker than a loose pancake batter, stir in a little more milk to loosen. Remove from the heat and stir in 2 tablespoons of the Parmesan until it melts into the sauce.

4. Stir the cooked mushrooms and spinach into the sauce and mix thoroughly to coat evenly. If using a pan, transfer the mixture to a wide, oven-safe baking dish. Sprinkle the remaining Parmesan evenly over the surface. Transfer to the oven and bake until the top has lightly browned, 20 to 30 minutes. Serve hot, fresh from the oven.

Tip: *You can prepare the gratin up to a day in advance of baking. Store the ready-to-bake gratin covered in the fridge and bake when you are ready to serve it.*

Mushroom Substitutions: I like to use chanterelles because of how well they complement a creamy sauce, but you can use almost any mushrooms or combination of mushrooms that you have on hand.

Mushroom and Scallion Pancakes

Serves 4 to 6

Scallion pancakes appear on seemingly every Chinese restaurant menu in the US, and various versions of this treat have been popular in several regions of China for hundreds of years. They are made from a rather unique dough using only flour and boiling water, the heat of the water partially cooking the flour. Though many versions exist, all tend to have a generous amount of scallions in the filling, and have a crispy outside layer. Some regions prefer thicker, chewier pancakes, and some add different spices, herbs, and even meats to the filling. Mushrooms add an almost meaty depth. I recommend weighing the flour to ensure the proper dough consistency.

2¼ cups (280 g) all-purpose flour

1 teaspoon porcini powder

½ cup plus 2 tablespoons (150 ml) boiling water

10 ounces (280 g) portabella mushrooms, cut into 1-inch (2.5 cm) pieces

3 tablespoons neutral oil

¼ cup (60 ml) dry sherry or Shaoxing wine

Sesame oil

1 large bunch scallions, green parts only, thinly sliced

Coarse salt

Chinese black vinegar

1. Mix the flour and porcini powder together in a heat-safe mixing bowl. Pour in the boiling water while mixing with chopsticks or a fork. When the dough starts to come together, turn it onto a floured surface and knead until it comes together into a very smooth, homogeneous dough, 4 to 5 minutes. You can add a few drops more water if needed to incorporate all of the flour, but the dough should not feel wet or sticky to the touch. Form into a ball, cover with plastic wrap, and let rest at room temperature for at least 30 minutes to cool and allow the gluten to relax.

2. Wet or dry sauté the portabella mushrooms (depending on their freshness and moisture level), following the instructions on page 31. Season lightly with salt, then add the sherry and scrape up any browned bits from the bottom of the pan. Purée to a paste with an immersion blender. Set aside to cool completely.

3. After the dough has rested, unwrap it and cut into 3 equal-size pieces. Take 1 piece and use a rolling pin to roll it out on a lightly floured surface into a very thin rectangular sheet, about 1⁄16-inch (1.5 mm) thick, dusting the rolling pin and surface with extra flour as needed to prevent sticking.

4. Brush a very thin layer of sesame oil over the surface of the dough. Spread one third of the mushroom purée over the dough in a single layer, leaving about ¼-inch (6 mm) margin around the perimeter. Sprinkle one third of the scallions on top, then a bit of the coarse salt. Starting from one edge, roll the sheet into a long, tight cylinder. Roll that cylinder into a tight spiral, tucking the end underneath. Set aside to rest. Repeat the rolling, filling, and rolling up into spirals with the remaining pieces of dough and the remaining filling.

5. One at a time, roll out the dough spirals into circles about ¼-inch (6 mm) thick. (This thickness will yield slightly chewy pancakes; for crispier pancakes, roll them a little thinner.) Be as gentle and cautious as possible when rolling them out to keep the dough from tearing a lot. (If they do tear a little, don't worry; they will still hold together, but they become messier to handle.) The pancakes are now ready to be fried; alternatively, at this stage, they can be stored in a plastic bag between layers of parchment paper and frozen for up to 3 weeks.

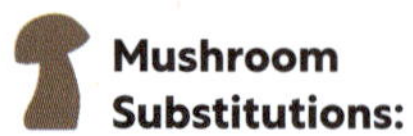

Mushroom Substitutions: Almost any mushrooms will work here. Use strong-flavored mushrooms, such as shiitake, mature porcini, slippery jacks, or hedgehogs, for maximum impact.

6. Heat a heavy-bottomed pan over medium-low heat. Add the remaining neutral oil. Carefully add 1 pancake and fry until golden brown, 3 to 4 minutes per side, being careful not to let it burn. Line a cooling rack or plate with a clean kitchen towel or paper towel. Transfer the pancakes to the cooling rack or plate to drain. Repeat with the other 2 pancakes. Cut each pancake into wedges and serve while hot with a bowl of black vinegar for dipping.

Black Trumpet–Potato Gratin

Serves 12

The black trumpet purée unevenly bleeding throughout the middle layer of this gratin gives it a beautiful, marbled look, while helping the mushrooms' deep, earthy flavor to penetrate every nook and cranny. Fresh or dried black trumpets work equally well here. If using dried, cook the strained soaking liquid down in the pan before puréeing. You will need a 7-by-10-inch (18 by 25 cm) baking dish for this recipe.

2 tablespoons neutral oil

2 large onions, cut into thin strips

2 tablespoons unsalted butter, plus extra for greasing

1 pound (450 g) fresh black trumpet mushrooms

2 pounds (900 g) russet potatoes, peeled and cut into ⅛-inch (3 mm) slices, preferably on a mandoline

1½ cups (170 g) shredded mozzarella

¼ cup (30 g) grated Parmesan

½ cup (120 ml) heavy cream

Mushroom Substitutions: Almost any mushrooms will work here, but the gratin's marbled appearance won't be as stunningly pronounced without the black trumpets.

1. Heat a large, heavy-bottomed pan over medium heat. Add 1 tablespoon of neutral oil, then add the onions. Sauté the onions, stirring regularly, until soft, 5 to 7 minutes. Reduce the heat to medium-low, add 1 tablespoon of the butter, and continue cooking until the onions caramelize to a medium brown color, 15 to 20 minutes. Season with salt, transfer to a large bowl, and set aside.

2. Dry sauté the black trumpets in the empty pan, following the instructions on page 31, using the remaining oil. Increase the heat to medium, season with salt, then add ½ cup (120 ml) water and scrape any browned bits from the bottom of the pan. Simmer until only about ¼ cup (60 ml) of liquid remains, 3 to 5 minutes, then remove from the heat. Transfer to a blender and purée until smooth, adding the remaining butter while blending. Add salt to taste.

3. Butter an oven-safe casserole dish or grease with nonstick cooking spray. Arrange one third of the potatoes in a single overlapping layer across the bottom of the dish. Season with salt and pepper. Spread half of the onions in a thin layer across the potatoes. Spread half of the black trumpet purée in a thin layer across that. Spread ½ cup (56 g) of the mozzarella in a thin layer over the surface. Repeat the layering with the potatoes, salt and pepper, onions, trumpet purée, and mozzarella. Finish with a third layer of potatoes, topped with the remaining mozzarella. Top with the Parmesan. Carefully pour the cream along the edge of the gratin without disturbing the layers. Cover the gratin with a piece of parchment paper, and place a weight on top to press the gratin flat. Let rest in the fridge for at least 30 minutes or up to 24 hours.

4. Preheat the oven to 325°F (160°C). Remove the weight and parchment from the baking dish and cover with foil. Once the oven is hot, bake for 60 to 90 minutes, until soft all the way through when probed with a paring knife or cake tester. Remove the foil and continue cooking uncovered for 10 minutes longer to lightly brown the cheese on top. Serve hot.

Tip: *If you want to remove the gratin from the baking dish after cooking to more easily cut clean portions, line the dish with parchment paper before layering the ingredients inside. After cooking, the gratin can be cooled overnight in the fridge and then inverted onto a cutting board. If intending to remove the gratin from the pan, add the mozzarella in two ¾-cup (84 g) additions, topping the final layer of potatoes with the Parmesan only.*

Catalan Beans and Mushrooms (Mongetes amb Bolets)

Serves 12

This hearty side really is not much more than beans and mushrooms. It's a classic Catalan dish for late autumn or early winter, when the wild mushroom season is in full swing. It goes great alongside almost any meat, and I often use it as a vegetarian main dish, served with good crusty bread. Catalans typically use white beans similar to those called cannellini beans in the US. Versions using chickpeas are also common. You can use any type of beans you like; just remember to soak them overnight before cooking. The recipe is extremely easy, but any favorite mushrooms will give you a big-flavored, satisfying dish. Most of the flavor comes from the mushrooms cooked with garlic and parsley.

1 pound (450 g) dried cannellini beans

1 onion, peeled and left whole

2 bay leaves

6 garlic cloves, 4 minced, 2 left whole

0.5 ounce (14 g) dried wild mushrooms such as porcini, yellow foots, or lobsters

2 tablespoons toasted pine nuts

2 pounds (900 g) saffron milk caps, left whole if small or roughly chopped if large

3 tablespoons extra virgin olive oil, plus extra for garnishing

2 to 3 tablespoons chopped fresh parsley, plus extra for garnishing

Mushroom Substitutions: Almost any mushrooms will work here. I love this recipe with saffron or bleeding milk caps (*Lactarius deliciosus* grp.), but you can use anything you like. Any favorite dried mushrooms can be substituted.

1. Add the dried beans to a large pot and cover with a generous amount of cold water. Leave covered at room temperature overnight. Drain the beans, give them a quick rinse, then cover them again with cold water. Add the onion, bay leaves, and the 2 whole garlic cloves. Bring to a boil over high heat, then reduce the heat to medium-low to simmer. Cook for about 90 minutes, periodically skimming off and discarding the scummy foam that rises to the top, until the beans are tender. Remove from the heat and season the liquid with a generous pinch of salt.

2. Add the dried mushrooms to a bowl. Measure out 1 cup (240 ml) of the bean cooking liquid and pour it over the dried mushrooms. Set aside to soak until needed.

3. Remove the boiled onion from the beans and add it to a blender with the pine nuts and 1 cup (240 ml) of the bean cooking liquid. Purée until smooth.

4. Heat a large, heavy-bottomed pot over medium-high heat. Wet sauté the saffron milk caps in batches, following the instructions on page 31, using 1 tablespoon of extra virgin olive oil per batch, until they are lightly browned. Remove each batch from the pan as it finishes cooking and set aside.

5. When the last batch of mushrooms is browned, still over medium-low heat, add all of the fresh mushrooms back to the pan. Strain the reconstituted dried mushrooms, reserving the liquid separately, and add them to the pan with the minced garlic, parsley, and the remaining extra virgin olive oil. Sauté for 2 minutes, stirring regularly to cook the garlic and parsley, then stir in the puréed onion. Add the reserved mushroom soaking liquid. Bring the sauce up to a simmer over medium-high heat, stirring occasionally, then stir in the cooked beans, after straining and reserving their liquid. Bring the contents of the pan back up to a simmer, then cook for about 2 more minutes, adding a little of the bean cooking liquid if the pan starts to dry out. And adjust the seasoning to taste.

6. Remove from the heat, stir in a generous amount of extra virgin olive oil, and serve immediately. Serve in bowls, with more extra virgin olive oil and chopped parsley for garnishing.

Tip: *The beans will continue to absorb liquid as they sit. If you have leftovers, stir in a bit more reserved bean cooking liquid before reheating them.*

Matsutake Chawanmushi

Serves 4 to 8

This take on a classic Japanese steamed custard makes a hip, sophisticated course on an upscale dinner party menu, or a light, satisfying meal served on its own. The matsutakes' aroma, flavor, and texture sing with every bite. The custard is usually made from a simple dashi mixed with eggs and then steamed until it sets. The matsutake and carrot pieces in the custard provide an interesting textural contrast with the impossibly silky base. Garnishing with herbs, citrus zest, and raw matsutake balances the smooth, rich flavor of the custard. For larger servings, use 4 coffee mug as molds. For smaller servings appropriate for dinner party appetizers, 8 smaller espresso cups work well.

MATSUTAKE CHAWANMUSHI

- 1 carrot, peeled and cut into ¼-inch (6 mm) slices
- 1 fresh matsutake, thinly sliced
- 3 eggs
- 1 tablespoon mirin
- 1 teaspoon soy sauce

MATSUTAKE DASHI

- 2 cups (480 ml) cold water
- One 4-inch (10 cm) piece kombu
- 1 small matsutake, cut or torn into pieces (use an older, less pretty, or previously frozen matsutake)
- 1 tablespoon bonito flakes

GARNISH

- Extra slices of fresh matsutake
- Zest of 1 yuzu, lemon, or lime
- Very thinly sliced scallions

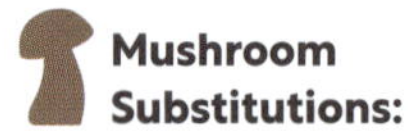

Mushroom Substitutions: There is no substitute for the matsutake here; this dish is all about their special aroma.

1. To make the matsutake chawanmushi, bring a saucepan of salted water to a boil over high heat. Add the carrot slices and boil for about 3 minutes, until just beginning to soften. Strain and let the carrots cool completely.

2. To make the matsutake dashi, add the cold water, kombu, and matsutake to a saucepan and soak for at least 30 minutes. Bring to a boil over medium-high heat, then immediately remove from the heat and discard the kombu. Strain and reserve the mushrooms, and add the bonito to the dashi. Let sit, uncovered, for about 1 minute, then strain out the bonito flakes. Stir the reserved matsutake back into the broth.

3. To continue making the matsutake chawanmushi, place a couple of carrot and matsutake slices in the bottom of each chawanmushi dish, coffee mug, or espresso cup.

4. Beat the eggs thoroughly, then whisk in the mirin, soy, and dashi. Season with salt, then divide the mixture between the molds.

5. Cover each cup with a tightly fitting lid or plastic wrap. Set up a large steamer either by placing a steamer basket inside of a large pot, or placing a large, perforated pan on top of another pan of boiling water. The steaming basket should sit above the surface of the boiling water. Set over medium heat, covered, and when ready, add the covered cups. Steam for about 13 minutes, or until the custard is entirely set.

6. Remove the cups from the steamer and uncover them, then top the custard with neatly fanned slices of matsutake garnish, the yuzu zest, and scallions. Serve immediately, while still hot.

Tip: *Kombu, a type of dried seaweed, and bonito flakes, shavings from a special dried and smoked fish, combine to make flavor bases for all kinds of traditional Japanese dishes. They can both be found in good Asian markets or ordered online, and keep well in the pantry for years.*

Rapini with Bacon and Butter Boletes

Serves 4 to 6

The crisp texture of the butter boletes takes center stage here, while their mild flavor takes a back seat to the richness of the bacon and pleasant bitterness of the rapini. This side dish is hearty enough to be a light meal, especially on top of your favorite grain.

1 bunch (about 1 pound/450 g) rapini

0.5 pound (225 g) slab bacon, skin removed, cut into ½-inch (1.25 cm) pieces

1 pound (450 g) butter boletes, cut into ½-inch (1.25 cm) pieces

2 garlic cloves, minced

Red pepper flakes

¼ cup (25 g) sliced almonds, toasted

Lemon wedges, optional

1. Bring a large pot of salted water to a boil over high heat. Add the rapini and cook just until it begins to soften, about 2 minutes. Using a slotted spoon, immediately transfer the rapini to a large bowl of ice water to stop the cooking. Drain well, then chop into 1-inch (2.5 cm) lengths and set aside.

2. Heat a large, heavy-bottomed pan over medium-low heat. Add the bacon. Stir regularly until the lardons are evenly browned, 7 to 10 minutes. Line a plate with a clean kitchen towel or paper towel. Transfer the bacon to the plate to drain, leaving just enough bacon fat in the pan to generously coat the bottom and reserving any extra fat separately.

3. Add the butter boletes to the pan and sauté in the bacon fat until lightly browned on all sides, 7 to 10 minutes. Season with salt, then transfer to a bowl and set aside.

4. Increase the heat to medium-high and, if the pan seems dry, add some of the reserved bacon fat. Add the garlic and red pepper flakes to the empty pan. Let the garlic sizzle for about 5 seconds, then stir in the rapini. Season with salt and cook for another 3 minutes, stirring regularly, until the rapini is heated through. Stir in the bacon and butter boletes and continue cooking until heated through, another 2 minutes. Adjust the seasoning, then serve topped with the toasted almonds and the lemon wedges on the side, if using.

Tip: *Slab bacon is simply bacon that has not been cut into slices. If you can't find slab bacon, just substitute the thickest sliced bacon you can find.*

Mushroom Substitution: Almost any mushroom will work here. Firm, dense, mild *Russula*, like *R. brevipes* or the charcoal burner (*R. cyanoxantha*), make an excellent substitute for the often scarce butter boletes, but you can use anything you like.

Chanterelle Croquetas with Rhubarb Sauce

Makes about 30 croquetas

A *croqueta* is a small, fried fritter that is delicate, creamy, and light on the inside, crispy on the outside, and filled with almost anything. Throughout Spain, croquetas show up on every tapas menu. Typical fillings include Spanish ham, chorizo, salt cod, and mushrooms—porcini are particularly popular. This traditional recipe uses an interesting technique, building an extra-thick béchamel sauce around the chanterelle filling. When cooled, the sauce becomes thick enough to portion, bread, and fry. I like to serve these croquetas with a pleasantly tart and refreshing rhubarb sauce. The sauce is not at all traditional, but it balances the richness of the croquetas beautifully.

RHUBARB SAUCE

2 rhubarb stalks (about 0.5 pound/225 g), thinly sliced crosswise

1 tablespoon granulated sugar

CROQUETAS

1 pound (450 g) chanterelles, cut into ½-inch (1.25 cm) pieces

1 tablespoon neutral oil

¾ cup (180 ml) sherry, Marsala, or dry white wine

3 tablespoons unsalted butter

1 yellow onion, minced

1½ cup (185 g) all-purpose flour

3 cups (720 ml) milk

Freshly grated nutmeg

4 to 5 fresh thyme sprigs, leaves only

½ cup (60 g) hazelnuts or almonds, toasted and roughly chopped, optional

2 cups (230 g) bread crumbs

2 eggs

Oil for frying such as canola, sunflower, or peanut

1. To make the rhubarb sauce, add the rhubarb, sugar, and a pinch of salt to a small saucepan. Add just enough water to cover and set over medium heat to bring to a boil. Reduce the heat to medium-low to maintain a gentle simmer. Simmer until the rhubarb completely breaks down, about 30 minutes. Add more water as necessary to keep the rhubarb covered. When the rhubarb has turned entirely to mush, cook for another 2 to 5 minutes, stirring regularly, until the sauce has the consistency of applesauce. Add salt or sugar to taste. Refrigerate until needed.

2. To make the croquetas, in a large, heavy-bottomed pan, dry sauté the chanterelles, following the instructions on page 31, using the neutral oil. When the chanterelles are lightly browned, 5 to 7 minutes after the liquid is completely cooked away, add the sherry and scrape up any browned on bits from the bottom of the pan. When the liquid has completely reduced, transfer the chanterelles to a cutting board. Let cool slightly, then chop into very small pieces and set aside.

3. Heat the empty pan over medium-low heat and add 1 tablespoon of the butter. When melted, stir in the onion. Sauté, stirring regularly, until the onion is softened but not browned, 5 to 7 minutes.

4. Add the remaining butter. Once melted, stir in ½ cup (60 g) of the flour to coat the onion. Continue to cook for 2 minutes, stirring constantly to avoid burning, until the flour is lightly toasted. Add about one third of the milk, whisking constantly to beat out any lumps. When fully incorporated, slowly whisk in the rest of the milk. Whisk vigorously until the sauce comes up to a simmer. Let the sauce simmer gently for about 2 minutes, stirring constantly, until the sauce is the consistency of thick pancake batter. (The thicker the sauce, the easier breading your croquetas will be, but also, the thicker the sauce, the easier it is to burn on the bottom of the pan, so be careful!) Season with a generous pinch of nutmeg, salt, and pepper.

continued ›

Mushroom Substitutions: Almost any mushrooms will work here.

5. Remove the sauce from heat, transfer to a casserole dish, and stir in the thyme, mushrooms, and hazelnuts, if using. Adjust the salt and pepper to taste. Let cool completely, then cover and refrigerate for at least 4 hours or up to 24 hours before proceeding.

6. Once the mushroom mixture is thoroughly chilled, spread the remaining flour in an even layer in a shallow baking dish or large plate and season with salt and pepper. Spread the bread crumbs in an even layer in a second baking dish or plate. Whisk the eggs together with 1 tablespoon water in a small bowl.

7. Using a small ice cream scoop or a couple of spoons, scoop about 1 tablespoon of the cold mushroom mixture into either a ball or a classic quenelle (oblong shape), and roll it gently in the flour until entirely coated. Carefully shake off any excess, then place it gently into the egg mixture, using your fingers or a slotted spoon to coat it completely. Let the excess egg drip off, then carefully roll in the bread crumbs to thoroughly coat. Place the croqueta on a clean tray or plate. Repeat with the remaining mushroom mixture, being careful not to let the breaded croquetas touch each other, as this will mar their coating. (You can bread the croquetas several hours in advance of cooking, or freeze them for longer storage. Freeze them in a single layer, without letting them touch. Once frozen, they can be transferred to a plastic bag or airtight container. They will keep for several weeks in the freezer, and can be fried directly from frozen.)

8. Fill a large, high-sided pan with at least 1 inch (2.5 cm) of oil. Bring the oil to 350°F (180°C) over medium-high heat. Once the oil is hot, carefully place the croquetas in the pan using a slotted spoon, being careful not to overcrowd the pan. Line a cooling rack or plate with a clean kitchen towel or paper towel. Turn the croquetas with a spoon or tongs while they fry to ensure they cook evenly. When they are a crispy and golden brown on all sides, 3 to 5 minutes, remove with a slotted spoon or spider skimmer, and transfer to the cooling rack or plate to drain. While still hot, sprinkle with a little salt. Continue frying in batches until all of the croquetas are cooked. Serve hot with the rhubarb sauce.

Morels Stuffed with Roasted Chiles and Cheese

Serves 4 to 6

East Coast morel hunters who celebrate finding a handful of morels around an old elm tree often have trouble comprehending just how productive the western burns can be for morels. I can often fill baskets, bags, and buckets with these prized mushrooms in only a few hours, so I'm always coming up with fun new ways to share them with friends. With their hollow bodies, morels practically beg to be filled with other ingredients. This recipe is inspired by my friend Jerry Kharitonov, who gave me the idea to stuff jalapeno poppers with morels. I loved the idea so much that I had to turn it on its head and refine it a bit. These stuffed mushrooms are also great served with the rhubarb sauce from page 137.

5 serrano chiles

¼ cup (60 g) plus 1 teaspoon unsalted butter

1 green garlic stalk or garlic scape, thinly sliced, or 2 garlic cloves and 1 scallion, minced

½ cup (115 g) cream cheese or mascarpone, room temperature

3 ounces (85 g) Manchego cheese, grated

½ cup (115 g) sour cream

1 to 2 tablespoons bread crumbs

Zest of 1 lemon

1 teaspoon salt

1 pound (450 g) large whole morels, ends of stems trimmed to create a larger opening for stuffing

1. Roast the chiles under the broiler or grill over high heat, rotating them periodically to ensure the skin chars evenly. Set the chiles aside to cool. Once cool enough to handle, carefully peel and discard the skin, then remove the stem, seeds, and ribs and discard, reserving the flesh.

2. Melt 1 teaspoon of the butter in a small pan over medium heat. Add the green garlic and sauté gently, stirring regularly, for about 3 minutes, until it has softened but not browned.

3. Add the green garlic, chiles, cream cheese, Manchego, sour cream, bread crumbs, lemon zest, and salt to a food processor, and pulse until smooth. Adjust the seasoning to taste. Using a spatula, transfer the cheese mixture from the food processor to a piping bag fitted with a round piping tip with at least ¼-inch (6 mm) opening.

4. Holding a morel in one hand, insert the piping tip into the stem opening and carefully pipe in enough filling to completely fill the entire hollow to the end of the stem. (This step is easier with a second person helping to hold the mushroom, as the filling will be stiff and take some strength to pipe. Alternatively, you can fill the mushrooms by pushing the stuffing in with a chopstick or other small utensil, but a piping bag is much more efficient.) Repeat until all of the morels are filled.

5. Preheat the oven to 350°F (180°C). Line a rimmed baking sheet or casserole dish with parchment paper. Gently melt the remaining butter in a small pan over low heat. Place the morels on the prepared baking sheet or with hollow ends upright in the casserole dish (this will ensure that less cheese oozes out during cooking), season with salt, and brush with the melted butter. Bake for 25 to 30 minutes, until the cheese is melted, and the morels are glistening, soft, and cooked through. Serve hot from the oven.

Tip: *If you don't like hot chiles, substitute one large poblano for the serranos. Any leftover filling is delicious spread on toasted crusty bread and baked in the oven until melted.*

Mushroom Substitutions: This filling works great with mild *Lactarius, Russula, Amanitas,* and various *Agaricus.* You can also try it with shiitakes, white buttons, or crimini. If substituting any non-hollow mushrooms for the morels, chop the stems into small pieces, sauté them, and then add the stems and another 2 tablespoons of bread crumbs to the stuffing mix.

Snowbank False Morels and Shishito Peppers

Serves 4 to 6

This dish makes a great side or a light meal on a hot day. The snowbank false morel (*Gyromitra montana*) is often maligned because people mistake it for some of its dangerous and rather different looking cousins. In fact, it's both a safe and delicious mushroom, that is quite common some years. They have a pleasant, somewhat chewy texture when cooked, and a rich, meaty flavor that plays nicely off the grassy, almost sweet, mildly spicy flavors of the peppers.

1 pound (450 g) snowbank false morels, stems discarded, caps cut into ½-inch (1.25 cm) pieces

2 tablespoons neutral oil

1 pound (450 g) Shishito or Padrón peppers, stems removed

Extra virgin olive oil

Coarse salt

10 to 12 fresh mint leaves, cut into ultra-thin strips

Lemon wedges

1. Wet sauté the snowbank false morels, following the instructions on page 31, using 1 tablespoon of the neutral oil. Season with salt, and when lightly browned, 5 to 7 minutes after the liquid is completely cooked away, remove from the heat and set aside.

2. Heat a large, heavy-bottomed pan over medium-high heat. Add the remaining neutral oil, then add the peppers in a single layer. If they don't fit in a single layer, cook in batches or use a second pan. Cook, stirring regularly, until the peppers begin to lightly blister and char on all sides, about 5 minutes. Reduce the heat to medium and add the mushrooms, stirring to mix them in. Cook just long enough to heat the mushrooms through, 2 to 3 minutes.

3. To serve, arrange the mushrooms and peppers on a wide plate. Top with a drizzle of extra virgin olive oil, sprinkle with a generous pinch of coarse sea salt, and garnish with the mint. Serve with the lemon wedges.

Snowbank false morels, Gyromitra montana

Mushroom Substitutions: Almost any mushrooms will work here. *Gyromitra caroliniana, G. korfii,* and *G. brunnea* would all be great if available.

Spanish Tortilla with Potatoes and Mushrooms (Tortilla de Patatas y Setas)

Serves 6

Tortilla de patatas is one of the most classic foods of Spain. It resembles what most Americans might call a frittata, but I like to say a frittata is eggs with a bunch of stuff mixed in, while a tortilla is a lot of stuff mixed with just enough egg to hold it together. One always fries the potatoes, and never finishes a tortilla in the oven. A deceptively simple dish, it works great in large portions as a very satisfying center of a meal, or in small squares as an appetizer. Many bars and restaurants serve them cold as a tapa, but in Spain they are just as likely to be served hot. Tortillas are also popular sandwich fillings, and in some places, common picnic foods. Mushrooms add a deep, earthy flavor and a chewy textural contrast to the classic tortilla. I strongly recommend using a nonstick pan here, as otherwise flipping the tortilla will be quite difficult.

1 pound (450 g) fresh mushrooms, cut into ¼-inch (6 mm) slices

1 tablespoon extra virgin olive oil

2 garlic cloves, peeled

3 russet potatoes (1.5 pounds/680 g), peeled, quartered lengthwise, quarters cut crosswise into ¼-inch (6 mm) slices

1 yellow onion, diced

9 eggs, beaten

1. Wet or dry sauté the mushrooms (depending on their type and moisture level), following the instructions on page 31, using the extra virgin olive oil, and season with salt and a little pepper. When finished cooking, set aside.

2. Fill a large pan with about ½ inch (1.25 cm) of neutral oil and place over medium-high heat. Add the garlic. When the garlic starts to aggressively sizzle, 3 to 5 minutes, scoop it out and add the potatoes. (The garlic serves as a temperature gauge and will add a bit of flavor to the oil.) Gently spread out and stir the potato slices. They should be completely submerged in the oil. After about 2 minutes, stir in the onion. Continue stirring occasionally until the potatoes are tender, but not browned, 7 to 10 minutes. Mix in the mushrooms and continue cooking just long enough to heat through.

3. Strain the potato-mushroom mixture, reserving the oil separately. Place a nonstick 10-inch (25 cm) pan over medium heat and add 1 tablespoon of the reserved oil.

4. While still hot, mix the potato-mushroom mixture together with the eggs in a large bowl. Let rest for 2 minutes, then pour into the nonstick pan. Gently stir to distribute the filling equally. Reduce the heat to medium-low to keep the eggs from browning too much. Use a spatula to push the middle around before it has set too much, to allow the uncooked eggs to fill in the bottom and start to solidify. After 3 to 4 minutes, scrape any egg down from the sides of the pan, and stop stirring to allow the tortilla to set. Without moving the tortilla, let it continue to cook for about 4 more minutes.

5. When the eggs have mostly set, you need to flip over the tortilla. Give the pan a gentle shake to help release the tortilla. If it is sticking, use a spatula to free it and add a few more drops of oil to the pan after flipping. Cover the pan with a plate, then invert the pan so the tortilla slides onto the plate. Then just slide the tortilla back into the pan, cooked side up.

6. Let the tortilla set and finish cooking, about 1 more minute, then slide it onto a plate, cut, and serve. It will be equally satisfying whether hot out of the pan, at room temperature, or cold.

Mushroom Substitutions: Almost any mushrooms will work here. Various Agaricus species and the shaggy parasol (*Chlorophyllum brunneum*) work especially well, as does everything from chanterelles to porcini to shiitakes.

Dane!

Empanadillas Stuffed with Salted Mushrooms, Raisins, and Pine Nuts

Makes 20 to 25 empanadillas

Empanadas originated in Galicia, on the Atlantic coast of Spain. In Spain, the smaller, individual-size version that you generally see in the Americas is called an empanadilla, while "empanada" refers to a larger stuffed pastry that fills a whole baking sheet and is cut up into smaller pieces to serve. This dough recipe comes from my wife Rosa's family. It is one of the simplest, most straightforward yeast dough recipes you will find. It also scales up very well. This particular filling is a vegetarian version of a traditional Catalonian stew in which I substitute salted mushrooms for the usual bacalao (salt cod). You can also get creative with other mushroom-based fillings. I highly recommended weighing the dry ingredients in the dough recipe to ensure the right consistency.

DOUGH

2¼ cups plus 2 tablespoons (300 g) all-purpose flour

1 teaspoon salt

1 packet (2¼ teaspoons) active dry yeast

1 teaspoon granulated sugar

¼ cup plus 3 tablespoons (100 ml) warm water (95°–100°F/35°–38°C)

1 egg

¼ cup plus 3 tablespoons (100 ml) extra virgin olive oil

STUFFING

½ cup (80 g) raisins

½ cup (120 ml) dry white wine

3 garlic cloves, crushed

5 fresh parsley sprigs

3 tablespoons extra virgin olive oil

4 cups (about 680 g) Salt-Preserved Mushrooms using *Lactarius* or *Russula* (page 52), soaked for 8 to 12 hours, rinsed, and cut into ½-inch (1.25 cm) pieces

1½ white onions, diced

1 cup (200 g) seeded, diced Roma tomatoes (about 3 tomatoes)

½ teaspoon pimentón de la vera (Spanish smoked paprika)

½ cup (65 g) pine nuts

2 eggs beaten with 1 tablespoon water

1. To make the dough, mix the flour and salt in a large mixing bowl. In another bowl, stir the yeast and sugar into the warm water. Let the yeast mixture sit until you see a large number of bubbles forming on top, 5 to 10 minutes.

2. Make a well in the middle of the flour, and add the egg, oil, and yeast mixture. Use a fork to mix the wet ingredients together, slowly incorporating the surrounding flour. When it starts to get too thick to mix with the fork, use your hands to incorporate all of the flour into the wet paste in the middle, being sure to scrape all the good bits off the fork. Knead the dough until it stops sticking to your hands and the bowl, 1 to 2 minutes. Form the dough into a ball, cover with a damp (not wet) towel inside the bowl, and let it rest in a warm place until it doubles in size, about 45 minutes.

continued ›

Mushroom Substitutions: Use boiled mushrooms if you don't have salted mushrooms (see page 52). Almost any mushroom will work here with different fillings.

3. To make the stuffing, cover the raisins with the wine in a small bowl, and set aside until needed, at least 20 minutes.

4. Process the garlic and parsley to a paste in small food processor or a mortar and pestle. Set aside.

5. Heat a large heavy-bottomed pan over medium heat and add 1 tablespoon of the extra virgin olive oil. Add the salt-preserved mushrooms and sauté until lightly browned, 7 to 10 minutes. Transfer the mushrooms to a bowl and set aside.

6. Reduce the heat to medium-low, add 2 tablespoons extra virgin olive oil, then add the onions. Sauté until the onions start to soften and turn translucent, 10 to 15 minutes, then add the tomatoes and pimentón and season with salt. Cook until the liquid from the tomatoes has completely reduced, about 10 minutes.

7. Add the garlic mixture to the pan and cook for about 2 minutes to take the raw flavor out of the garlic. Stir in the mushrooms, then add the raisins and wine and cook until only a tablespoon or two of liquid remains, 5 to 8 minutes. Stir in the pine nuts and adjust the seasoning to taste. If the mix gets very dry, you can stir in 1 to 2 more tablespoons water. Remove from the heat.

8. Preheat the oven to 350°F (180°C). Line 2 rimmed baking sheets with parchment paper. Tear or cut off a fist-size piece of dough. Roll the dough out into a flat sheet about 1⁄16 inch (1.5 mm) thick on a lightly floured surface. Use a coffee cup, cookie cutter, or ring mold to cut out pieces 3 to 4 inches (7.5–10 cm) in diameter. Form the scrap dough back into a ball and set aside; scraps can be combined and rerolled 2 times before getting too tough to work.

9. Place a generous spoonful of filling in the center of the dough circle. Using a finger or small brush, spread a little egg wash around the outer rim of the circle. Fold one half of the dough circle over the filling and press down to form a semicircle. Seal the edge by pinching well with your fingers or pressing down with the tines of a fork. Place the empanadillas on the prepared baking sheets, leaving 1 inch (2.5 cm) between each. If the cut dough circles shrink a bit, give each a quick roll with the rolling pin before filling. Repeat the rolling, filling, and sealing until all of the dough and filling is used up.

10. Using a sharp knife or fork, poke a couple of small holes on the top of each empanadilla. Brush the tops with more egg wash, then bake for 15 to 25 minutes, until golden brown. Serve hot from the oven or at room temperature. (Leftovers will keep in the fridge for 3 days; warm them gently before serving.)

Mushroom Pakora

Serves 6 to 8

Pakora are classic Indian fritters made with gram (chickpea) flour. This simple, sparse batter is meant to just barely coat and hold the ingredients together. I love how pakoras fry up in odd, abstract shapes. The moisture in this batter comes from the water the mushrooms and vegetables release, but if it is too dry, you can add a few extra drops. The flavors of the spices in the pakora pop against the earthy mushrooms, sweet vegetables, and spicy citrusy kick of the chutney. If you like, you can experiment with adding different spices and even some different vegetables to the mix. The little bit of cornstarch helps crisp up the finished pakora.

CILANTRO CHUTNEY

1 large bunch fresh cilantro

½ yellow onion, roughly chopped

Juice of 5 limes

1 serrano chile, stem removed, roughly chopped

1 teaspoon salt

PAKORA

4 cups (500 g) fresh mushrooms, cut into ¼-inch (6 mm) slices

2 cups (125 g) cauliflower florets, cut or broken into small pieces

1 onion, quartered and cut into ¼-inch (6 mm) slices

One 1-inch (2.5 cm) piece ginger, peeled and grated

1 garlic clove, minced

¾ cup (75 g) gram (besan) flour

3 tablespoons cornstarch

2 tablespoons fresh chopped mint

1 teaspoon ground fennel

½ teaspoon ground cumin

1 teaspoon salt

1 teaspoon freshly ground black pepper

Oil for frying such as canola, sunflower, or peanut

1. To make the cilantro chutney, combine the cilantro, onion, lime juice, serrano, and salt in a blender and blend until smooth. Adjust the seasoning to taste.

2. To make the pakora, mix the mushrooms, cauliflower, and onion together in a large bowl, then season with a generous pinch of salt to draw out their water. Squeeze the vegetables a little as you mix to help release their moisture. Let sit for 30 to 45 minutes to let the flavors meld.

3. Mix the ginger and garlic into the mushroom mixture, then mix in the gram flour, cornstarch, mint, ground fennel, ground cumin, salt, and pepper. The mushrooms and onions should have released enough water in Step 2 to hydrate the flour and make a very thick batter. If the batter is runny, add another 1 to 2 tablespoons of gram flour. If the batter looks dry, add a few drops of cold water at a time until the batter is moistened and coats the vegetables like a thick paste.

4. Fill a large, high-sided pan with at least 1 inch (2.5 cm) of oil. Heat the oil over medium-high heat to 350°F (180°C), then use a large spoon to scoop out a small amount of the pakora mix, and carefully drop into the pan from just above the surface of the oil. Line a cooling rack or plate with a clean kitchen towel or paper towel. Fry the test pakora until crispy and lightly browned on all sides, 3 to 4 minutes, then remove with a slotted spoon or spider skimmer and transfer to the cooling rack or paper plate to drain. Let cool slightly, then adjust the seasoning of the batter for the remaining pakoras to taste.

5. Fry in batches, adding as many pakora at a time as will fit without crowding the pan, and transferring to the prepared cooling rack or plate as they finish cooking. Season with a small pinch of salt as soon as they leave the oil. Serve hot, with the cilantro chutney on the side for dipping.

Tip: *Gram (also called "besan") flour is made from a certain kind of chickpea. Purchase it at Indian markets or online; there really isn't a good substitute to achieve the right texture and flavor of the pakoras.*

Mushroom Substitutions: Almost any mushroom will work here. Crimini are great, as are chanterelles, hedgehogs, and maitake. Be sure to parboil any mushrooms that require thorough cooking to be eaten safely for 3 to 5 minutes before using. The brief frying time might not be enough time to get them well-cooked.

6

Soups and Stews

Cold, rainy weather dominates the heart of mushroom season where I live, putting a craving for comforting soups and stews at the center of my relationship with mushrooms.

One rainy January, a couple of good friends invited Rosa and me to join them where they were house-sitting on the Mendocino coast for a weekend of mushrooms, beer, and food. That Saturday, in the midst of a rather surreal weekend, we went out hunting in the middle of a deluge of heavy rains. For hours, water flowed down the trails like small creeks, and cold winds blew the rain sideways as we sloshed and smiled our way along. In between the moments of torrential downpour, we focused on hunting in the less sheltered areas around the forest edges, and in the grassier spots where candy caps were out in huge numbers. These open areas seemed more like swamps during this storm, where a wrong step could land you in a puddle halfway to your knee. When the rain dumped harder, we would duck under denser tree cover, where chanterelles and various milk caps and *Russula* also sheltered. Despite wearing layers of raingear, we all quickly became soaked to the bone. Nevertheless, we had a grand old time and found lots of mushrooms.

After returning to the house and showering the day's mud away, we all huddled by the warmth of the now roaring fireplace. Beers were passed around, several toasts were made, and attention soon turned to cooking dinner on that same fire. The meal began with a salad of homegrown citrus tossed with beets we had roasted in the fire's embers. Next we cooked a sampling of several different "weird" mushrooms that none of us had ever tried before. Then we rounded it off with a hearty stew of sausage, Japanese pumpkin, and fresh candy caps (page 25).

As we sat around the fire, we scooped the stew directly out of the cast iron Dutch oven still sitting in the embers and devoured it with a crusty loaf of bread. Great conversation was had, many beers were shared, and we all wound up quite happy and sated. The storm still raged outside, but it was far from the concerns of our cozy arc around the hearth. It remains one of the simplest, and most memorable mushroom dinners I have ever cooked.

Rosa, with a cute trio of Ruby Porcini

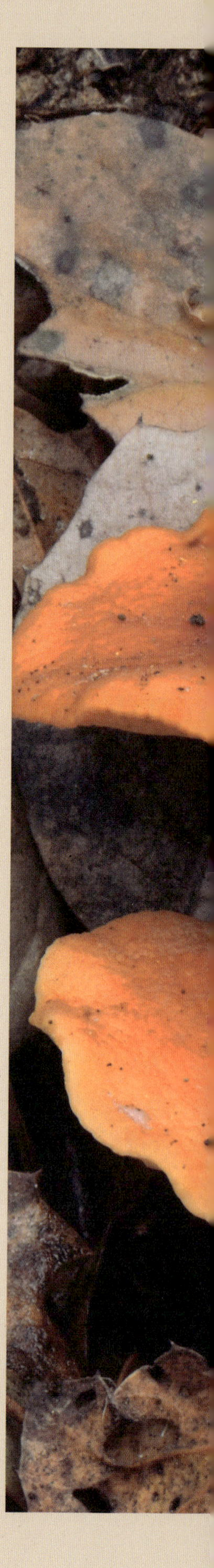

Mushroom Scrap Broth

Makes 3.5 quarts (3.3 L)

Now and then you will be left with a lot of unsightly mushroom scraps. Sometimes an earnest porcini hunt leaves you with only past-prime, overly mature mushrooms that may not even seem good enough to slice up and put in the dehydrator. On the other hand, a productive hunt can fill the dehydrator while still leaving a pile of mushrooms too ripe to keep for long. A basket full of shrimp *Russula* can easily leave behind a mass of broken cap fragments. This rich, versatile broth is an excellent recipe to have in your back pocket for using up these mushroom odds and ends. It can replace chicken or vegetable stock in all kinds of recipes in which you want an earthy, mushroomy kick.

4 cups (500 g) fresh mushroom scraps, roughly chopped

1. Place the mushrooms in a stock pot. Cover with 1 gallon (3.8 L) water and bring to a boil over high heat. Reduce the heat to medium to bring to a simmer and let cook for 30 to 45 minutes to allow the flavor to develop.

2. Strain through a fine-mesh strainer, discarding the solids, and let cool completely. Extra broth can be portioned into airtight containers and frozen for up to several months.

Tip: *If you have only a small amount of stock-worthy scraps, start a bag or container of them in your freezer. Every time you have a few bits, you can add them to the pile. When the stash gets big enough, make the stock.*

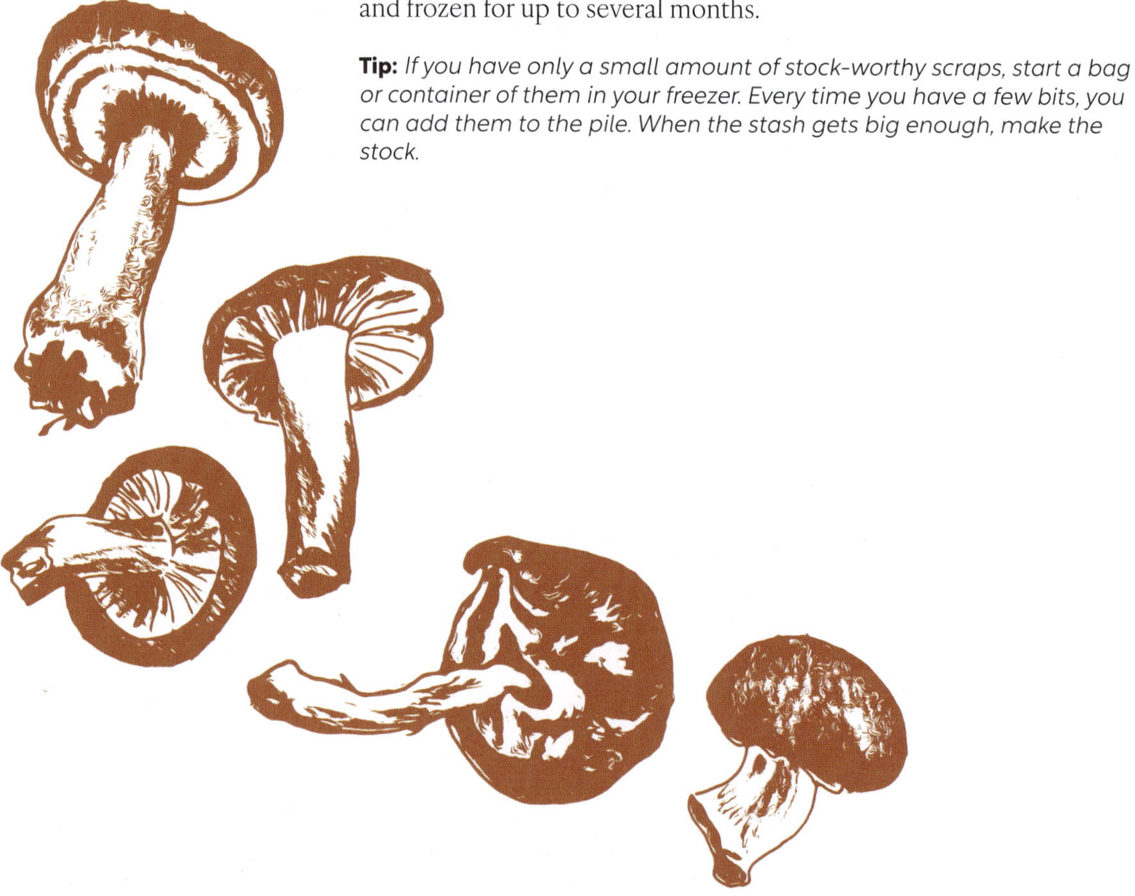

Mushroom Substitutions: Almost any mushrooms will work here. Because the mature members of the porcini clade, and especially the mature pores (the spongy layer under the caps), are intensely flavored, all of them make an excellent broth. Don't limit yourself to porcini, though. Any flavorful mushrooms, from Agaricus to Xerocomellus, will work great.

Sri Lankan-Style Mushroom Curry

Serves 4 to 6

This recipe evolved from a traditional Sri Lankan dal I was taught many years ago. It uses coconut milk and a wonderfully aromatic spice blend, which cannot be substituted with premade spice mix or curry powder. The spice balance of this simplified garam masala differs from that of store-bought curry powders, and it's absolutely worth the few minutes of effort to make your own. The cauliflower mushroom's many nooks and crannies trap lots of the sauce, and its mild flavor lets the spice mix take the spotlight.

GARAM MASALA

1 tablespoon whole coriander seeds

1 tablespoon whole cumin seeds

1½ teaspoons whole fennel seeds

15 whole cloves

13 to 15 green cardamom pods

1 teaspoon fenugreek seeds or ¼ teaspoon candy cap powder

1 tablespoon ground cinnamon

½ to 2 teaspoons cayenne pepper

CURRY

1 large cauliflower mushroom (about 2 pounds/900 g), cut into 1-inch (2.5 cm) pieces

1 tablespoon ghee or unsalted butter

1 yellow onion, thinly sliced

1 cinnamon stick

One 1½-inch (4 cm) piece fresh ginger, peeled and minced

1 tablespoon grated fresh turmeric or 1 teaspoon ground turmeric

2 garlic cloves, minced

1 Roma tomato, quartered

15 curry leaves

1 serrano chile, halved lengthwise

One 14-ounce (400 g) can coconut milk, shaken well before opening

1 teaspoon neutral oil

1 teaspoon black mustard seeds

Juice of 1 lime

Cooked basmati rice

Fresh cilantro leaves

1. To make the garam masala, one spice at a time, toast the coriander seeds, cumin seeds, fennel seeds, cloves, cardamom pods, and fenugreek seeds in a small, dry pan over medium heat, stirring regularly to prevent burning, until very fragrant, 2 to 3 minutes per spice. Let cool completely, then finely grind all the whole spices together in a spice grinder. Mix in the cinnamon and cayenne. (The garam masala will be at its best when freshly made, but it will keep for a few months in an airtight container.)

2. To make the curry, dry sauté the cauliflower mushroom pieces, following the instructions on page 31, using the ghee, until lightly browned. Season with salt.

3. Adjust the heat to medium, add half of the onion, 2 tablespoons of the garam masala, the cinnamon stick, and the ginger, turmeric, and garlic. Cook for 3 minutes to soften the onion a bit, then add the tomato, curry leaves, and chile and continue to sauté for another 3 to 5 minutes to bring out the spices' aromas.

continued ›

Mushroom Substitutions: Good choices include butter boletes, blewits, crimini, and maitake. Hawk's wings, giant sawgill, your favorite *Russula* or milk caps, and meaty *Amanitas* like the coccora or southwest Caesar's Amanita will also work well.

4. Increase the heat to medium-high and add 1 cup (240 ml) water. Once it comes to a boil, reduce the heat to medium-low to simmer for 5 minutes to infuse the spices into the broth. Stir in the coconut milk and gently simmer for 1 to 2 more minutes, until the mixture looks very saucy but not soupy. Adjust the consistency as needed by simmering longer if too thin, or adding more water if too thick. When the desired consistency is reached, turn off the heat.

5. While the curry simmers, heat a small pan over medium heat. Add the oil and the mustard seeds. Cook until the mustard seeds finish popping, 2 to 3 minutes. Add the remaining onion and cook until soft and somewhat brown, 10 to 15 minutes, being careful not to burn. Add 1 tablespoon of the garam masala and season with salt. Sauté for another 2 minutes to cook the raw flavor out of the spices.

6. Bring the curry back to a simmer over medium-high heat, stirring often. Add the onion mixture to the curry and simmer for 2 to 3 minutes over medium-low heat. Add the lime juice and adjust the seasoning to taste. Serve over the cooked basmati rice, garnished with the cilantro.

Tip: *Curry leaves can be found at specialty Asian or Indian markets, fresh or frozen. If you can't find curry leaves, simply omit them from the recipe. There really is no substitute. For a vegan curry, substitute oil for the ghee.*

Porcini-Lentil Stew

Serves 4

The layered, earthy flavors from the dried and fresh mushrooms, balanced by the juicy turnips and refreshing high notes of the dill, turn this stew into the perfect antidote for a dreary winter day. Even better, this simple, comforting dish is more than hearty enough to serve as a meal on its own. To make the stew into a soup, simply add a bit more water to thin it out. I prefer to use black lentils, often called beluga lentils, here. They are beautiful and hold up texturally, not disintegrating as they cook, but you can substitute any lentils you like. If desired, you can use mushroom or vegetable stock in place of the water.

1 pound (450 g) fresh porcini

2 tablespoons oil

1 onion, diced

3 celery ribs, diced

½ teaspoon dried dill

1 ounce (28 g) dried porcini

3 tablespoons chopped fresh parsley

2 garlic cloves, minced

7 baby turnips, quartered, or 1 large turnip, peeled and cut into ½-inch (1.25 cm) pieces

1½ cups (300 g) black lentils

½ cup (120 ml) dry red wine

1. Wet or dry sauté the fresh porcini, following the instructions on page 31, using 1 tablespoon of the oil, until lightly browned. Season with salt and set aside.

2. Heat a pot over medium-low heat. Add the remaining oil, then add the onion and celery. Sauté, stirring occasionally, until the vegetables are very soft but not browned, 7 to 10 minutes. Season with salt, then add the dried dill and the dried porcini. Add the parsley and garlic and cook another 3 to 5 minutes, stirring regularly, until fragrant and well incorporated into the vegetables.

3. Stir in the turnips and lentils and increase the heat to medium-high. Pour in the wine and scrape up any browned bits stuck to the bottom of the pan. When the wine has mostly reduced, 1 to 2 minutes, add enough water to barely cover the lentils. Adjust the heat to medium-low to allow the liquid to simmer slowly. When lentils are almost fully softened, 20 to 30 minutes, stir in the cooked mushrooms, taste, and add salt to taste.

4. Continue cooking at a gentle simmer until the lentils are very tender, but not mushy, another 5 to 10 minutes, adding water as needed to keep the lentils covered. Serve hot.

Tip: *The leftovers are delicious, but the lentils tend to soak up all the liquid, so you will probably need to add more water the next day.*

Mushroom Substitutions: Almost any mushrooms can take the place of the fresh porcini. Dried *Suillus*, *Leccinum*, shiitake, or morels will make good substitutes for the dried porcini. If using mushrooms that were dried dirty, soak them first, then clean them, straining and reserving the soaking liquid for use in the stew.

Stewed Mushrooms in Peanut Sauce

Serves 4 to 6

A couple friends of mine who've spent time in different parts of Africa told me about regularly eating local stews made with peanut sauces—including mushroom stews. The idea sounded so good to me that I came up with a mushroom and peanut stew of my own. The flavors are comforting, familiar, and homey, despite being far from those I grew up with. I have made variations of this recipe with a wide variety of mushrooms, wild and cultivated, and enjoyed them all a lot. Traditionally, many of these stews would be based on some sort of meat, but I don't miss the meat at all when eating this mushroom-filled stew. You probably won't see lime with these dishes in Africa, but the small spike of acidity adds a lot of depth and balances the richness. Serve with long grain rice for a satisfying, complete meal.

0.5 ounce (14 g) dried porcini

2 pounds (900 g) mixed fresh mushrooms

¼ cup (60 ml) neutral oil

2 yellow onions, finely chopped

1 green bell pepper, diced

One 2-inch (5 cm) piece of ginger, peeled and minced

1 habanero chile, halved and seeded for a milder stew or minced for a spicier stew

1 garlic clove, chopped

2 bay leaves

¼ cup (66 g) tomato paste

3 cups (720 ml) puréed tomatoes, canned or fresh

2 large carrots, peeled and cut into 1½-inch (4 cm) pieces

1 cup (250 g) creamy natural peanut butter

2 sweet potatoes, peeled and cut into 2-inch (5 cm) pieces

Cooked long-grain rice

Roughly chopped fresh cilantro

Lime wedges

Mushroom Substitutions: Almost any mushrooms will work here. I recommend using a mix of different mushrooms for the pleasantly contrasting textures and flavors.

1. Cover the dried porcini with 2 cups (480 ml) water and let soak for at least 10 minutes to soften.

2. Heat a large heavy-bottomed pot over medium-high heat. Cook the mushrooms in batches using a dry or wet sauté (depending on their type and moisture level), following the instructions on page 31, with 1 tablespoon of the neutral oil per batch, until lightly browned. Season with salt. Transfer the mushrooms to a large bowl and set aside.

3. Return the pot to the stove and, with the heat still at medium-low, add the remaining oil, then add the onions. Season with salt and sauté, stirring regularly, until the onions are soft and translucent but not browned, 7 to 10 minutes. Add the bell pepper, ginger, chile, garlic, bay leaves, and another pinch of salt and continue to cook, stirring regularly, until the bell pepper is just starting to soften, 5 to 7 minutes. Add the tomato paste, stir to coat the vegetables, and continue cooking, stirring constantly, for about 1 minute to cook off the paste's raw flavor.

4. Add the rehydrated porcini and their soaking liquid and scrape up any browned bits from the bottom of the pot. Add the cooked mushrooms along with any liquid released during cooking and the tomato puree. Add the carrots and increase the heat to high to bring the liquid to a boil, then immediately reduce the heat to medium-low to keep the stew at a gentle simmer.

5. Meanwhile, whisk the peanut butter in a bowl with ¼ cup (60 ml) water until emulsified, then whisk it into the stew, making sure that there are no lumps of peanut butter left. Again, adjust the heat to keep the stew at a simmer. Adjust the salt to taste.

6. Let the stew simmer for about 5 minutes to allow the flavors to come together, then add the sweet potatoes. Continue simmering, stirring regularly to make sure that nothing burns on the bottom, until the vegetables are soft, the liquid is slightly thickened, and the oil begins to separate and float on top of the liquid, 15 to 25 minutes. Adjust the seasoning to taste. Serve hot on a bed of rice, topped with the fresh cilantro, with the lime wedges on the side.

Tip: *You can substitute a milder chile for the habanero, if desired.*

Matsutake with Clams, Kale, and Chorizo

Serves 4

In 2015, a few friends and I celebrated the holidays with some very fruitful matsutake hunting. On Christmas morning, we took a two-hour drive to check a previous year's honey hole. Where we were expecting to see a hillside of matsus high up above Mendocino County; instead, we wound up playing in the snow, running between patches of frozen, mushroomless ground. Despite not finding mushrooms, we all had a great time, knowing that we had collected fifteen pounds of matsutake at another hunting ground the day before. I made this memorable dish for our Christmas dinner when we got back home, and it's still a special-occasion treat to this day. Matsutake love seafood, and the richness and spices from the chorizo, along with the chewy greens, turn this into a hearty, satisfying one-pot meal. Make sure to use Mexican-style chorizo here. Spanish-style chorizo is made with a totally different spice mix. Serve this with crusty bread to soak up the delicious juices left in the bowl.

2 pounds (900 g) live Manila clams or other small clams

1 heaping tablespoon salt

1 pound (450 g) fresh matsutake, cut into ¼-inch (6 mm) slices

2 tablespoons neutral oil

1 pound (450 g) chorizo, casings removed, crumbled

3 garlic cloves, chopped

½ cup (120 ml) dry white wine or non-hoppy beer

1 bunch kale, destemmed and roughly chopped

1. Rinse the clams under cold running water until the water runs off clear to remove any sand stuck to their shells. Discard any clams with broken shells or ones that don't close when tapped. Place the clams in a large bowl and cover with cold water. Stir in the salt. Let sit for 30 minutes to allow the clams to purge themselves of any sand inside of them. Drain and give another quick rinse in cold water. Store, drained, in the fridge until ready to use.

2. Heat a large pan over high heat. Add the mushrooms. They will start giving off a lot of water within about 10 seconds. Wait for them to release as much water as possible, which will usually take about 1 minute, then reduce the heat to medium and drain, reserving the liquid separately.

3. Add 1 tablespoon of the oil, season the mushrooms with salt, and continue cooking until they are just starting to brown, 5 to 7 minutes. Transfer to a bowl and set aside.

4. Add the remaining oil and the chorizo to the pan. Cook, breaking up the chorizo with a spatula, until lightly browned, 7 to 10 minutes.

5. Stir in the garlic and let it cook for about 30 seconds, until fragrant. Pour in the wine and scrape up any browned bits from the bottom of the pan. Add the clams and kale, stirring to mix thoroughly. Season lightly with salt and pepper. Pour in the reserved liquid from the matsutake. Cover the pan and let steam just until all the clams open up, 3 to 5 minutes. Serve piping hot.

Mushroom Substitutions: There is no substitute for matsutake in this dish. Very mature, open matsutake work well here.

White Button Ajoblanco

Serves 4

Ajoblanco, which literally translates to "white garlic," is the precursor to Spain's other cold soups, such as gazpacho. Almonds, along with stale bread, garlic, a little bit of vinegar, cold water, and olive oil form the base of the traditional version. It almost certainly traces its roots to similar soups made by the Moorish conquerors who ruled Spain for centuries. The almonds give it a flavor and texture almost reminiscent of tahini-based sauces from the African side of the Mediterranean. In this version, boiled white button mushrooms replace the almonds. It's amazing, and almost inexplicable, how similar the flavor and texture are to those of more traditional recipes. Traditionally, sweet green muscatel grapes garnish ajoblanco, and help to balance the rich, creamy, acidic soup. Instead of the grapes, I like to top my myco-version with small mushrooms that have been candied in grape juice. You can always use green grapes if you prefer.

3 cups (300 g) stale crusty bread, crusts removed and discarded, torn into pieces

12 ounces (340 g) white button mushrooms, left whole

1 tablespoon sherry vinegar

2 garlic cloves

¼ cup plus 2 tablespoons (90 ml) extra virgin olive oil

2 to 3 tablespoons beech (shimeji) mushrooms, sweet poached in white grape juice (see page 242)

Coarse salt

Extra virgin olive oil

1. Add the bread to a large bowl, cover with a generous amount of cold water, and soak for at least 30 minutes or up to 2 hours.

2. Bring a large pot of salted water to a boil over high heat. Add the button mushrooms, let the water return to a boil, then cook for 6 to 7 minutes, until cooked through. Drain and let cool completely. (This step can be done up to 1 day in advance; store the cooked mushrooms in an airtight container in the fridge.)

3. Drain the bread, gently squeezing out the excess water. Add the bread, mushrooms, vinegar, garlic, and a pinch of salt to a blender. Add just enough cold water to engage the blades, then blend until very smooth. Add a little more cold water if needed to keep the blades spinning, but note that the soup should be thick. With the blender running, slowly stream in the olive oil and continue blending until emulsified. Adjust the salt to taste. Transfer to an airtight container and refrigerate for at least 1 hour to chill and allow the flavors to meld.

4. Serve cold, topped with the sweet poached mushrooms and a few drops of their syrup, along with a little coarse salt and a few generous glugs of extra virgin olive oil.

Mushroom Substitutions: To keep the color light and the flavor similar to a classic ajoblanco, use tight white button mushrooms that haven't begun to open, with gills that haven't yet turned chocolate brown. You can also play with almost any other mushrooms to introduce other flavors and darker colors. Regardless of which mushrooms you use, boil them first, as indicated in the recipe.

Vegan Cream of Mushroom Soup

Serves 8

Cream of mushroom soup is a luxurious treat to make when you have a lot of fresh mushrooms on hand and want them to be the center of attention. This simple, updated vegan version will pleasantly surprise you with its deep flavor and aroma and rich, creamy mouthfeel. The mushrooms themselves, not a roux, thicken this soup, and it will be some shade of buff tan or brown, not white, because the soup is mainly mushrooms. For a sinfully rich dairy version, cook the mushrooms with butter instead of oil and substitute heavy cream for the extra virgin olive oil. Turn this into a decadent sauce for pasta, chicken, or fish by reducing the liquid a bit more before blending. This soup keeps well for several months in the freezer, and it's a great way to consolidate and preserve a big harvest.

2 pounds (900 g) chanterelles, cut into ½-inch (1.25 cm) pieces

1 tablespoon oil

¼ cup (60 ml) brandy, dry sherry, or dry white wine

6 fresh thyme sprigs, leaves only

Zest of 1 lemon, optional

½ cup (120 ml) extra virgin olive oil

1. Dry sauté the chanterelles in a large, heavy-bottomed pot, following the instructions on page 31, using the oil. Cook until lightly and evenly browned, then season with salt. Do not crowd the pot; if necessary, cook the mushrooms in batches, and when the last batch is browned, transfer all the mushrooms back into the pot.

2. Turn the heat up to medium-high. Wait 20 to 30 seconds for the pot to get hot, then pour in the brandy and scrape up any browned bits stuck to the bottom. When the liquid has almost completely reduced, pour in 8 cups (1.9 L) water and bring up to a simmer. Add the thyme and a pinch of salt and continue cooking until the liquid has reduced by about one quarter, 20 to 30 minutes.

3. Carefully transfer the contents of the pan and the lemon zest, if using, to a blender and blend, starting on low speed and gradually increasing the speed to high. Blend on high speed for 30 to 60 seconds, until very smooth. With the blender still running, slowly drizzle in the olive oil until emulsified. When all of the olive oil is incorporated, adjust the seasoning to taste. Serve hot.

Tip: *If you prefer, blend in a more mild-flavored oil, or even cream if you don't care if the soup contains dairy, instead of the extra virgin olive oil. Extra virgin olive oil tends to be strongly flavored, which can compete with the flavors of some mushrooms.*

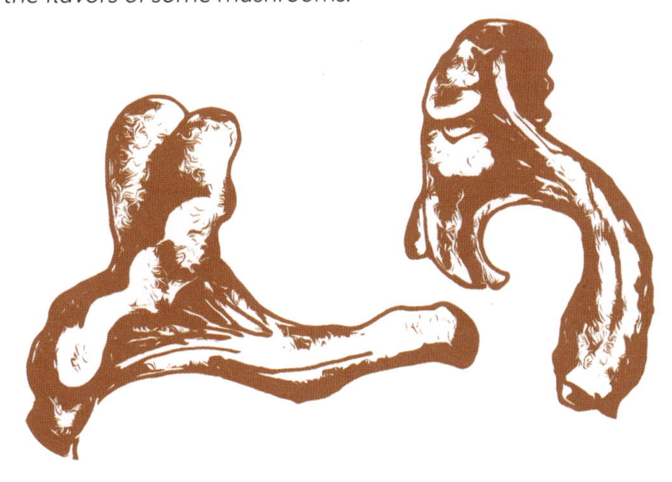

Mushroom Substitutions: Almost any mushrooms will work here; just use a variety with a flavor you enjoy when concentrated.

Porcini-Chestnut Soup

Serves 16

The sweet flavor of chestnuts marries beautifully with the deep earthiness of porcini in this crowd-pleasing soup. In Italy and Spain, where porcini grow with chestnut trees, the two are often paired on the plate. You won't see a lot of heavy cream in this book, but this soup is worth the indulgence. If you want to make a thicker purée, simply reduce the water a little further before blending. Roasting and peeling chestnuts is tedious, and sometimes painful. However, this soup is super easy to make and comes out great using prepackaged, peeled, roasted chestnuts. But if you are motivated to roast and peel your own, it will taste even better.

1.5 ounces (40 g) dried porcini

4 cups (960 ml) warm water

1 tablespoon neutral oil

3 large yellow onions, halved and thinly sliced

3 cups (450 g) roasted and peeled chestnuts, plus extra, chopped, for garnish

1¼ cups (300 ml) dry sherry

A few drops of fresh lemon juice

2 cups (480 ml) heavy cream

1. Cover the dried porcini with the warm water and set aside to soak for at least 20 minutes.

2. Heat a large, heavy-bottomed saucepan over medium heat. Add the oil, then the onions, along with a pinch of salt. Cook, stirring regularly, until the onions just barely start to brown, 7 to 10 minutes. Reduce the heat to medium-low and continue cooking, stirring regularly to prevent burning, until the onions are caramelized to a light brown color, 15 to 20 minutes.

3. Strain the porcini, reserving the soaking liquid separately. Add the mushrooms and chestnuts to the onions, turn the heat up to medium-high, and continue to sauté for another 2 to 3 minutes to release their aromas.

4. Add the sherry and scrape up any browned bits from the bottom of the pan. When the sherry has reduced to about ¼ cup (60 ml), add the reserved mushroom soaking liquid along with another 2 cups (480 ml) water. Season with salt. Bring to a boil, then reduce the heat to medium-low to keep at a gentle simmer for 20 to 30 minutes to concentrate the flavors into the stock.

5. Working in batches, transfer to a blender, add the lemon juice, and blend, starting on low speed and gradually working your way up to high speed. Blend on high speed for 30 to 60 seconds, until very smooth. With the blender still running, slowly stream in the cream until emulsified. When all of the cream is incorporated, adjust the seasoning to taste. Serve hot, garnishing each portion with the extra chestnut pieces.

Mushroom Substitutions: You can substitute other strongly flavored dried mushrooms here. I like using various pored mushrooms (those with a spongy layer under the cap rather than gills) such as chestnut boletes (*Gyroporus* spp.) or bicolor boletes (*Baorangia bicolor*).

Candy Cap, Italian Sausage, and Kabocha Squash Stew

Serves 4

John Pisto is an Italian American chef from the Monterey, California, area who ran successful restaurants, had a TV show, and published multiple cookbooks. He also is a lifelong mushroom hunter and a hell of a nice guy. Many years ago, I ate a risotto he made with candy caps and Italian sausage, which very much inspired this dish. It is simple comfort food for a cold night. Rich, fatty, fennel-heavy Italian sausage plays nicely with the maple aroma and earthy flavor of the candy caps. The squash's natural sweetness also helps to emphasize the candy caps' maple notes. I like to eat this as a stew with crusty bread, but it could just as easily be tossed with your favorite pasta.

1 tablespoon oil

1 pound (450 g) bulk Italian sausage

1 teaspoon minced fresh rosemary

1 pound (450 g) fresh candy caps, smaller mushrooms left whole, larger mushrooms halved

1 fennel bulb, diced

1 small yellow onion, diced

2 garlic cloves, chopped

Red pepper flakes

1 pound (450 g) kabocha squash or peeled butternut squash or pumpkin, seeded and cut into ½-inch (1.25 cm) pieces

1 cup (240 ml) wheat beer or other mild, non-hoppy beer or dry white wine

2 tablespoons extra virgin olive oil

1. Heat a large, heavy-bottomed pot or Dutch oven over medium heat. Add the oil, then add the sausage and rosemary. Stir the sausage, breaking it into bite-size pieces as it cooks. Continue cooking, stirring regularly, until the sausage is broken up and well browned, 10 to 15 minutes.

2. Add the candy caps and continue cooking, stirring regularly, until the moisture they release has been completely reduced, about 5 minutes. Add the fennel, onion, and garlic and continue to cook until the onion and fennel start to soften, 3 to 5 minutes. Season with the red pepper flakes and salt and pepper.

3. Add the squash and cook for 5 minutes to soften, stirring often to ensure that nothing burns on the bottom of the pan.

4. Add the beer and scrape up any browned bits stuck to the bottom of the pan. When the liquid has reduced to about ¼ cup (60 ml), taste a piece of squash, and if still not cooked through, add ½ cup (120 ml) water and continue to cook until the liquid is again reduced to ¼ cup (60 ml), and the squash is tender. Repeat if necessary. Remove from the heat, adjust the seasoning to taste, and stir in the extra virgin olive oil. Serve hot with crusty bread.

Tip: *If you choose to use this as a pasta sauce, stir the cooked pasta in along with a few tablespoons of the pasta cooking water just before removing from the heat.*

Mushroom Substitutions: Almost any mushrooms will work here, although leaving out the candy caps will come at the cost of their maple flavor. Various milk caps and *Russula* would work particularly well. You could add 1 teaspoon of candy cap powder to the stew if you substitute other mushrooms for the fresh candy caps.

Chicken-of-the-Woods and Shrimp Étouffée

Serves 4 to 6

Chicken-of-the-woods takes the place of actual chicken in this dish, and its texture and flavor might fool some of your friends. An étouffée is really just a stew done in a uniquely Louisianan style, with a medium-dark roux, about the color of peanut butter, to give it a rich color, flavor, and body, and the holy trinity of onion, green pepper, and celery providing the vegetable base. Often, these stews will include andouille sausage, but I prefer to leave it out and instead let mushrooms and shrimp provide all the substance, with smoked paprika (pimentón) replacing the smoke from the andouille. The flavor of the étouffée will be driven, more than anything, by the quality of your stock, so use homemade if you can.

2 tablespoons plus 1 teaspoon oil

1 pound (450 g) cleaned shrimp, shells and heads reserved

4 cups (960 ml) fish, vegetable, mushroom (page 36), or chicken stock

1.5 pounds (680 g) chicken-of-the-woods, cut into ¼-inch (6 mm) slices

1 yellow onion, diced

3 large celery ribs, cut into ¼-inch (6 mm) pieces

1 green bell pepper, cut into ¼-inch (6 mm) pieces

1 jalapeno, minced

1 bunch fresh parsley, roughly chopped, plus 2 to 3 tablespoons, for garnish

3 garlic cloves, minced

½ teaspoon smoked paprika

¼ teaspoon dried thyme

¼ teaspoon dried oregano

¼ cup (60 g) plus 1 tablespoon unsalted butter

½ cup (65 g) all-purpose flour

½ cup (120 ml) non-hoppy beer or dry white wine

1 tablespoon Louisiana-style hot sauce such as Crystal or Tabasco

1 bunch scallions, sliced very thin

Cooked long-grain rice

1. Heat a pot over medium-high heat. Add 1 teaspoon of the oil, then the shrimp shells and heads. Sauté, constantly stirring, until the shrimp scraps turn bright red, 2 to 3 minutes. Add the stock, then increase the heat to high to bring to a boil. Reduce the heat to low, cover the pot, and simmer gently for 20 to 30 minutes to incorporate the shrimps' flavor into the stock. Remove from the heat and strain, discarding the solids. (You should have about 4 cups/960 ml of stock. If you have less, add water to make up the difference.)

2. Wet sauté the chicken-of-the-woods, following the instructions on page 31, using 1 tablespoon of the oil. When lightly browned, season lightly with salt and pepper, then transfer the mushrooms to a bowl and set aside.

3. Return the pan to medium heat, and when hot, add the remaining oil. Add the onion, celery, green pepper, and jalapeno and sauté,

Mushroom Substitutions: Substitute maitake (hen-of-the-woods), your favorite *Russula* or *Lactarius*, crimini, or other *Agaricus* buttons. You could use king trumpets (*Pleurotus eryngii*) or hawk's wings (*Sarcodon* spp.), though their texture will not be as firm.

stirring regularly, until the vegetables soften, and the onion becomes translucent, 7 to 10 minutes. Season with salt and pepper, then add the parsley, garlic, paprika, thyme, and oregano and cook for another 3 to 5 minutes, stirring as needed, to develop the aromas and combine the flavors. Transfer the vegetables to a bowl and set aside.

4. Clean the pan thoroughly (any stuck bits will burn and give the roux a bitter flavor). Return the pan to medium-low heat, and when hot, add the butter. Once the butter has melted, add the flour, stirring to make a homogenous paste. Continue stirring constantly with a wooden spoon to prevent burning, until the roux has turned a light brown color like peanut butter, 10 to 15 minutes.

5. Add the vegetables, stirring to coat thoroughly with the roux, then slowly add the beer, stirring constantly until completely incorporated and absorbed into the roux. Increase the heat to medium-high and add 1 cup (240 ml) of the shrimp stock, whisking until completely incorporated and the mixture is smooth like pancake batter, with no lumps. Immediately add the remaining stock, slowly pouring while whisking to remove any lumps, and bring up to a simmer. Adjust the heat to medium-low to keep the étouffée gently simmering for 10 minutes, until the stock has thickened, and the flavors have melded.

6. Stir in the chicken-of-the-woods, shrimp, and hot sauce and let cook for another 2 to 3 minutes to bring the flavors together.

7. Adjust the seasoning to taste. Serve over the cooked rice, garnished with parsley and scallions, with additional hot sauce on the side.

A beautiful cluster of chicken-of-the-woods

French Onion Soup with Mushroom Toast

Serves 8

I stumbled onto the incredible utility of mushroom soaking liquid quite accidentally, while making soups every day for a large group that included many vegetarians. I had regular requests for classic French onion soup, but couldn't use the traditional veal stock as a base. I was working with dried porcini for another dish and realized that soaking them in extra water would leave enough liquid for a soup base. The vegetarian French onion soup that resulted got rave reviews all around, and ultimately changed the way I did a lot of my cooking. Not only does this make a traditional meat-based dish vegetarian friendly, but it also makes it sit a lot less heavy in your stomach. I have made this version dozens of times in professional kitchens, and nobody has ever missed the meat broth. The soup is all about the caramelized onion flavor, and the mushrooms elevate the cheesy crouton.

1 ounce (28 g) dried porcini

3 quarts (2.8 L) cold water

2 tablespoons oil

1 tablespoon unsalted butter

3 pounds (1.3 kg) red onions, halved and thinly sliced

1 large bunch of fresh thyme, leaves only

½ cup (120 ml) brandy or cognac

1 tablespoon sherry vinegar or red wine vinegar

Pinch of sugar, optional

¼ cup (60 ml) dry red wine

Eight ½-inch-thick (1.25 cm) slices good crusty bread, trimmed to fit inside the serving vessels, toasted

0.5 pound (225 g) grated Gruyère

1. Add the dried porcini to a large bowl, cover with the cold water, and set aside to soak for at least 20 minutes.

2. Set a large, heavy-bottomed pot over medium heat and add 1 tablespoon of the oil, then add the butter. Once the butter has melted, add the onions. Stir regularly to prevent burning and cook for 5 to 7 minutes, until they being to soften and release their moisture, then reduce the heat to medium-low and continue to cook, stirring regularly, until deeply caramelized. This may take 1 hour, or even longer. Remember, this soup is all about the love you give to the onions, so do not rush.

3. Add half of the thyme leaves and season with salt, increase the heat to medium-high, and add the brandy and vinegar, scraping up any browned bits from the bottom of the pot. (The alcohol may flame up, so be careful! Do not try to scrape up the browned bits until after any flames burn out.)

4. When only about 1 tablespoon of liquid remains, strain the mushroom soaking liquid into the pot, reserving the rehydrated mushrooms separately. Increase the heat to high and bring to a boil. Reduce the heat to medium-low to keep the soup at a simmer, and cook until the liquid has reduced by about one third, 20 to 30 minutes. When almost done simmering, taste and season well with salt and add the pinch of sugar, if using. Stir in the remaining thyme leaves and then remove the pot from the heat.

5. Heat a heavy-bottomed pan over medium-high heat. Add the remaining oil, then add the reserved soaked mushrooms. Season with salt and cook, stirring regularly, until lightly browned, 2 to 3 minutes. Add the wine and scrape up any browned bits from the bottom of the pan, then continue cooking until the wine has almost completely

Mushroom Substitutions: Any big-flavored dried mushroom, especially pored mushrooms like *Suillus* or bicolor boletes (*Baorangia bicolor*), will work here. If using mushrooms that need thorough cooking to be safe to eat, such as morels, cook them well after soaking; refer to the list on pages 10–26 for appropriate cooking methods.

reduced, 1 to 2 minutes. Transfer the mushrooms to a cutting board, let cool slightly, then chop finely. Arrange the chopped mushrooms on top of the toasts and top each toast with a generous layer of grated Gruyère.

6. Preheat the oven to 400°F (200°C). Divide the soup between 8 oven-safe crocks or bowls and cover each with one of the toasts. (If you don't have any oven-safe crocks or bowls, you can bake the toasts on a rimmed baking sheet and place them on top of the soup at the table.) Carefully place the crocks on a rimmed baking sheet and transfer to the oven. Bake until the cheese melts and starts to brown, 5 to 10 minutes. Serve hot, straight from the oven.

Tip: *For a vegan soup base, just omit the butter. You can also use a vegan cheese substitute to make the croutons vegan.*

Saffron Milk Cap Stew with Pork Belly and Potatoes

Serves 4 to 6

Years ago, I whipped up a batch of this stew with saffron milk caps right before Rosa was set to travel to Barcelona to visit her family. She got the idea to bring a portion home for her mother to try—a decision that, considering I had yet to meet my eventual mother-in-law, had me feeling extremely nervous! Similar stews appear throughout Spain. What if her mom concluded that I didn't understand the food of her people? Thankfully, shortly after arriving in Barcelona, Rosa sent me an email with her mom's post-meal comment: *Es un estofado como es de ley.* ("This is a stew as it's supposed to be.") Attached was a picture of her mother smiling, thumbs up, in front of a bowl of my stew. Whew!

0.5 pound (225 g) braised pork belly (see page 226), cold, cut into 1-inch (2.5 cm) squares, ¼-inch (6 mm) thick

1 pound (450 g) saffron milk caps, cut into ½-inch (1.25 cm) pieces

1 bunch of fresh parsley, roughly chopped

5 garlic cloves, crushed

1 yellow onion, diced

1 pound (450 g) fingerling potatoes, cut into bite-size pieces

1 tablespoon pimentón de la vera (Spanish smoked paprika)

½ cup (120 ml) white wine

Extra virgin olive oil

Toasted crusty bread

1. Heat a large, heavy-bottomed pan over medium heat. Add the pork belly in a single layer. (If it doesn't all fit in a single layer, cook it in batches.) Cook until the pieces have browned on the bottom, then turn them over to brown the other side, about 3 minutes per side. Transfer to a bowl and set aside. Spoon about half of the rendered fat into a small bowl and reserve, leaving the rest in the pan.

2. Add the saffron milk caps to the pan. Sauté, stirring regularly, until the mushrooms are just lightly browned, 5 to 10 minutes. (Depending on how much water they release, they may need to cook for a little longer to reduce the liquid before they start to brown.) Transfer to a bowl and set aside.

3. Grind all but a small handful of the parsley, the garlic, and a pinch of salt to a coarse paste, using either a mortar and pestle or a food processor with a small bowl. Set aside.

4. Add the reserved fat to the empty pan, then add the onion. Reduce the heat to medium-low and sauté, stirring regularly, until soft but not browned, 7 to 10 minutes. Stir in the potatoes and saffron milk caps, and then stir in the pimentón and season with salt. Cook for another 2 minutes, stirring regularly, to bring out the aroma and flavor of the pimentón.

5. Stir in the parsley mixture and sauté, stirring regularly, just long enough to cook the raw taste out of the garlic, about 2 minutes. Add the wine and scrape up any browned bits from the bottom of the pan. Pour in just enough water to barely cover all of the ingredients, increase the heat to high to bring to a boil, then reduce the heat to medium low to simmer.

Mushroom Substitutions: Any of your favorite *Russula* or milk caps, beech (shimeji) mushrooms, white buttons, crimini, or other *Agaricus* buttons will work here. Hawk's wings, giant sawgill (*Neolentinus ponderosus*), and corals (*Ramaria* spp.) also are a great option.

Saffron milk caps really shine in stews.

6. Simmer the stew gently, adding more water as necessary to keep the vegetables mostly submerged, until the potatoes are fork-tender, but not falling apart, 15 to 20 minutes. Adjust the seasoning to taste.

7. Serve immediately, garnished with the remaining parsley, a drizzle of olive oil, and toasted crusty bread. The stew keeps well for 4 or 5 days in the fridge. If needed, add a little water when reheating.

Tip: *When I cook pork belly at home, I always freeze portions after cooking for easy use in dishes like this one. The Candy Cap Brined and Braised Pork Belly (page 226) works excellently here. If you don't have leftover pork belly, a piece of slab bacon can be portioned and treated exactly the same. If your butcher doesn't have slab bacon, just substitute the thickest sliced bacon you can find.*

Sordid Waxy Cap, Potato, and Pea Curry (Aloo Matar)

Serves 4

David Arora's *Mushrooms Demystified* taught my entire generation about mushrooms. His funny editorial comments, especially in edibility discussions, soften dives into deep science and cultural lore. In one note, Arora bemoans the sordid waxy cap (*Hygrophorus sordidus*) for ruining a potato and pea curry by becoming "gummy, amorphous masses of slime that coagulated around or completely engulfed the peas and savory chunks of potato, rendering the entire dish inedible (though unforgettable)." He, unsurprisingly, advised against eating waxy caps. Years later, I learned David had become a proponent of eating these mushrooms, along with many other less-appreciated edibles. Meanwhile, Rosa and I had begun sampling all the waxy caps we could find after learning how popular they were in Catalonia, where she's from. David's sordid villain was one of our favorites. My friend Jonathan Frank and I decided to redeem David's infamous curry, which evolved into this recipe. The mushrooms are not a traditional part of Indian potato (aloo) and pea (matar) stews, but I love the texture and earthy, meaty flavor they add.

GARAM MASALA

- 1 tablespoon plus 1½ teaspoons whole coriander seeds
- 1 tablespoon whole cumin seeds
- 13 to 15 whole green cardamom pods
- 15 whole cloves
- 1 teaspoon black peppercorns
- ½ teaspoon fennel seeds
- 2 bay leaves
- 1 teaspoon ground cinnamon
- ½ teaspoon cayenne pepper

ALOO MATAR

- 1 pound (450 g) waxy potatoes such as Yukon Gold, red, or fingerling, peeled and cut into ¾-inch (2 cm) pieces
- 1 pound (450 g) sordid waxy caps (about 3 large mushrooms), cut into ½-inch (1.25 cm) pieces
- 2 tablespoons oil
- 1 tablespoon whole cumin seeds
- 1 large yellow onion, diced
- One 2-inch (5 cm) piece ginger, peeled and minced
- One 2-inch (5 cm) piece fresh turmeric, peeled and grated, or 1 tablespoon ground turmeric
- 3 garlic cloves, minced
- 6 Roma tomatoes, puréed
- 6 cashews, ground using a mortar and pestle or a spice grinder, optional
- 2 cups (280 g) shelled and blanched green peas or thawed frozen peas
- Fresh cilantro sprigs

1. To make the garam masala, one spice at a time, toast the coriander seeds, cumin seeds, cardamom pods, cloves, peppercorns, and fennel seeds in a small, dry pan, stirring often to prevent burning, until very fragrant, 2 to 3 minutes each. Let cool completely, then add the toasted spices and bay leaves to a spice grinder and grind to a fine powder. Transfer to a small bowl and stir in the cinnamon and cayenne. (The garam masala will be at its best when freshly made, but it will keep for a few months in an airtight container.)

continued ›

Mushroom Substitutions: The subalpine waxy cap (*H. subalpinus*), a spring montane species, is a great substitute for the sordid waxy caps, as are butter boletes and any meaty, mild *Russula* or *Lactarius*. White button or crimini mushrooms work great, too. Cauliflower mushrooms (*Sparassis* spp.) add a fun texture, and any mushroom that cooks well in big chunky pieces is worth a try.

The sordid waxy cap, Hygrophorus sordidus

2. To make the aloo matar, add the potatoes to a saucepan and cover with water. Salt the water generously and bring to a boil over high heat, then reduce the heat to keep the water at a gentle simmer until the potatoes are just barely tender, about 10 minutes. Drain immediately and set aside.

3. Dry sauté the sordid waxy caps, following the instructions on page 31, using 1 tablespoon of the oil, until the mushrooms are lightly browned, then season with salt, remove from the heat, and set aside.

4. Place a large, heavy-bottomed pan over medium heat and add the remaining oil, then add the cumin seeds. When the seeds have just started to sizzle, about 30 seconds, stir in the onion, then add the ginger, turmeric, garlic, and 1½ teaspoons garam masala. Continue sautéing, stirring regularly, until the onions are soft, 5 to 7 minutes. Season with salt, then stir in the tomatoes.

5. Adjust the heat to keep at a gentle simmer and continue cooking, stirring regularly, until the puréed tomatoes have reduced to about ½ cup (120 ml). Stir in the ground cashews, if using, and continue cooking for 1 to 2 more minutes to help thicken the remaining liquid. Stir in the peas, potatoes, and sordid waxy caps, and bring back to a simmer for 3 minutes to heat through and harmonize the flavors. If the stew ever gets too dry, stir in a small amount of water. You want to finish with just enough sauce to coat all of the ingredients. Adjust the salt to taste. Serve, garnishing each portion with cilantro sprigs.

Sweet Corn Soup with Huitlacoche

Serves 8

I have been making versions of this corn soup for decades, and people always love it. It is all about sweet corn, so make it at the height of the season with the freshest corn you can find. The huitlacoche adds an incredible depth of flavor along with a fun textural contrast to the creamy soup. The first time I used huitlacoche with this soup, it elevated it to such levels that my diners were practically fighting with each other to get more. Ever since, it's regularly appeared on the summertime menus of my formal mushroom dinners.

8 ears sweet corn, shucked

¼ cup (60 g) unsalted butter

2 large shallots or 1 small sweet onion, roughly chopped

1 recipe Huitlacoche Purée (page 72), prepared through Step 2

1. Use a serrated knife to strip the corn kernels off the cobs and into a large bowl. Place the stripped cobs in a large pot and cover with cold water. Bring to a boil over high heat, then reduce the heat to medium-low to simmer for 45 to 60 minutes to make a flavorful stock. Set the corn stock aside.

2. Heat a large, heavy-bottomed pan over medium-low heat. Add the butter, and when melted, add the shallots and a pinch of salt. Cook, stirring regularly, until soft but not browned, about 5 minutes. Stir in the corn kernels and another pinch of salt, increase the heat to medium, and continue cooking, stirring regularly, for 5 to 10 minutes, until the kernels are tender and glossy.

3. Remove the corn cobs from the corn stock and discard, then add 2 quarts (1.9 L) of the corn stock to the pan. (You do not need to strain it.) If you have less than 2 quarts (1.9 L) of stock, make up the difference with water. Increase the heat to high to bring to a boil, then adjust the heat to keep the soup at a simmer. Let it simmer for 20 to 30 minutes, adding more water if the water level ever dips below the top of the corn, to allow the flavors to concentrate. Adjust the salt to taste.

4. Working in batches, carefully transfer the soup to a blender. Blend, starting on low speed and working your way slowly up to high speed, for at least 1 minute, until smooth and creamy. (The longer you blend, the stronger the sweet corn flavor will be.) Adjust the salt to taste. If the soup is too thick for your liking, add water while blending. If the soup is thinner than preferred, leave some of the liquid behind in the pan during blending. For the smoothest, creamiest texture, pass the soup through a fine-mesh strainer.

5. Serve hot, with a generous portion of the prepared huitlacoche spooned on top of individual portions.

Mushroom Substitutions: There is no substitute for huitlacoche in this recipe.

7

Pasta and Rice

I love fresh pasta. I love the feel of the dough coming together in my fingers, feeling it smooth out and firm up while kneading, the process of rolling it out, and the joy of getting friends together to laugh at our attempts to form classic shapes. The act of making pasta always draws people in as if hypnotized, building up anticipation for the meal that will follow. Even in professional kitchens, when someone starts making pasta, everyone strays from their overly busy to-do list to watch for a moment. A well-made, fresh, from-scratch pasta dish is about as comforting as comfort food gets, and it's hard to imagine a better use for homemade pasta, and mushrooms, of course, than some of the dishes that follow.

You'll notice that many of the recipes in this chapter are a bit more involved than in other chapters. I am confident that you can already cook mushrooms, cook a package of dried pasta in boiling water, and then toss the mushrooms with the pasta without any help from me. This chapter challenges you to expand your pasta repertoire. Mushrooms present us with great opportunities to learn some more advanced techniques, like creating filled pastas, and pasta provides an excellent backdrop for some cool mushroom cooking techniques.

Imagine your next family pasta night featuring Lion's Mane Cannelloni (page 182), or inviting your friends over for Hen-of-the-Woods and Broccoli Pierogi (page 191). I hope you'll look at pasta in totally new ways after exploring this chapter.

Fresh, handmade cavatelli, ready for cooking

Cauliflower Mushroom Carbonara

Serves 2 as an entrée or 4 as a starter

This may be my favorite recipe in this entire book, and it has been an absolute home run every time I've served it at a dinner or class over the years. Traditional carbonara takes humble eggs, guanciale, and Parmesan cheese and transforms them into a rich, creamy sauce. Despite their name, cauliflower mushrooms (*Sparassis* spp.) look much more like a bundle of egg noodles than a head of cauliflower, and many people like to use them as a noodle replacement with beef stroganoff or as the "noodles" in chicken noodle soup. Following their lead, in this recipe, I replace the pasta with cauliflower mushroom "noodles." The pleasantly mild flavor and uniquely crisp texture of the mushroom is, in my opinion, an improvement on the usual spaghetti. Guanciale are pork jowls that are cured in a similar way as pork belly is for pancetta. The results will be just as delicious if you use pancetta or bacon instead.

4 ounces (115 g) guanciale, skin removed, finely diced

1 teaspoon extra virgin olive oil

1 large garlic clove, minced

¼ teaspoon minced fresh rosemary

Generous pinch of red pepper flakes

2 eggs

1 cup (120 g) finely grated Parmesan

1 pound (450 g) cauliflower mushrooms (about 4 to 5 cups), torn into "noodles"

1. Add the guanciale, olive oil, garlic, rosemary, red pepper flakes, and a few grinds of black pepper to a large pan. Cook over low heat until all of the fat has rendered from the guanciale and the meat is crispy, 10 to 15 minutes. Keep warm over low heat.

2. Beat the eggs with 1 tablespoon water in a large bowl, then thoroughly mix in a little more than ¾ cup (90 g) of the Parmesan, along with salt and a generous amount of freshly ground black pepper.

3. Bring a large pot of salted water to a rolling boil over high heat. Add the cauliflower mushrooms and let boil for 5 minutes to cook through, then drain, reserving a few tablespoons of the cooking water separately.

4. Immediately toss the mushrooms into the pan with the guanciale mixture. While still very hot, as soon as the cauliflower is well-coated in the fat, add it all to the bowl of egg and Parmesan and mix very well to coat evenly. Add a couple tablespoons of the mushroom cooking water as needed to thin the sauce.

5. Serve immediately, topped with the remaining Parmesan and more freshly ground black pepper.

Tip: *It is absolutely essential to mix the "noodles" with the egg mixture while the "noodles" are still steaming hot. They will cook the eggs and cheese together, turning them into a sauce.*

Mushroom Substitutions: There's no substitute for the cauliflower mushrooms here.

Suillus Agnolotti with Fennel-Shallot Broth and Hideous Gomphidius Garnish

Serves 6 to 8

Despite looking extremely fancy and fussy, these agnolotti—small stuffed pasta pillows—are the quickest and easiest filled pasta shape I know how to make. If you can roll out pasta sheets, you can quickly learn to make this elegant pasta. This agnolotti method is a variation on a technique popularized in professional circles after appearing in *The French Laundry Cookbook*. It's a perfect opportunity to showcase good flavored but texturally problematic mushrooms like *Suillus* by puréeing them into the filling. This dish is also a bit of an esoteric ecological joke, as the *Gomphidius* are thought to be parasites of *Suillus*, but you need not use obscure mushrooms. This dish will impress with just about any mushrooms you have on hand. You will need a pasta machine for this recipe.

AGNOLOTTI DOUGH

2 cups (250 g) all-purpose flour

1 teaspoon salt

2 eggs plus 1 yolk

1 tablespoon extra virgin olive oil

MUSHROOM FILING

1 cup (220 g) Duxelles made from *Suillus* spp. (page 70), blended fairly smooth

FENNEL-SHALLOT BROTH

3 shallots, roughly chopped

1 garlic clove, crushed

1 tablespoon whole fennel seeds

1 tablespoon whole coriander seeds

GARNISH

4 young, firm slime spikes, cut into ¼-inch (6 mm) slices

1 tablespoon oil

Fresh chervil leaves

Extra virgin olive oil

1. To make the agnolotti dough, heap the flour in a wide circular mound on your cutting board and mix in the salt. Make a well in the center, and add the eggs and yolk, olive oil, and 1 tablespoon water. Using a fork, carefully beat the eggs, slowly incorporating flour from the edges of the depression. When the egg mix starts becoming too thick to mix with the fork, scrape all of the doughy bits off the fork with your fingers and add back to the dough. Use your hands to knead the dough, folding in a little of the remaining flour with each fold until it comes together as a solid piece. Continue working in the flour only until the dough is no longer sticky. At that point, use a scraper or knife to push the rest of the flour to the side.

2. Continue kneading for at least 5 minutes, until the dough becomes very smooth and homogeneous. If the dough feels a bit dry, sprinkle your hands with a couple of drops of water and continue kneading; the water will get incorporated into the dough as you work it. If the dough is too wet or sticky, work in a bit more flour. When the dough is smooth, wrap it tightly in plastic and let sit for at least 30 minutes, or up to 24 hours, to relax the gluten. If leaving the dough for more than 1 hour, rest it in the fridge.

3. Before rolling the pasta, clear a large work surface and divide the pasta ball in half, keeping one half wrapped in plastic. Roll out one half to the thickness of the second-lowest setting on your machine. The sheet should be thin and pliable, but not so thin that it becomes fragile and can easily tear.

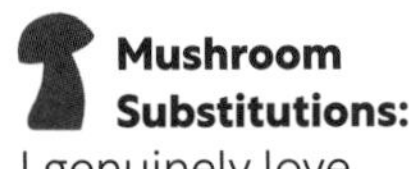

Mushroom Substitutions: I genuinely love using slippery jacks (*Suillus* spp.) and slime spikes (*Gomphidius* spp.) here, but almost any mushrooms will work in the pasta filling or for the garnish.

continued ›

4. To make the mushroom filling, place the duxelles into a piping bag with a round ¼-inch (6 mm) tip, or a disposable piping bag with a ¼-inch diameter hole cut in the tip.

5. Lay the pasta sheet on the clean, dry work surface and pipe a long line of filling, ¼ inch (6 mm) from the end, along the whole length of the sheet, leaving ¼-inch borders on both ends. Fill a small bowl with water. Using your finger or a brush, paint a very light and thin line of water down the length of the sheet, right next to the filling. Carefully fold the edge of the sheet over the filling, down the length, gently pressing the pasta edge down against the moistened line to seal it closed. Make sure the entire length is sealed well, like a long, thin tube.

6. Working from one end of the tube to the other, seal off individual agnolotti. First, push down on the end of the tube using your fingertip. Holding your fingertip down to keep the end sealed, place another fingertip ½ inch (1.25 cm) up the tube, and press firmly to seal it off. This should leave a ½-inch by ¼-inch (1.25 cm by 6 mm) stuffed pillow at the end of the tube. Keeping one fingertip pressed down, press down another ½ inch away from the first pillow to create another little pillow. Repeat this process, working down the whole length of the sheet. (To make a fancier version of the shape, slightly lift and tilt the filled tube up at a 90-degree angle as you pinch off the little pillow shapes. When you cut them in the next step, a tiny little pocket will form along the sealed edge of each agnolotti.)

7. Using a fluted or straight cutting wheel, cut down the whole length of the sheet parallel to the row of agnolotti, leaving about ¼-inch (6 mm) border. Then, use the cutting wheel to cut through the seam between each of the agnolotti to separate them. Carefully place them on a floured sheet until ready to cook. Make sure they are not touching each other, or they will stick together. You should be able to fit at least a second row of agnolotti on each pasta sheet, and if your pasta machine is very wide, a third. Repeat the rolling, filling, shaping, and cutting with the second piece of dough and the remaining filling. (You can lightly

cover and refrigerate the agnolotti for up to 24 hours or freeze them in a single layer for longer storage. Once frozen, they can be tossed together in an airtight bag and stored for several weeks in the freezer.)

8. To make the fennel-shallot broth, heat a small saucepan over medium-high heat. Add the shallots and garlic to the dry pan and cook, stirring occasionally, until they are well browned but not burned, 2 to 3 minutes. Add the fennel and coriander seeds and toast, stirring constantly, for 10 to 15 seconds.

9. Add ¼ cup (60 ml) water and scrape up any browned bits from the bottom of the pan. Add another 1¼ cups (300 ml) water and bring to a boil over high heat. Reduce the heat and let the mixture simmer for about 5 minutes to flavor the broth. Season with salt, then strain, discard the solids, and keep the broth warm over low heat.

10. To make the garnish, dry sauté the slime spikes, following the instructions on page 31, using the oil, until lightly browned. Season with salt and set aside until needed.

11. While the mushrooms cook, bring a large pot of salted water to a boil over high heat. Spread a few drops of olive oil over a rimmed baking sheet. Working in batches to avoid overcrowding the pot, add the agnolotti to the water, stirring to keep them from sticking to the bottom and each other. They will sink to the bottom at first, then start to float to the surface as they cook. Let them cook for about 1 minute after they float up to the top, then use a spider skimmer or slotted spoon to carefully transfer the agnolotti from the water to the oiled tray. Repeat with the remaining agnolotti.

12. To serve, spoon about ½ cup (120 ml) of the fennel-shallot broth into individual bowls. Gently place a generous portion of the agnolotti in the broth, then spoon the sautéed mushrooms on top in a tight, neat mound. Garnish with the fresh chervil leaves and a few drops of extra virgin olive oil.

Tip: *I strongly recommend forming agnolotti from one pasta sheet before rolling out the second to prevent the sheets from drying too much while you work.*

Lion's Mane Cannelloni

Serves 6 to 8

Cannelloni, popular in both Italy and Catalonia (where they are called *canelons*), are large tubes of pasta stuffed with a filling and then covered in sauce and baked. In Catalonia and parts of Italy, you most commonly see them made with a meat filling and a béchamel sauce, but the filling and sauce combinations are limited only by your imagination. The crabmeat-like texture and rich flavor of the lion's mane filling complement the classic béchamel sauce. You will need a pasta machine for this recipe. If you don't want to make fresh pasta, you can roll the filling in cooked lasagna noodles, though you will likely need to cut the noodles a bit smaller.

FILLING

1 tablespoon plus 1½ teaspoons oil

4 cups (560 g) butternut squash or pumpkin, peeled, seeded, and cut into ¼-inch (6 mm) pieces

2 pounds (900 g) lion's mane or comb tooth mushrooms, cut into ½-inch (1.25 cm) pieces

2 tablespoons unsalted butter

2 leeks, white parts only, cleaned, halved lengthwise, and cut into ¼-inch (6 mm) wide strips

Red pepper flakes

BÉCHAMEL SAUCE

¼ cup (60 g) unsalted butter

½ cup (65 g) all-purpose flour

4 cups (960 ml) milk, plus extra as needed

Freshly grated nutmeg

¼ cup (30 g) freshly grated Parmesan

Double recipe of Agnolotti Dough (page 179), prepared through Step 3 and cut into 4-inch (10 cm) squares

1 cup (120 g) freshly grated Parmesan

Olive oil

1. To make the filling, heat a large, heavy-bottomed pan over medium-high heat. Add the oil, then add the squash. Sauté, stirring often, until the squash is soft, 7 to 10 minutes. Season with salt and pepper and set aside in a large bowl.

2. Add the lion's mane mushrooms to the empty pan and dry or wet sauté (depending on their moisture level), following the instructions on page 31. You will likely need to cook them in 2 or 3 batches. When their moisture has reduced away, cook the mushrooms in the butter until they are lightly browned. Add the leeks and continue cooking on medium-low heat, stirring regularly, until the leeks are soft but not browned, 5 to 7 minutes. Season with salt and pepper, then transfer to the bowl with the squash. Season everything with the red pepper flakes. Adjust the salt to taste. Set aside.

3. To make the béchamel sauce, heat a heavy-bottomed saucepan over medium heat. Add the butter, and when melted, whisk in the flour until thoroughly combined. Continue cooking, whisking the roux constantly for about 2 minutes to lightly toast the flour.

4. While whisking, pour in 1 cup (240 ml) of the milk. When it has been incorporated with no lumps, add another 1 cup milk, again whisking constantly until it is incorporated and being sure to whisk out any lumps. Whisk in the remaining milk, then stir in the nutmeg and season with salt. Continue whisking regularly as the sauce heats

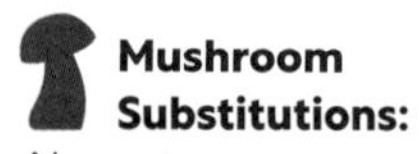

Almost any mushrooms will work here. The mild, creamy sauce and other filling ingredients play nicely with just about everything.

Lion's mane looks like a pom-pom growing out of a tree!

up to ensure it doesn't burn on the bottom of the pan. When the sauce begins to boil, reduce the heat to medium-low to simmer, still whisking regularly, for 5 to 10 minutes, to thicken the sauce until it's just thick enough to cling to the back of a spoon. If the sauce gets too thick, you can whisk in a little more milk to thin it out. Remove the béchamel from the heat, season with pepper, and whisk in the Parmesan until fully melted and the sauce is again smooth. Adjust the seasoning to taste.

5. Bring a large, generously salted pot of water to a boil over high heat. While the water is heating up, cover a flat, clean surface with a clean sheet or large towel. When the water is boiling, cook the pasta sheets a few at a time, boiling for about 1 minute, then immediately remove from the water with a spider skimmer, or slotted spoon, drizzle with a few drops of olive oil, and spread them out flat on the sheet. Continue until you have cooked all of the pasta sheets.

6. Preheat the oven to 375°F (190°C). If the béchamel has cooled and gotten too thick to easily work with, reheat it gently while whisking. Spread a generous layer of béchamel in the bottom a casserole or baking dish. Spoon a substantial line of mushroom filling across the middle of each pasta sheet. Carefully roll each sheet into a tube around the filling as tightly as possible without causing filling to spill out the ends, and place seam-side down in the casserole dish. Repeat with the rest of the pasta and filling, arranging the cannelloni tightly against each other in the baking dish.

7. When the casserole dish is full, spoon a generous layer of béchamel over the top of the cannelloni, and then spread the Parmesan in an even layer on top (it's OK if you have some béchamel left). Bake until hot all the way through and lightly browned on top, 30 to 45 minutes. Serve hot, straight from the oven.

Tip: *You can assemble individual portions of cannelloni in smaller baking dishes, or you can cook them family style in a larger casserole or baking dish. My wife's Catalan family always cooks them in a large casserole, and they layer the cannelloni two or three layers deep. If you have more than one layer of cannelloni, you will need to add a layer of sauce and a bit of cheese between each pasta layer.*

Rethinking the Shaggy Mane

Most mushroom hunters are familiar with the extremely widespread and common shaggy mane (*Coprinus comatus*). They can be found pushing up through very tough, compacted soil and even breaking through asphalt immediately after a rainstorm, but they're also ephemeral, beginning to melt away before the end of the day. Rows of them often pop up along the edges of roads, though they can appear just about anywhere, whether forest, waste, or field.

Another "inky" species, the mica cap (*Coprinellus micaceus*), is also incredibly common and widespread, but not as frequently eaten. Mica caps are small mushrooms that don't have much, if any, texture when cooked, but they have a strong flavor comparable to their shaggy mane cousins.

Mushroom hunters consistently hear that they need to "hurry up and eat these mushrooms before they start to turn, because they're no good once they start getting inky." I want to challenge this conventional wisdom by saying that not only should you not worry if they're getting inky, but that they actually become a really cool and unique weapon in your kitchen arsenal once they turn, or deliquesce. Deliquescing is an enzymatic process that happens quickly as a natural part of these mushrooms' life cycle, usually beginning within a few hours of sprouting. It causes the mushroom to begin to digest its own tissue and to slowly disintegrate into an inky black liquid, but it does not make the mushrooms any less edible. Inky specimens provide a powerful, mature mushroom taste, and they can give an amazingly deep black color to dishes. You can eat shaggy manes and mica caps just like any other mushrooms, of course, but the inked-out mushrooms open up an exciting set of culinary possibilities.

When collecting shaggy manes and mica caps, especially for turning into an inky purée, it is best to use a rigid, watertight container or a sealable plastic bag. Because the deliquescing process happens so quickly, even very nice, clean specimens can quickly start disintegrating and making a mess of your basket or bag. Collect only mature or nearly mature mushrooms for ink; any beginning to show a little of the black color on the edge of the cap are perfect. Immature mushrooms still in button stage will usually not deliquesce after you collect them, so cook them fresh.

As soon as you get them home, rinse the mushrooms clean. Leaving them damp helps accelerate the process.

Inky Purée

Makes about 2 cups (480 ml)

By allowing shaggy manes to follow their natural process of melting into an inky mess, you can transform them into a black mushroom purée that will give dishes a stark black color and an intense but pleasant mushroom flavor. It's simple to make, tastes and looks great, and is very versatile. Now, whenever I come across substantial numbers of worthy mushrooms, I collect them, make this purée, and throw it in the freezer, where it keeps for many months.

1 pound (450 g) "overripe" shaggy manes or mica caps

1. Place the mushrooms in a bowl and let rest on the counter for 1 to 2 hours to get the deliquescing process started, then move to the fridge. The deliquescing process takes anywhere from a few hours to overnight. When the contents of the bowl look like a black soup of mushroom scraps, proceed with Step 2.

2. Place all the mushroom scraps, along with their inky black liquid, into a small saucepan. Add a pinch of salt, bring to a boil over medium-high heat, then quickly reduce the heat to medium-low to simmer gently.

3. The mushrooms will release a bit more moisture as they cook. Continue to simmer the liquid in the pan for 2 to 5 minutes, until reduced by about one quarter. Remove from the heat, then blend until very smooth. The purée should have a consistency slightly thinner than that of applesauce. If the purée is too thin, reduce it further on the stove. If it is too thick, dilute to the desired consistency with water. The purée can now be used or frozen. It will keep for 5 to 6 months, frozen in an airtight container.

Tip: *Defrosting the frozen purée can sometimes cause it to separate a little. Once completely thawed, you can buzz it with an immersion blender to recombine. It helps to emulsify the purée with some fat (especially butter) to make sauces.*

Mushroom Substitutions: There really is no substitute for shaggy manes or mica caps. I do not eat the "true" inky cap (*Coprinopsis atramentaria*) because it contains a compound, coprine, that causes severe negative reactions if you consume any alcohol within a couple of days before or after eating the mushrooms. Neither shaggy manes nor mica caps contain this compound, and both are thus safe to consume with alcohol. There are many other, mostly tiny or uncommon, inky species, but I'm not aware of anyone eating any of them, nor am I certain which of them do or do not contain coprine.

Black Inky Pasta

Serves 4 to 6

This dish was inspired by both black-colored squid ink pastas and sauces. Though it may look just like the seafood-filled versions, this vegetarian dish focuses completely on deep mushroom flavor. The inky purée has a far more dramatic impact on the flavor and appearance of the sauce than it does on the pasta, so use the ink for just the sauce if you have a limited amount of purée and must choose. You will need a pasta machine for this recipe.

INKY PASTA

2 cups (250 g) all-purpose flour

2 egg yolks

Generous pinch of salt

½ cup (120 ml) Inky Purée (page 185)

INKY SAUCE

1 cup (240 ml) Inky Purée (page 185)

1 tablespoon unsalted butter

1 cup (175 g) fresh porcini, cut into ½-inch (1.25 cm) pieces

1 tablespoon neutral oil

8 cherry tomatoes, halved or quartered

Fresh basil leaves

1. To make the inky pasta, make a mound of flour on a large cutting board and make a bowl-shaped depression in the middle of the mound. Add the yolks, salt, and inky purée into the depression. Using a fork, carefully whisk the wet ingredients together, aiming for a fairly smooth, homogeneous mixture. Slowly start to work bits of flour from the sides of the depression into the wet mix. Keep working in more flour until the mixture gets too thick to mix with the fork.

2. Use your fingers to pull all the clinging bits off the fork, and add them to the wet mix. Use your hands to fold in the remaining flour, little by little, as you knead and rotate the dough. (Many factors, including the humidity of the air and the moisture content of your inky purée, will affect how much flour you need. If the dough starts to get dry, don't try to incorporate all of the flour. Simply scrape the extra flour to the side of the board and continue kneading. If the dough is too wet and sticky, add a bit more flour.)

3. Continue kneading for 5 to 10 minutes to develop the gluten and produce a very smooth dough. Wrap the dough in plastic wrap and let rest for at least 30 minutes, or up to 24 hours, to relax the gluten. If leaving for more than 1 hour before rolling, refrigerate. Remove the dough from the fridge and let it sit at room temperature for 15 minutes to soften before you roll it out.

4. Cut the pasta dough into two pieces, leaving one half wrapped in plastic. Roll out one half to the thinnest setting on your machine and cut long flat noodles like linguine, around ⅛-inch (3 mm) wide, or fettuccine, around ¼-inch (6 mm) wide, as they hold the simple inky sauce beautifully. The mushrooms make the pasta dough retain a lot of

Mushroom Substitutions: Almost any mushrooms will do in place of the porcini garnish. There are no substitutes for the shaggy manes or mica caps used to make the inky purée.

moisture, so you may need to hang your freshly cut noodles on a pasta drying rack, or over the back of a chair or a clean broomstick, for a few minutes to dry them and keep them from sticking together. Repeat with the second half of the dough.

5. To make the inky sauce, heat the inky purée in a pan large enough to accommodate the cooked pasta over medium heat. Simmer until it has the consistency of heavy cream, 2 to 5 minutes. Turn off the heat and whisk in the butter until completely melted and well incorporated. Add salt to taste. Keep warm.

6. Dry sauté the porcini, following the instructions on page 31, using the neutral oil, until lightly browned. Season lightly with salt, and set aside on low heat to keep warm.

7. Bring a large pot of generously salted water to a boil over high heat. Add the pasta and cook for about 1 minute, until just al dente. Drain the pasta (do not rinse), reserving some of the cooking water, then add the pasta directly to the pan with the sauce. Gently stir it into the sauce to evenly coat. If the sauce looks too thick, use a little bit of the pasta cooking water to thin it out.

8. Spoon some sauce from the pan into individual dishes, then top with the pasta. Garnish with the porcini, cherry tomatoes, and basil.

Black Risotto

Serves 4 to 6

The black ink from shaggy manes turns this simple mushroom risotto into a visually stunning, intensely flavored dish that will grab even the most jaded diner's attention. In several kitchens where I worked as a line cook, cooking risotto using a metal spoon was a big no-no. I've never really believed it to make much of a difference, but the standard folklore is that metal spoons can break the rice grains while you stir. This is one taboo I don't have the heart to break, and as a result, I have several wooden spoons with flattened out edges from countless hours of stirring risotto. The ingredient list calls for more stock than you are likely to need for this recipe, but a lot of variables will affect exactly how much you use, so it is better to start with a bit extra. Only use as much as you need to get the rice cooked properly. Reserve the remaining stock for another use.

1 pound (450 g) fresh fairy ring mushrooms

1 tablespoon neutral oil

1 tablespoon extra virgin olive oil

1½ tablespoons unsalted butter, cut into pieces

1 large shallot, minced

2 garlic cloves, minced

1½ cups (310 g) Arborio or Carnaroli rice

½ cup (120 ml) dry white wine

3½ cups (840 ml) hot mushroom (page 36), vegetable, or chicken stock

1 cup (240 ml) Inky Purée (page 185)

4 or 5 fresh thyme sprigs, leaves only

¼ cup (45 g) pomegranate seeds

1. Dry sauté the fairy ring mushrooms, following the instructions on page 31, using the neutral oil, until lightly browned. Set aside in a bowl.

2. Heat the empty pan over medium heat. Add the extra virgin olive oil and ½ tablespoon of the butter. Once the butter has melted, add the shallot and garlic. Stir and let sizzle for about 1 minute, then add the rice and cooked fairy ring mushrooms, stirring to coat evenly in the fat.

3. Add the wine and continue to stir constantly until the liquid has almost completely reduced, 1 to 2 minutes, then add a couple of ladlesful of the stock. Continue stirring, making sure all of the rice stays beneath the surface of the liquid, until the liquid is mostly absorbed, 3 to 4 minutes, then add another ladleful of stock. Season with salt, and repeat cooking and adding more stock, adding slightly less stock with each addition, while constantly stirring until the rice is almost done. You'll need to taste a couple grains as you go to check its doneness. At this stage, it's better to be a little undercooked. You can always add more stock later to finish. Overcooked rice cannot be fixed.

4. When the rice is nearly al dente, but still a little too hard, instead of adding more stock, stir in the inky purée. Cook and stir until mostly absorbed, then check the rice for doneness again and add more stock if needed. (Most restaurants prepare risotto in advance, so it takes only a few minutes to finish when an order comes in. To do the same at home, stop right before adding the purée—when the rice is a ladleful or two of stock from finished. Spread it in a thin layer on a rimmed baking sheet to cool completely, then store it in a sealed container in the fridge for up to 3 days. To finish cooking, transfer the cold risotto to a pan, stir in a small ladleful of hot stock, and proceed with this step of the recipe.)

Mushroom Substitutions: Almost any mushrooms will do in place of the fairy ring mushrooms (*Marasmius oreades*). There isn't any substitute for the shaggy manes or mica caps in the inky purée that will still give you the deep, dark color, though any good mushroom purée will make a delicious risotto.

Fairy ring mushrooms in the wild

5. When the rice is just about al dente, remove from the heat and stir in the thyme leaves and the remaining butter. Keep stirring until the butter is completely melted and evenly distributed. Adjust the seasoning to taste. Serve immediately, garnished with the pomegranate seeds. If necessary, add a small amount of stock to keep the risotto from getting too "tight" or dry.

Tip: *The rice in risotto should still be very slightly al dente. Too often the rice is overcooked, making for a gummy texture that isn't very enjoyable to eat. Another common risotto error is making it too thick. Risotto should be just slightly runny, not quite thick enough to hold a fork upright or a heavy protein on top of. If your risotto is too thick, stir in a small amount of hot stock to loosen it up before serving. Both of these issues can be caused by letting the risotto sit too long; risotto should be served immediately after it finishes cooking.*

Hen-of-the-Woods and Broccoli Pierogi

Serves 6

In this book full of sentimental recipes, this one may mean the most to me. Growing up, and even into my middle age, pierogi have always been a special treat for me and the rest of my family. Right before the first edition of this book went to print, I made pierogi for my ninety-plus-year-old grandmother using this recipe and the very first wild hen-of-the-woods (Grifola frondosa) that I had ever collected. It was the last time I cooked for my grandmother, and she went back for seconds and thirds at a time in her life where she would rarely finish her first portion.

PIEROGI DOUGH

2¾ cups plus 1 tablespoon (350 g) all-purpose flour

Generous pinch of salt

1 cup (230 g) sour cream

2 egg yolks

1 tablespoon canola oil

1 tablespoon unsalted butter, melted

HEN AND BROCCOLI FILLING

0.5 pound (225 g) broccoli, cut into florets

1 pound (450 g) hen-of-the-woods (maitake), cut into ½-inch (1.25 cm) pieces

1 tablespoon oil

2 garlic cloves, minced

½ cup (120 ml) dry white wine

1 tablespoon unsalted butter

GARNISH

2 large yellow onions, thinly sliced

2 tablespoons oil

1 tablespoon butter

Sour cream

1. To make the pierogi dough, place the flour in a large bowl and mix in the salt. In another bowl, mix the sour cream, egg yolks, canola oil, and melted butter together.

2. Tip the flour onto a clean surface and make a well in the center. Add the wet ingredients to the well and use a fork to gradually work the flour into the wet ingredients. Work as much flour into the mix as possible with the fork, then use your fingers to pull the sticky dough bits off the fork and add them back to the dough. Use your hands to knead until it comes together to form a very smooth dough. This shouldn't take more than a few minutes. If it feels a bit too wet and sticky, you can knead in a little more flour.

3. Cover the dough tightly with plastic wrap, and let it rest at room temperature for at least 30 minutes or up to 4 hours to relax the gluten. If leaving the dough for more than 1 hour, refrigerate it. Let the dough come to room temperature before rolling out.

4. To make the hen and broccoli filling, bring a large pot of salted water to a boil over high heat. Add the broccoli florets and cook until the color sets to a deep dark green and the broccoli is crisp-tender, 1 to 2 minutes. Drain the broccoli and immediately plunge it into a large bowl filled with ice water to stop the cooking process. When cool, drain the broccoli well and set it aside.

5. Dry or wet sauté the hen-of-the-woods (depending on their moisture level), following the instructions on page 31, using the oil. When lightly browned, increase the heat to medium, toss in the garlic, and cook for another 30 seconds, until fragrant. Pour in the wine and scrape any browned bits from the bottom of the pan. When the wine is almost all evaporated, turn off the heat and stir in the butter to coat the mushrooms. Add salt to taste. Let cool slightly.

6. Pulse the mushrooms and broccoli in a food processor until minced and thoroughly mixed, but not puréed. Adjust the seasoning to taste.

continued ❯

Mushroom Substitutions: Almost any mushrooms will work here, but it works best with very flavorful mushrooms like mature porcini, various *Suillus*, *Leccinum*, and portabella.

7. Cut off a large piece of the dough ball and dust your work surface and the dough with a little bit of flour. Roll out the dough into a rectangle 1⁄16-inch (1.5 mm) thick, dusting the work surface, rolling pin, and dough with flour as needed to prevent sticking. If your dough is snapping back too much to finish rolling out, cover and let rest another 15 to 30 minutes. Use a cookie cutter, ring mold, or coffee cup to cut circles out of the dough about 3 inches (7.5 cm) in diameter.

8. Put a generous spoonful of filling in the center of each circle. Carefully fold the circle in half over the filling. Seal the edge by pinching the dough firmly between your thumb and forefinger or pressing with the tines of a fork, starting at one corner and working your way around to the other corner. Do your best to gently press out any air pockets as you seal up each pierogi. Set the pierogi on a floured tray, or a piece of parchment paper, making sure they don't touch each other to prevent sticking. Repeat the rolling, filling, and sealing until all the dough is used up. The dough scraps can be kneaded back together and rerolled up to 3 times. (You can freeze the pierogi at this point if you like. Freeze in a single layer, being careful not to let them touch, until they are completely frozen, then transfer to an airtight container. They will last for up to 1 month in the freezer and can be boiled from frozen.)

9. To make the garnish, heat a heavy-bottomed pan over medium heat. Add 1 tablespoon of the oil, then add the onions. Sauté, stirring regularly, until the onions are lightly browned, about 10 minutes. Season with salt, and set aside.

10. Generously oil a rimmed baking sheet or large plate. Bring a large pot of salted water to a boil over high heat. Boil the pierogi in batches of 4 to 7 at a time, being sure not to crowd them too much. When they float to the top, cook about 20 seconds longer, then scoop them out with a spider skimmer or slotted spoon, drain well, and transfer to the prepared baking sheet or plate.

11. Heat a large, heavy-bottomed pan over medium heat. Add the butter and the remaining oil. Cooking in batches, add some of the pierogi to the pan in a single layer. When the bottoms are golden brown, carefully flip each pierogi and brown the other side, about 3 minutes per side. Wipe out the pan and add more oil and butter between each batch. Serve hot with a dollop of sour cream and a generous helping of sautéed onions.

A Tale of (A Lot More Than) Two Hedgehogs

Hedgehog mushrooms (*Hydnum* spp.) get their name from the spiny little teeth adorning the bottom of the cap instead of the gills that adorn so many mushrooms. For many years, mushroom people divided the hedgehogs in North America into just two species, the big chunky sweet tooth (*Hydnum repandum*), and the smaller, more delicate bellybutton (*H. umbilicatum*). Some folks also occasionally talked of another hedgehog or two in some parts of the country. Recently, though, DNA work has revealed that the two or three species we all thought we knew are now believed to be more than a dozen species in North America alone. Thankfully, you can leave sorting through all these species to the academics. And when it comes to cooking and collecting for the table, thinking in terms of the sweet tooth versus the bellybutton still works as well as it ever has.

Bellybuttons, the smaller of the hedgehogs, cook up deliciously with a simple sauté. If they are on the wet side, use a dry sauté (page 31); if a bit drier, use a wet sauté (page 31). Their flavor is nutty and almost sweet, and they need very little help beyond a bit of salt. Bellybuttons also pick very clean—often requiring no further cleaning if harvested carefully. Unfortunately, because they are quite small, it can take a good amount of effort sometimes to find enough for a large meal. I love using them in just about any applications that let sautéed mushrooms shine.

The large and meaty sweet tooth hedgehog: Note how small the needles look that are embedded in the flesh.

Sweet tooths, the larger of the hedgehogs, have a wonderful texture that I've found is best brought out by a wet sauté. The flavor can be a bit variable, and occasionally, a little on the bland side. Years ago, it was a revelation to me when my friend Tom Jelen told me how well the bigger hedgehogs absorb other flavors, especially when roasted or sautéed with meats and herbs. They also maintain a meaty texture after fairly long cooking times, so I often add them to roasting pans with meats, and into stews.

The large hedgehogs can be quite a pain to clean. They don't typically get that dirty, but because they grow very slowly, it is common for pine needles and small twigs to get embedded thoroughly in the flesh. My best advice is to use a sharp paring knife and patience, also useful for scraping or trimming off the dirt from the base of the stem. If dirt gets into the teeth, it's usually easiest to just scrape the teeth off with a knife.

The much more dainty bellybutton hedgehogs are shown here next to small huckleberry leaves.

Cavatelli with Bellybutton Hedgehogs and Pine Nuts

Serves 4

This simple dish showcases the wonderful flavor and texture of the bellybutton hedgehogs and takes barely more time to make than it does to boil water and cook the pasta. The cavatelli's ridges and hollow centers are perfect for catching the chunky sauce and pine nuts, but a wide tubular pasta like rigatoni will also work. The bellybuttons' flavor stands powerfully on its own. If you want to make this recipe using their cousin, the sweet tooth hedgehog, I suggest cooking them in the fat rendered from a couple of slices of diced bacon to add a meatier flavor (saving the bacon to mix in at the end), before proceeding with the recipe.

1 pound (450 g) bellybutton hedgehogs, larger mushrooms halved, smaller mushrooms left whole

1 tablespoon plus 1 teaspoon oil

1 tablespoon minced fresh rosemary

1 shallot, minced

1 garlic clove, minced

½ cup (120 ml) dry white wine

½ cup (120 ml) mushroom (page 36), vegetable, or chicken stock

1 tablespoon unsalted butter, cut into pieces

1 pound (450 g) fresh or 0.5 pound (225 g) dried cavatelli

½ bunch fresh parsley, chopped

¼ cup (35 g) pine nuts, toasted

2 tablespoons good extra virgin olive oil

Finely grated Parmesan or Pecorino Romano

1. In a large, heavy-bottomed pan, dry sauté the hedgehogs, following the instructions on page 31. Add the rosemary after adding 1 tablespoon of the oil, then season with salt and continue cooking until evenly browned.

2. With the heat still on medium-low, clear a small space in the pan by pushing the mushrooms to the sides, add the remaining oil, and then add the shallot and garlic and cook for 1 to 2 minutes, stirring to prevent burning, to bring out their aromas.

3. Stir to combine the shallot and garlic with the mushrooms, increase the heat to medium-high, then add the wine and scrape up any browned bits from the bottom of the pan. When the wine is almost entirely reduced, add the stock, and reduce by half, 3 to 5 minutes. Remove from the heat, stir in the butter, and adjust the seasoning to taste. Set aside until the pasta has finished cooking.

4. Bring a large pot of generously salted water to a boil over high heat. Add the cavatelli and cook until al dente, 2 to 3 minutes for fresh or 8 to 12 minutes for dried, depending on the brand.

5. When the pasta is ready to drain, return the pan with the mushrooms to medium heat. Swirl in a tablespoon or two of the pasta cooking water if the pan is looking dry, then drain the pasta, reserving a little of the water. Mix the pasta into the mushroom mixture, remove from the heat, then stir in the parsley, pine nuts, and extra virgin olive oil. If it seems too dry to you, stir in another tablespoon or two of the pasta water. To serve, garnish with the grated Parmesan and a few grinds of black pepper.

Mushroom Substitutions: Almost any mushrooms will work here. Chanterelles are great if you don't have hedgehogs. Maitake (*Grifola frondose*), shiitake, oysters, and crimini will all work well, though they'll each impart their own unique textures and flavors to the dish.

Orecchiette with Sweet Tooth Hedgehogs and Braised Lamb Shanks

Serves 4

2014 started out quite dry in California, but somehow, the sweet tooth hedgehogs still managed to have a fairly good season. I was working as the Executive Sous Chef at a very high-end country club on the San Francisco Peninsula at the time, making trips up to the Mendonoma coast to picking pounds and pounds of hedgehogs any time I could get a day off. Many of my harvests wound up on the menu. Variations of this braised lamb shanks and hedgehog pasta dish appeared as luxurious specials on the menu for weeks, and it remains one of my absolute favorite things to make with hedgehogs. Both orecchiette and cavatelli have a size well-suited to the lamb pieces, and lots of nooks and crannies to hold on to the sauce. They also both have an excellent chewiness to them that works well here. Both store-bought dried and fresh homemade versions work equally well.

BRAISED LAMB SHANKS

2 pounds (900 g) bone-in lamb shanks

1 tablespoon oil

1 yellow onion, roughly chopped

4 celery stalks, roughly chopped

1 large carrot, peeled and roughly chopped

4 garlic cloves, crushed

1 small fresh rosemary sprig

1 bay leaf

1 cup (240 ml) dark, non-hoppy ale or dry red wine

½ bunch fresh thyme

1 to 2 quarts (1 to 1.9 L) unsalted meat stock or mushroom broth (page 152)

PASTA AND SAUCE

1 pound (450 g) fresh sweet tooth hedgehogs, cut into ½-inch (1.25 cm) pieces

2 tablespoons oil

2 shallots, minced

1 pound (450 g) fresh or 8 ounces (225 g) dried orecchiette or cavatelli

2 tablespoons extra virgin olive oil

Freshly grated Pecorino Romano or Parmesan

Freshly ground black pepper

Chopped fresh parsley

Mushroom Substitutions: Substitute maitake, your favorite mild milk caps or *Russula*, hawk's wings, or even crimini. Butter boletes also work well.

1. To make the braised lamb shanks, preheat the oven to 375°F (190°C). Heat a heavy-bottomed pot over medium-high heat. Season the lamb shanks generously with salt and pepper, add the oil to the pot, then add the shanks and sear, turning as necessary to get a dark brown crust on all sides, 3 to 5 minutes per side. When all sides are browned, remove the lamb from the pan, set aside, and pour off any extra fat, leaving just enough in the pan to barely coat the bottom.

2. Reduce the heat to medium and add the onion, celery, carrot, garlic, rosemary, and bay leaf to the empty pan. Season well with salt and pepper and sauté, stirring regularly, until the vegetables start to brown and soften, 7 to 10 minutes. Increase the heat to medium-high, add the ale, and scrape up any browned bits from the bottom of the pan. When the liquid has almost entirely evaporated, add the lamb shanks and thyme, then add just enough stock to cover the top of the lamb shanks.

3. Adjust the seasoning to taste, then bring the liquid to a boil. Later, the liquid will reduce, concentrating the flavors, so go very light on the salt to begin with. Turn off the heat, cover the pot, and transfer to the oven. Braise for 2 to 3 hours, until the lamb is tender enough to flake apart with a fork. Remove from the oven, leaving the heat on.

4. When the lamb is done, remove it from the liquid and set aside to cool. Strain and reserve the braising liquid separately. Let it sit for a few minutes to allow fat to rise to the top, then carefully skim it off with a spoon. When the lamb has cooled enough to handle, tear, flake, or cut it into bite-size pieces.

5. To make the pasta and sauce, in an oven-safe pan, dry sauté the sweet tooth hedgehogs, following the instructions on page 31, using 1 tablespoon of the oil. Add the braising liquid and scrape up any browned bits from the bottom of the pan. Cover and transfer to the oven to bake for 15 minutes, until the flavors have melded.

6. Heat a large pan over medium-high heat. Add the remaining oil, then add the shallots, stirring often to prevent burning. After about 45 seconds, add the lamb pieces and stir regularly, for 1 to 2 minutes, to heat through. Add the mushrooms along with half of their liquid, reserving the rest. Cook, stirring regularly, until the contents of the pan comes to a simmer, 1 to 2 minutes. (This sauce should be very thin. If it seems a bit dry, add as much of the lamb braising liquid as necessary to dilute it. If you run out of braising liquid, add some of the pasta water before serving.)

7. Bring a large pot of well-salted water to a boil over high heat. Add the pasta and make sure the water returns to a rolling boil. (Try to time this step so that the pasta is finished cooking about the same time as Step 6 is complete.) Cook the pasta just until slightly firmer than al dente, 2 to 3 minutes for fresh or 9 to 12 minutes for dried, depending on the brand, then drain, and add to the pan with the sauce, and mix thoroughly.

8. Let the pasta finish cooking in the sauce, about 1 more minute. The pasta will absorb more of the sauce's flavor this way. Add a couple spoonfuls of braising liquid as needed to keep the sauce from getting too thick. When the pasta is finished cooking, remove it from the heat, adjust the seasoning to taste, and stir in the extra virgin olive oil. Serve immediately, topping individual portions with cheese, a couple of grinds of black pepper, and chopped parsley.

Tip: *The braised shanks provide a sumptuous mouthfeel and rich flavor that is hard to replicate any other way. If you don't like lamb, you can substitute pork or veal shanks. Don't be afraid to cook the meat ahead of time. Braising the meat a day or two in advance will, if anything, make it better. Simply warm up the precooked lamb a bit to make it easy to pull the meat apart before proceeding with Step 5.*

Potato Gnocchi with Butter Boletes and Porcini Cream Sauce

Serves 4 to 6

I've been a fan of gnocchi since before I knew the word for them. One of my earliest food memories is eating a homemade Ashkenazi gnocchi analog called "shlishkes" at my Great Aunt Mona's house. I couldn't have been older than five, yet more than four decades later, the taste and texture of those little potato dumplings fried in butter still stand out in my mind. This creamy, deeply mushroomy dish is all about the contrast of the pillow soft, melt-in-your-mouth texture of the gnocchi with the chewy, crisp boletes. Cut the mushroom pieces a little larger than the size you will make the gnocchi, so they end up a similar size after shrinking as they cook, which plays up the textural contrast.

POTATO GNOCCHI

3 pounds (1.3 kg) Yukon Gold potatoes

1½ teaspoons salt

2 egg yolks

1½ cups (190 g) all-purpose flour, plus more for rolling and cutting the gnocchi

Olive oil

MUSHROOMS AND SAUCE

0.5 ounce (14 g) dried porcini

1 cup (240 ml) dry white wine

1 pound (450 g) butter boletes, cut into pieces slightly larger than the gnocchi

1½ teaspoons extra virgin olive oil

1 tablespoon unsalted butter

1 tablespoon chopped fresh parsley

1 garlic clove, minced

1 cup (240 ml) heavy cream

6 or 7 fresh sage leaves, chopped

A pinch of freshly grated nutmeg

Freshly grated Parmesan

Freshly ground black pepper

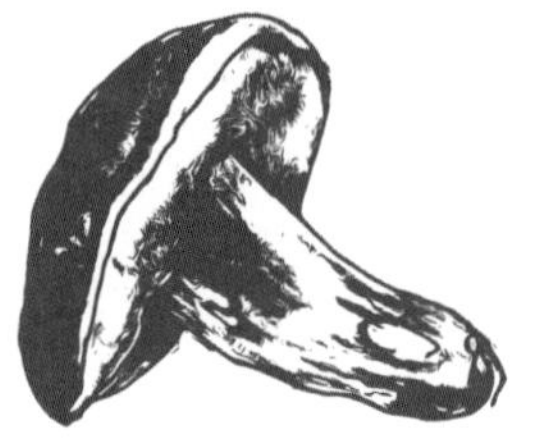

1. To make the potato gnocchi, preheat the oven to 375°F (190°C). Prick the potatoes a few times with a fork, then set them on a rimmed baking sheet and, when the oven is hot, bake for about 45 to 60 minutes, until tender, testing for doneness by poking them with a paring knife or cake tester. Remove from the oven, cut a slit along the top of each potato, and press the ends toward the middle to create an opening so steam can escape.

2. When cool enough to handle, remove the peels. Push the potato flesh through a ricer or food mill, leaving it in a loose mound on a clean work surface. Season with the salt and let cool for another 5 minutes.

Mushrooms Substitutions: You can use any fresh or dried mushrooms you like here, but fresh mushrooms with a firm, crisp texture, like maitake, crimini, or shrimp *Russula*, will make the most interesting, fun-to-eat dish.

3. When the potatoes are still warm but not hot enough to cook the egg, add the egg yolks to the top of the mound and sprinkle ½ cup (65 g) flour over the potatoes. Use one hand to fold the potatoes over on themselves, incorporating the egg and flour, while using the other hand to sprinkle on more flour with each fold. Continue this process until the dough just starts to come together. At this point, start adding a little bit of flour only every few folds, to any sections that feel more like mashed potatoes and less like dough. When the dough no longer feels sticky to the touch, it has incorporated enough flour, and the dough is done. (Use the 1½ cups/190 g flour in the ingredient list as a rough estimate; a million variables will determine how much you really need.)

4. Cut off a fist-size piece of dough. Lightly dust it and your work surface with flour, then roll to the dough into a long, smooth rope about ½ inch (1.25 cm) in diameter. Cut it into pieces about ¾-inch (2 cm) long using a bench scraper or knife.

5. Gently pick up each gnocchi and push and roll them down the back of a fork's tines and onto a floured tray, creating an indent in the opposite side with your thumb as you roll. Don't let the finished gnocchi touch, or they will stick together.

6. Generously oil a baking sheet. Bring a large pot of salted water to a boil over high heat and carefully add the gnocchi in batches of 15 to 20, stirring gently. The gnocchi will sink to the bottom at first and then float to the surface of the water as they cook. Let them cook for about 15 seconds after they float to the top, then remove with a slotted spoon or spider skimmer and place on the prepared baking sheet to cool, rolling them around a little to coat them with the oil and keep them from sticking. Repeat until all of the gnocchi are cooked. (Gnocchi are best made the same day they are to be eaten, though they will keep in the fridge for a couple of days if you have extras. The texture gets denser and less soft and light as they are stored.)

7. To make the mushrooms and sauce, break the dried porcini into small pieces in a bowl. Cover them with the wine and let soak at least 10 minutes to soften.

8. Dry sauté the butter boletes, following the instructions on page 31. When the water released from the mushrooms is gone from the pan, lightly brown the mushrooms using the olive oil and butter.

9. With the heat still on medium-low, add the parsley and garlic to the pan and cook for another 1 to 2 minutes, stirring often, until the garlic is fragrant but not

continued ›

An array of boletes—clockwise from top: butter, king, queen, fib king, and manzanita

browned. Increase the heat to medium-high, add the rehydrated porcini and wine, and scrape up any browned bits from the bottom of the pan. Adjust the heat to allow the liquid to simmer gently, stirring occasionally, until reduced to 1 to 2 tablespoons, about 5 minutes.

10. Stir the cream into the pan, and adjust the heat to medium to simmer. Add the gnocchi and sage. Season with nutmeg, salt, and pepper, and gently stir to coat everything with the sauce. Let simmer, stirring regularly, until the sauce begins to thicken, about 2 minutes. Remove from the heat, taste, and adjust the salt and pepper to taste. Serve immediately, garnished with the Parmesan and freshly ground pepper.

Tip: *The ideal gnocchi dough contains enough flour to keep the potatoes together in fluffy, light dumplings, but no more. Don't knead the dough any more than necessary to incorporate the flour; you do not want to develop too much gluten, because more gluten development means chewier gnocchi.*

Mixed Mushroom Paella

Serves 4

Paella comes from Valencia in the eastern part of Spain, and Valencians take paella very seriously. Paella is always cooked in a thin layer, ideally only the thickness of two or three cooked grains of rice, and the bottom layer should form a crispy crust called the *socarrat*. This otherwise traditional recipe substitutes mushrooms for rabbit and seafood and is every bit as delicious as the original. Thanks to the mushrooms, purists would never call this a paella—but we don't have to tell them. You do not need to use a traditional paella pan here, but you do need to use a pan that's wide enough to cook the paella properly in a thin layer—this recipe perfectly fills a pan with a 14½ inch (37 cm) diameter. Cook the paella on the grill or over your largest burner to heat the entire bottom of the pan evenly and develop the socarrat.

PICADA

1 bunch fresh parsley, roughly chopped

6 garlic cloves

1 generous pinch kosher salt

1 generous pinch saffron strands

½ cup (120 ml) dry white wine

PAELLA

3½ cups (840 ml) mushroom (page 152), vegetable, or chicken stock

1 ounce (28 g) dried mixed mushrooms

2 to 3 mushrooms for grilling, cut into ¼-inch (6 mm) slices

1 tablespoon oil

6 cups (800 g) mixed fresh mushrooms for sautéing

1 tablespoon extra virgin olive oil

1¼ cups (250 g) Bomba rice

¼ cup (35 g) green peas, shelled and blanched if fresh, thawed if frozen

3 canned piquillo peppers or 1 roasted red bell pepper, thinly sliced

SOFRITO

1 tablespoon extra virgin olive oil

1 large yellow onion, cut into ¼-inch (6 mm) pieces

1 green bell pepper, cut into ¼-inch (6 mm) pieces

2 Roma tomatoes, seeded and cut into ¼-inch (6 mm) pieces

1½ teaspoons to 1 tablespoon pimentón de la vera (Spanish smoked paprika)

1. To make the picada, combine the parsley, garlic, and kosher salt in a mortar and pestle or small food processor and grind or pulse to a paste, then add the saffron and continue to grind or pulse while slowly streaming in ¼ cup (60 ml) of the wine.

2. To make the paella, heat the grill to medium-hot. Add the stock and dried mushrooms to a saucepan and set aside to soak. Brush the mushrooms for grilling with the oil and sprinkle with salt. Grill until cooked through and lightly browned, 3 to 5 minutes per side. Cut into 1- to 2-inch (2.5–5 cm) slices, then set aside.

continued ›

Mushroom Substitutions: Almost any dried or fresh mushrooms will work here. I recommend using a mix of types with different textures and flavors for the best results. For the dried mushrooms, use a mix of any of your favorites. For the grilled mushrooms, try large shrimp *Russula*, porcini, or portabella. For the sautéed mushrooms, try lobsters, oysters, saffron milk caps, maitake, or crimini.

3. Dry or wet sauté the mixed fresh mushrooms (depending on their type and moisture level) in a paella pan or your largest wide-mouth pan, with the extra virgin olive oil until browned, seasoning only with salt, following the instructions on page 31. Transfer to a bowl and set aside.

4. To make the sofrito, reduce the heat to medium-low and add the extra virgin olive oil to the empty pan. Add the onion, bell pepper, and a good pinch of salt. Cook, stirring regularly, until the vegetables are soft but not browned, 7 to 10 minutes. If they start to pick up color, reduce the heat. Add the tomatoes and another pinch of salt, and continue to cook until the liquid from the tomatoes is mostly gone, 5 to 7 minutes, then add the pimentón and continue cooking, stirring as needed, for about 2 more minutes. When the sofrito is almost finished cooking, set the saucepan of stock with the reconstituted mushrooms over medium heat to warm through.

5. To continue making the paella, add the rice and the sautéed mushrooms to the pan with the sofrito, then add the picada and stir until everything is thoroughly combined. Let cook for 1 to 2 minutes, until the wine has completely reduced.

6. Increase the heat to medium-high, swirl the remaining wine into the mortar or food processor bowl to clean out any remaining bits, then pour the wine into the pan. When the liquid is completely absorbed, add the stock and reconstituted mushrooms, stirring gently to combine and evenly distribute the rice across the bottom of the pan. Add a generous pinch of salt, and let the liquid come up to a simmer, adjusting the heat to medium-low to keep it gently simmering, then stop stirring to allow the rice to settle on the bottom to eventually form the socarrat.

7. Continue cooking at a gentle simmer until the liquid is mostly absorbed, 15 to 20 minutes. If the rice is still a little undercooked (taste a few grains) by the time the liquid is mostly absorbed, poke a few holes in the layer of rice using a spoon and add ½ to 1 cup (120–240 ml) hot water. The holes will allow the liquid to penetrate the rice rather than sit on the surface. Arrange the grilled mushrooms on top, followed by the peas, then continue cooking for another 4 to 5 minutes after the last of the liquid has been absorbed to develop the socarrat.

8. Remove the paella from the heat and arrange the piquillo peppers on top. Let rest for 3 to 5 minutes before serving.

Tip: *Bomba rice is the standard choice, and its size, shape, and texture are a big part of the traditional look and feel of a traditional paella. If you can't find it, substitute Arborio rice, which is similar in shape, but a bit larger.*

8

Hearty Entrees

In the summer of 2015, I found myself at a loose end and in desperate need of a good mushroom hunting trip to raise my spirits, after a very bad ending to an executive chef job. So, after hearing a tip that the White Mountains of Arizona were having a tremendous season, Rosa and I jumped in the car and embarked on the thousand-mile drive eastward into the Arizona desert.

We left in the wee hours of the morning, and by the time lunchtime rolled around, we had climbed far up into the mountains, Flagstaff looming a short way in front of us. Happy to be surrounded by beautiful forest after driving through the desert for hours, we decided to pull off at a random exit and stretch our legs in the woods. Only about fifty yards from the road, a flash of red caught my eye, then another, and another. We had struck a vein of lobster mushrooms! I ran back to the car and grabbed a basket. Within half an hour we had filled the basket and a grocery bag to overflowing. We could likely have filled many more, but a sudden lightning storm chased us back to the safety of the car.

That quick stop in Flagstaff was just a tease of the riches awaiting us at our destination. The White Mountains of Arizona held seemingly endless forests bursting with chanterelles, red porcini, white porcini, southwest Caesar's Amanita, aspen boletes, cauliflower mushrooms, and many more! We had several days of incredible hunting in beautiful, largely untouched woods. Every new grove of trees seemed to have its own embarrassment of riches—so much so that we decided not to go out hunting again on the final morning of our trip because we dreaded the thought of having to process another ten pounds of whatever great edibles we might find.

On the way back from the White Mountains, already forgetting our earlier misgivings about collecting more mushrooms and in need of a break after a couple hours of driving, we decided to take another look in the same ponderosa pine forest outside of Flagstaff. We weren't intending to collect much, but in less than an hour, without really trying, we'd easily filled a few bags and baskets with more lobsters. It's tough to explain how plentiful the lobsters were without it sounding like an exaggeration. No sooner had we walked away from one patch than we were stumbling into another. The way back to the car still had us tromping through patch after patch of lobsters. It was disorienting—so much so that we managed to get a bit lost and wound up coming out of the woods almost a mile up the road from where we had parked! We must have made a funny sight to the occasional passing car: two

A big ol' basket of lobsters

confused and dirty tourists trudging down a back forest road, overburdened with mushrooms, swiveling our heads in search of our parking spot, and most disconcertingly, with wide grins plastered over our faces.

That desperate road trip to escape a failed restaurant gig evolved into a new tradition for Rosa and me. Almost every summer, when the monsoon rains bring up the mushrooms, we head to Arizona, and each trip is better than the last.

I always come home from Arizona inspired and weighed down with mushrooms—a perfect combination for coming up with new recipes, like the Lobster Mushroom Enchiladas on page 217. Every time I make them, I think back to that first trip, that one week of almost surreal bounty that turned around my entire state of mind and put me on the path that I am still, happily, on today.

Polenta with Mixed Mushroom Ragout

Serves 6 to 8

I have cooked a million variations of polenta with mushrooms, but I had to choose just one favorite recipe to share here. The tart sweetness of the tomatoes and the freshness of the herbs balance out all the earthy mushroom flavors. Grilling the polenta keeps this recipe casual and breezy, perfect for a late summer dinner. If you find yourself craving a more stick-to-your-ribs version some cold winter evening, substitute your favorite soft, creamy polenta for the grilled polenta cakes.

GRILLED POLENTA

Nonstick cooking spray

1 tablespoon salt

1½ cups (240 g) polenta

¼ cup (30 g) freshly grated Parmesan

MIXED MUSHROOM RAGOUT

2 pounds (900 g) mixed fresh mushrooms (about 8 cups), cut into ½-inch (1.25 cm) pieces

2 tablespoons oil

1 yellow onion, finely diced

2 garlic cloves, minced

One 28-ounce (830 ml) can peeled, diced tomatoes

1 bunch fresh thyme, leaves only

0.5 ounce (14 g) dried mushrooms, broken into ½-inch (1.25 cm) pieces

1 cup (240 ml) dry red wine

12 fresh sage leaves, finely chopped

2 tablespoons unsalted butter, cut into pieces

3 fresh parsley sprigs, leaves only, chopped

Freshly grated Parmesan

1. To make the grilled polenta, grease a 13-by-18-inch (33 by 45 cm) rimmed baking sheet with nonstick cooking spray, then line it with parchment paper.

2. Bring 3 cups (720 ml) water to a boil in a heavy-bottomed pot and stir in the salt. Pour in the polenta in a steady but slow stream, whisking the entire time. Reduce the heat to medium-low and continue whisking, breaking up any clumps, until smooth. When the polenta starts to thicken, stir in the Parmesan, turn off the heat, and continue whisking for a few seconds to melt and incorporate all of the cheese.

3. Immediately pour the polenta onto the prepared baking sheet and use a spatula to spread into an even layer between ¼ and ½ inch (6 mm–1.25 cm) thick. (Dip the spatula in water to keep the polenta from sticking too much while spreading it.) Let cool and set at room temperature for 1 to 2 hours.

4. When the polenta has set, flip it off the sheet onto a cutting board and remove the parchment paper. Cut into 12 to 16 pieces in your preferred shape and store in a single layer until ready to grill.

5. Clean the grill and then grease it with nonstick cooking spray. Heat the grill to high heat. Pat the polenta cakes dry, then transfer to the grill and cook on both sides. Depending on how hot your grill is, the cakes should only need 1 to 2 minutes per side. (Alternatively, sear them with a little oil in a heavy-bottomed pan over medium-high heat.) Set aside.

6. To make the mixed mushroom ragout, wet or dry sauté the fresh mushrooms in two batches (depending on their type and moisture level), following the instructions on page 31, using 1 tablespoon of the oil per batch, until lightly browned, then

continued ›

Mushroom Substitutions: Almost any mushrooms will work here. Use a mix of fresh mushrooms for a complex variety of aromas, flavors, and textures, and try to include at least one variety with a good substantial texture. For the dried mushrooms, I prefer a mix of meatier-flavored varieties like porcini, Suillus, lobsters, or hawk's wings.

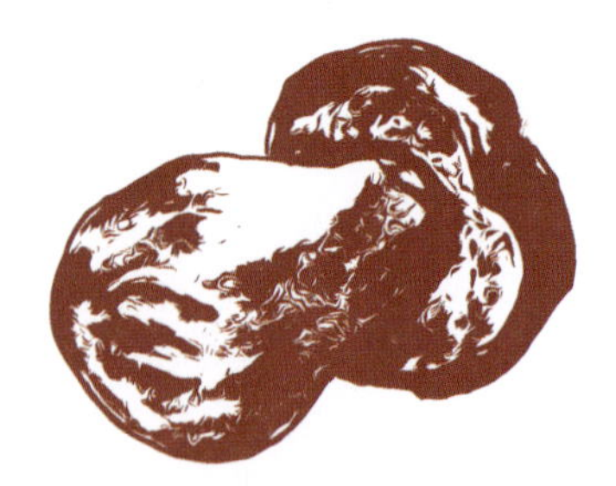

season with salt. After the last batch is cooked, return all of the mushrooms to the pan.

7. With the heat still on medium-low, add the onion and garlic, and continue cooking, stirring regularly, until the onion is soft, about 7 minutes. Add the tomatoes, half of the thyme, and the dried mushrooms, season with salt and pepper, then adjust the heat to keep the mixture at a simmer, stirring occasionally to prevent burning, until only a couple tablespoons of the tomato liquid remains, about 10 minutes.

8. Add the wine, return to a simmer, and continue cooking until about ¼ cup (60 ml) of liquid remains, about 5 minutes.

9. Remove from heat, stir in the sage and remaining thyme, then stir in the butter until melted and emulsified. Adjust the seasoning to taste. Serve immediately on top of the polenta, garnished with the parsley and Parmesan.

Banana Leaf–Wrapped Chilean Sea Bass with Matsutake and Rice

Serves 4

Matsutake are a natural pairing for all kinds of mild-flavored seafood, like the Chilean sea bass used here, which soaks up the mushrooms' aroma and flavor. For the best presentation and maximum aroma appreciation, let each diner open their own packet at the table. Chilean sea bass is an amazingly rich, firm, flaky white fish. If not available, choose another fatty, mild-flavored fish like monkfish or sablefish (black cod). You can find banana leaves frozen at your local Asian market. Thaw them at room temperature for an hour or two before use. They infuse a subtle flavor and aroma of their own into the fish and are worth seeking out, but if not available, wrap the bundles in parchment and tie with twine instead.

8 large banana leaves, plus scraps for making ties

¾ cup (180 g) jasmine rice

½ teaspoon salt

0.5 pound (225 g) fresh matsutake, cut into ⅛-inch (3 mm) slices

Soy sauce

1 pound (450 g) Chilean sea bass, portioned into four 4-ounce (115 g) fillets

1 lime, thinly sliced

Mushroom Substitutions: There is no substitute for matsutake here, as their unique aroma is key to this dish.

1. Tear several long, ⅛- to ¼-inch-wide (3–6 mm) strands from the banana leaf scrap pieces to make stringlike ties. Set aside.

2. Rinse the rice in a fine-mesh strainer under cold water until the water runs clear. Add 1 cup (240 ml) water and the salt to a small saucepan, cover, and bring to a boil over high heat. Stir in the rice, reduce the heat to medium, and re-cover. Cook until the liquid is completely absorbed, about 15 minutes, then remove from the heat. (The rice will be slightly undercooked; this is intentional because it will finish cooking later in the assembled packets.)

3. Lay 1 banana leaf flat, and then lay another perpendicularly on top. Place ½ cup (90 g) of the cooked rice in a tight pile in the center of the top leaf. Place one quarter of the matsutake slices on top of the rice, then season with a few drops of soy sauce. Season both sides of each fish fillet lightly with salt and pepper. Place 1 fillet on top of the mushrooms, then arrange a couple of slices of lime on top of the fish.

4. Fold the top banana leaf tightly over the mound, then fold the other leaf tightly over the first at a 90-degree angle to make a neat bundle. If there are any tears in your bundle, wrap a third banana leaf over them at a 90-degree angle. Use one of the banana leaf "strings" to tie the bundle securely. Repeat the layering and bundling with the remaining ingredients.

5. Fill a large pot with about 1 inch (2.5 cm) of water and heat over medium-high heat. When the water is simmering, either place a steamer basket on top of the pot or set a rack inside to sit just above the surface of the water. Carefully arrange the banana leaf bundles inside in a single layer, seam-side down. Cover and steam for 10 minutes, until cooked through, then remove carefully, letting any excess liquid drain back into the steamer before plating.

6. Serve with soy sauce for drizzling at the table.

Collard-Wrapped Monkfish with Leeks and Black Trumpets

Serves 4

This makes an elegant and light but satisfying entrée thanks to the meaty chew of the monkfish and mushrooms. The leeks' creaminess and the black trumpets' earthiness also play well with the mild and citrusy pop from the lemon. If you can't find monkfish, substitute another fatty, mild white fish. Look for collards with very large leaves to make the wrapping easier; if you can't find any especially large leaves, you can roll two leaves together around the fish instead of one.

0.5 pound (225 g) black trumpets

2 teaspoons oil

1 tablespoon unsalted butter

1 large leek, white part only, cleaned, halved, and cut into 1⁄8-inch (3 mm) slices

4 large collard leaves, thickest part of stem removed with a sharp knife

Four 5-ounce (140 g) monkfish fillets

1 lemon, thinly sliced

1. Dry sauté the black trumpets, following the instructions on page 31, using the oil. Season with salt, remove from the heat, and set aside.

2. Heat a pan over medium heat. Add the butter and then, when melted, add the leek. Reduce the heat to medium-low and season with a pinch of salt. Sauté, stirring regularly, until the leek is very soft but not browned, about 5 minutes. Add salt to taste. Remove from the heat and set aside.

3. Lay the collard leaves flat with the cut-stem ends facing away from you. (If you need to double 2 medium leaves, "scissor" their stem openings together.) Season both sides of the fish fillets with salt and a small amount of black pepper. Leaving about ½-inch (1.25 cm) border from edge of the collard leaf closest to you, place one quarter of the trumpets on each leaf, spreading slightly to make a mound about ½ inch larger in diameter than the fish fillets. Top each mound with 1 fish fillet, then top each fillet with one quarter of the leek. Finally, cover the leeks with a few slices of lemon.

4. Working with one bundle at a time, gently place 1 finger from each hand on top of the lemon slices to hold the stack together, then lift and fold the sides of the collard leaf inward with your other fingers while carefully rolling the bundle up and away from you to close up the top. Finish by placing each bundle seam-side down and trimming away any scrappy-looking pieces of the collard leaf with a sharp knife.

5. Fill a large pot with about 1 inch (2.5 cm) of water and heat over medium-high heat. When the water is simmering, either place a steamer basket on top of the pot or set a rack inside to sit just above the surface of the water. Carefully arrange the collard bundles inside in a single layer, seam-side down. Cover and steam for 10 minutes, until cooked through, then carefully remove, letting any excess liquid drain back into the steamer before plating. Serve hot.

Mushroom Substitutions: Almost any mushrooms will work here, but you'll have the best results with strongly flavored ones like yellow foots, fairy ring (*Marasmius oreades*), or beech (shimeji).

Clams with Mushrooms (Almejas con Setas)

Serves 4

This dish comes from Galicia, on the Atlantic coast of Spain. You won't find any better seafood anywhere in the world, and Rosa and I always pick mushrooms in the chestnut and oak forest when visiting family there. This simple recipe makes a great one-pot meal and showcases an interesting cooking technique for the mushrooms. The vegetables are first slow cooked into a sofrito, and then mushrooms are added to pick up their flavor but not brown. The salty sweetness of the clams and acidity from the wine turns this into a well-balanced, deeply flavored dish.

2 pounds (900 g) live clams

1 heaping tablespoon salt

2 tablespoons oil

1 large onion, finely diced

3 garlic cloves, minced

1 generous pinch saffron threads

1 green bell pepper, seeded and finely diced

½ red bell pepper, seeded and finely diced

2 pounds (900 g) saffron milk caps, cut into large pieces

2 tablespoons chopped fresh parsley, plus more for garnish

1 small pinch red pepper flakes

1½ cups (360 ml) dry white wine

Crusty bread

1. Rinse the clams under cold running water until the water runs off clear to remove any sand stuck to their shells. Discard any clams with broken shells or ones that don't close when tapped. Place the clams in a large bowl and cover with cold water. Stir in the salt. Let sit for 30 minutes to allow the clams to purge themselves of any sand inside of them. Drain and give another quick rinse in cold water. Store, drained, in the fridge until ready to use.

2. Heat a cazuela (a traditional shallow ceramic pan used in Spain) or large, heavy-bottomed pan over medium-low heat. Add the oil, then add the onion, garlic, and a pinch of salt. Sauté, stirring regularly, until the onions are just beginning to soften, about 5 minutes, then stir in the saffron threads and continue to sauté until the onions are very soft but not browned, another 5 to 7 minutes. Add the bell peppers and another small pinch of salt, and continue to cook, stirring regularly, over low heat until the peppers are meltingly soft but not browned, about 7 to 10 minutes.

3. Add the saffron milk caps along with another small pinch of salt. The mushrooms will give off some liquid. Cook, stirring regularly, until the liquid has completely reduced, about 10 minutes. You can add a little more oil if necessary to prevent sticking. Stir in the parsley and the red pepper flakes and cook for another 1 to 2 minutes, to release their flavor and aroma into the other ingredients.

4. Increase the heat to medium-high and pour in the wine, then scrape up any browned bits from the bottom of the pan and bring the wine up to a simmer. Let the wine simmer for 1 to 2 minutes to cook off the alcohol.

5. Stir in the clams and cover the pan. Adjust the heat to keep the mixture simmering gently, and cook just until the clams open, about 5 minutes, uncovering and stirring things around once or twice to make sure all of the clams are getting cooked in the liquid. As soon as all the clams have opened, remove from the heat, taste, and adjust the salt to taste. Garnish with a bit more freshly chopped parsley, and serve immediately with crusty bread. You shouldn't need anything else!

Mushroom Substitutions: Almost any mushrooms will work here. Try shrimp *Russula*, shrimp-of-the-woods (*Entoloma abortivum*), or any big, meaty, mild-flavored *Russula* or milk cap. The slimy waxy caps (*Hygrophorus* spp.) also do well. For cultivated mushrooms, use a mix of nameko, beech (shimeji), and crimini, or even white buttons. Try to use a mix of strongly flavored and firm-textured mushrooms.

Clams with Matsutake and Sake

Serves 2

When I first started collecting matsutake, I shared some with a Japanese chef friend of mine, Shingo Katsura. He enthusiastically told me that his favorite way to use them was to steam clams in sake and shave the matsutake directly on top. This three-ingredient dish is one of the easiest recipes in the entire book, and also one of the most delicious, bursting with so much flavor you may not need anything else alongside it. I am happy to drink any flavorful juice leftover straight out of my bowl, but you can also spoon it over rice.

2 pounds (900 g) live Manila clams or other small clams

1 heaping tablespoon salt

½ cup (120 ml) dry sake

2 matsutake buttons

1. Rinse the clams under cold running water until the water runs off clear to remove any sand stuck to their shells. Discard any clams with broken shells or ones that don't close when tapped. Place the clams into a large bowl and cover with cold water. Stir in the salt. Let sit for 30 minutes to allow the clams to purge themselves of any sand inside of them. Drain and give another quick rinse in cold water. Store, drained, in the fridge until ready to use.

2. Heat a large, heavy-bottomed pan over medium-high heat. Add the clams, then add the sake and cover the pan. Cook, briefly lifting the lid to check the clams about every minute, until the clams have all opened, 4 to 5 minutes, then uncover and remove from the heat. Shave the matsutake very thinly, directly on top of the clams using a mandoline or a sharp knife. Serve immediately, so the matsutake aroma is fresh and prominent.

Mushroom Substitutions: There is no substitute for the matsutake because of the special aroma they give to this dish.

Lobster Mushroom Enchiladas

Serves 4 to 6

These enchiladas make a very satisfying vegetarian entrée. The lobsters' crisp texture holds up after cooking, while the chiles and spices in the sauce balance the mushrooms' strong flavor and aroma. If you are finding lobsters in the fall or winter, use diced and roasted winter squash or pumpkin instead of the corn in this recipe. Dried guajillo and ancho chiles are available in Mexican markets or online. You can play with the ratio of guajillos to anchos if you like, but there is no substitute for authentic chiles if you want to make good Mexican sauces.

ENCHILADA SAUCE

9 dried guajillo chiles, stemmed and seeded

5 dried ancho chiles, stemmed and seeded

1 white onion, peeled and quartered

3 garlic cloves

2 tablespoons tomato paste

1 tablespoon toasted sesame seeds

1 teaspoon ground cumin

½ teaspoon dried oregano

½ teaspoon ground cinnamon

Small pinch ground cloves

MUSHROOM FILLING

2 pounds (900 g) lobster mushrooms, cut into ½-inch (1.25 cm) pieces

1 tablespoon oil

½ yellow or white onion, diced

4 ears corn, kernels cut off the cob, or about 3 cups (500 g) thawed frozen corn

Juice of 1 lime

1 bunch fresh cilantro, roughly chopped

4 ounces (115 g) shredded Monterey Jack

ENCHILADAS

Oil, for frying

Fifteen 6-inch (15 cm) corn tortillas

2 ounces (60 g) shredded Monterey Jack

Sour cream

Avocado, sliced or diced

1. To make the enchilada sauce, add the guajillo chiles, ancho chiles, onion, and garlic to a large saucepan with enough water to cover. Bring to a boil over high heat, then reduce the heat to medium-low and simmer for 10 minutes, until the chiles begin to soften. Remove from the heat and let stand for 30 minutes, until the chiles are very soft and the flavors have begun to meld.

2. Purée the chiles, onion, and garlic with just enough of the cooking liquid to make the blending effortless, about 1½ cups (360 ml). Add the tomato paste, sesame seeds, cumin, oregano, cinnamon, and cloves, and season with salt. Blend, starting on low speed and working your way up to high speed, until very smooth. Adjust the seasoning and spices to taste. It should be just thick enough to coat the back of a spoon. If it's too thick, blend in extra cooking liquid until the desired consistency is reached. Return the sauce to the pan and keep warm over very low heat.

continued ›

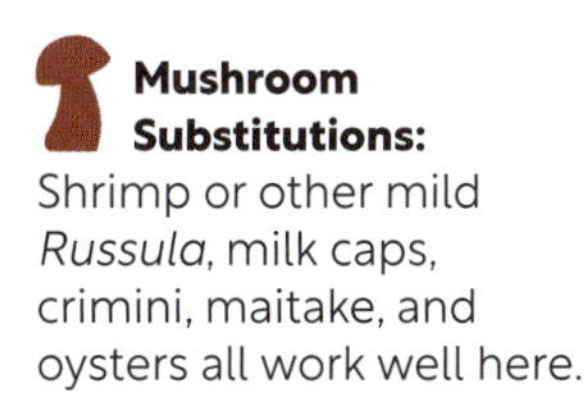

Mushroom Substitutions: Shrimp or other mild *Russula*, milk caps, crimini, maitake, and oysters all work well here.

3. To make the mushroom filling, cook the lobster mushrooms with a wet sauté, following the instructions on page 31, using the oil. Season with salt and continue cooking until the mushrooms are lightly browned, stirring regularly. With the heat still on medium-low, add the onion and cook until soft and just starting to brown, 7 to 10 minutes.

4. Increase the heat to medium-high and add the corn. Cook for 3 to 4 minutes, stirring regularly, until the corn is cooked through, then remove from the heat, add the lime juice, and adjust the seasoning to taste. Let cool completely, then mix in the cilantro, Monterey Jack, and a few spoonfuls of the enchilada sauce.

5. To make the enchiladas, fill a pan with about ¼ inch (6 mm) of oil and heat over medium heat until a small piece of tortilla sizzles immediately when added, 1 to 2 minutes. Using tongs, place 1 tortilla in the oil, fry for 5 seconds, then flip it and fry for another 5 seconds. Remove from the oil, letting as much oil drip off as possible, then set on a plate and repeat with the remaining tortillas. (Note that the goal is not to get the tortillas crispy; you want to just soften them enough to make them pliable.)

6. Preheat the oven to 350°F (180°C). Coat the bottom of a 9-by-13-inch (23 by 33 cm) baking dish with about one third of the enchilada sauce. Dredge 1 of the tortillas lightly in the sauce, flipping to cover both sides, then place a generous amount (slightly less than ¼ cup/40 g) of filling in a line across the center of the tortilla. Roll it up tightly around the filling, being careful to not spill it out the ends, and place the enchilada seam-side down, snuggly against one side of the baking dish. Repeat the dredging, filling, and rolling, placing each enchilada seam-side down and firmly against the prior enchilada, in two rows, until the baking dish is full, and you've used all the tortillas and filling. This is a messy process if you're doing it right!

7. Spoon another one third of the sauce over the enchiladas, then sprinkle the remaining cheese evenly over the top. Cover tightly with foil and bake for 15 to 20 minutes, until heated through and the cheese is melted.

8. Uncover the enchiladas and spoon a little more warmed sauce on top just before serving. (The baking can dry them out a little bit, so finishing with a little extra sauce makes for much better eating.) Serve with sour cream and avocado on the side.

Pheasant with Almondy Agaricus Pan Sauce

Serves 4

One springtime in the Sierra Nevada, my friends and I snuck down a private mountain road to a campground we knew, still closed from the winter. It was a perfect area to cook a picnic lunch, surrounded by towering firs and pines, deep in the quiet forest. In a couple weeks, the campground would be loudly buzzing with dozens of families, but for now, it was just us. We cooked up several new-to-us species of mushrooms we had collected that day—a favorite ritual. The following recipe, featuring the amber-staining agaricus (*A. moronii*), a mushroom with a delicious almond extract flavor and aroma, was the main dish at that memorable lunch. The almond flavor makes a really special pan sauce.

4 pheasant or chicken airline breasts (skin-on, with wing joint attached)

1 tablespoon oil

0.5 pound (225 g) almondy *Agaricus*, cut into ¼-inch (6 mm) slices

¾ cup (180 ml) Dunkel Weisse or other malty, non-hoppy, beer or dry fruity white wine

3 tablespoons unsalted butter, cut into pieces

10 to 12 fresh sage leaves, roughly chopped

1. Preheat the oven to 400°F (200°C). Pat the pheasant breasts dry, then season well with salt and pepper. Heat a large, heavy-bottomed pan over medium-high heat. Add the oil and place the breasts skin side down in the pan. After about 1 minute, reduce the heat to medium and continue to cook, untouched, for another 4 to 5 minutes, or until the skin is lightly browned and crispy.

2. Flip the breasts, place the pan in the oven, and continue to cook for 4 to 8 more minutes, until the pheasant breasts are barely cooked through. (Very large chicken breasts may take up to 15 minutes in the oven.) They are done when they are still juicy, but no longer pink inside. Set the cooked breasts aside on a plate, skin side up.

3. Pour any excess fat out of the pan, leaving just enough to coat the bottom. If there's not enough fat to coat the bottom, add more oil. Return the pan to medium heat and add the mushrooms. Season with salt and sauté just until slightly softened, about 2 minutes. (It's more important here to preserve as much of the delicate almond flavor and aroma as possible than to brown the mushrooms thoroughly.)

4. Increase the heat to high, add half of the beer, and scrape up any browned bits from the bottom of the pan. Add the rest of the beer and cook until reduced by half, about 2 minutes, then turn off the heat.

5. Add the butter and sage, swirling or stirring constantly to emulsify the sauce as the butter melts. Adjust the salt and pepper to taste. Spoon the sauce over the pheasant to serve.

Mushroom Substitutions: Almost any mushroom will work here, including other *Agaricus* like white buttons and crimini, but you'll lose the almond aroma and flavor.

Mushroom and Buckwheat-Stuffed Cabbage

Serves 6 to 8

Some of my earliest memories are of my Polish great-grandmother, Jenny, cooking for my brother and me. My love affair with food almost certainly began with her cooking, and her stuffed cabbage was always one of my favorites. My childhood memories very much inspired this recipe, and the smell of it baking in the oven always reminds me of her. Most traditional recipes use a ground meat and rice filling. I enjoy the more well-rounded flavor I get by substituting a mix of different mushrooms for the meat—and as a bonus, I can serve this to my vegetarian loved ones. The cabbage rolls are as good after a day or two in the fridge as they are fresh out of the oven.

SWEET AND SOUR TOMATO SAUCE

1 tablespoon neutral oil

1 small white onion, halved and thinly sliced

2 bay leaves

One 28-ounce (830 ml) can puréed tomatoes or puréed, whole peeled tomatoes

1 cup (240 ml) vegetable stock, mushroom soaking liquid, or water

¼ cup (60 ml) apple cider vinegar

2 tablespoons light brown sugar

½ teaspoon dried dill or 1 teaspoon fresh chopped dill

STUFFED CABBAGE

½ cup (85 g) buckwheat groats (untoasted buckwheat, not toasted groats called "kasha")

1 pound (450 g) bellybutton hedgehogs, finely diced

0.5 pound (225 g) yellow foots, finely diced

1½ tablespoons unsalted butter

½ yellow or white onion, finely diced

1 garlic clove, minced

1 tablespoon chopped fresh parsley

1 egg, beaten

1 large head green cabbage, core carefully removed with a sharp knife

1 cup (125 g) all-purpose flour

1 tablespoon oil

1 tart apple, such as Granny Smith, peeled and cut into ¼-inch (6 mm) slices

Mushroom Substitutions: Almost any mushrooms will work here. Use a combination of two or more different mushrooms for a deeper flavor and varied texture.

1. To make the sweet-and-sour tomato sauce, heat a heavy-bottomed saucepan over medium-high heat. Add the oil, then add the onion and bay leaves. Season with salt and sauté, stirring regularly, until the onion is softened and just starting to get a little color, about 5 minutes. Add the tomatoes, vegetable stock, vinegar, brown sugar, and dill and stir regularly until the sauce comes to a simmer. Reduce the heat to maintain a gentle simmer and season lightly with salt and pepper. Simmer gently for about 20 minutes, to reduce a bit and let the flavors come together, then remove from the heat and adjust the seasoning to taste.

2. To make the stuffed cabbage, bring a saucepan of salted water to a boil over high heat. Add the buckwheat, reduce the heat to medium-high, and boil until almost tender, but still a little al dente, about 5 minutes. Drain, then set aside.

3. Dry sauté the bellybuttons and yellow foots, following the instructions on page 31, using the butter. When lightly browned, season with salt and pepper, then, with the heat still on medium-low, add the onion and garlic and continue to sauté until the onions are softened but not browned, 5 to 7 minutes. Remove from the heat and stir in the parsley.

4. Add the cooked buckwheat to the mushroom mixture, and adjust the salt and pepper to taste. Let cool completely, then stir in the egg and refrigerate until ready to use.

5. Bring a large pot of salted water to a boil over high heat. Carefully place the whole head of cabbage in the water and cook for 5 minutes, until slightly soft, then drain and let sit until cool enough to handle. Peel off each individual leaf, being careful not to tear them. Use a sharp knife to remove the thick, tough part of the vein at the bottom center of each leaf.

6. Lay 1 leaf flat on a clean surface with the outer side of the leaf facing down and the edge with the stem end of the leaf facing away from you. Place 3 to 4 tablespoons of mushroom stuffing in a tight mound, leaving about ½-inch (1.25 cm) border from the side closest to you. Fold the edges of the leaf over the filling, roll tightly to seal it in, then set aside with the seam-side down. Repeat the stuffing and rolling until you've used up all the leaves and/or filling.

7. Add the flour to a wide dish or shallow bowl and season with a generous pinch of salt and pepper. Heat a large, heavy-bottomed pan over medium heat. Add the oil. One at a time, dredge each roll in the flour, tapping off any excess, and place seam-side down into the pan. Repeat until the pan is full, leaving at least 1 inch (2.5 cm) between them. Cook until the bottoms have browned, then gently flip the rolls to brown the other side, about 3 minutes per side. When both sides have browned, transfer the cabbage rolls seam-down to a 9-by-13-inch (23 by 33 cm) baking dish. Repeat the cooking with the remaining cabbage rolls, adding more oil to the pan as needed.

8. Preheat the oven to 350°F (180°C). Bring the tomato sauce back up to a simmer over medium heat. Meanwhile, arrange the apple slices between the cabbage rolls. When the sauce is hot, pour it over the rolls and apple slices to cover completely. Bake uncovered for 30 minutes, until just beginning to brown. Serve immediately.

Savory Mushroom Galette

Serves 4

This galette looks beautiful as a centerpiece and makes the mushrooms and vegetables the stars of the meal. It's deceptively easy for such an impressive-looking dish. The cherry tomatoes provide a natural sweetness to balance out the mushrooms' earthiness, while the creamy goat cheese helps to marry the various flavors. Feel free to play with different vegetables or adding fresh herbs. I highly recommend weighing the flour for the crust because the volume varies depending on a number of hard to predict factors. Weighing will guarantee consistently good results.

CRUST

2¼ cups plus 2 tablespoons (300 g) all-purpose flour

1 cup plus 1 tablespoon (245 g) unsalted butter

¼ cup plus 1 tablespoon (75 ml) cold water

FILLING

3 cups (400 g) fresh mushrooms, cut into bite-size pieces

3 cups (210 g) broccoli, cut into bite-size florets

2 cups (300 g) cherry tomatoes, halved

1 zucchini, halved lengthwise and cut into ⅛-inch (3 mm) slices

1 tablespoon fresh thyme leaves

Zest of 1 lemon

2 tablespoons extra virgin olive oil

½ cup (85 g) crumbled goat cheese

½ cup (60 g) grated Parmesan

1 egg, beaten

1. To make the crust, combine the flour and a pinch of salt in the bowl of a food processor. Add the butter and pulse until the mixture has the consistency of coarse sand (a few pea-size pieces are OK). With the processor running, stream in just enough of the cold water to form a dough. Flatten the dough into a disk, wrap in plastic wrap, and refrigerate for 1 to 2 hours to allow the dough to fully and evenly hydrate and to relax the gluten.

2. To make the filling, toss the mushrooms, broccoli, cherry tomatoes, zucchini, thyme, and lemon zest together in a bowl, then stir in the extra virgin olive oil until the vegetables are thoroughly coated. Stir in the goat cheese and season with salt and pepper. Let sit at room temperature for 30 to 60 minutes; you want the filling at room temperature when the galette goes into the oven.

3. Line a rimmed baking sheet with parchment paper. Remove the dough from the fridge and allow it to soften for 5 to 10 minutes, then roll it into a thin circle about 17 inches (43 cm) in diameter. (It is much easier to roll the dough if you do so on a sheet of plastic to keep it from sticking to the work surface.) Carefully center the dough on the prepared baking sheet, letting the edges overhang slightly if necessary.

4. Preheat the oven to 375°F (190°C). Spread half of the Parmesan in a thin layer over the crust, leaving a 3-inch (7.5 cm) boarder. Arrange the filling on top of the Parmesan, again being careful to leave a 3-inch border. Starting from one side and working around the galette in a circle, fold the outer edge of the crust over the periphery of the filling, making a new fold or pleat about every 1 inch (2.5 cm) to create a rim. (Note that the crust should not fully cover the filling.)

5. Brush the beaten egg over the crust, then sprinkle the remaining Parmesan over the exposed filling. Transfer to the oven and bake until the crust is well browned, and the filling is soft and beginning to lightly caramelize, 45 to 60 minutes. Remove from the oven, cut into wedges, and serve hot or at room temperature.

Mushroom Substitutions: Almost any mushrooms will work here, but if using mushrooms that require thorough cooking to be safe to eat, be sure to par cook them before adding them to the vegetable mixture. For very wet mushrooms, give them a dry sauté (page 31) before mixing with the other ingredients to prevent the tart from being soggy.

Stuffed Blue Knight "Ravioli"

Serves 4

The blue knight (*Albatrellopsis flettii*) glows a beautiful, deep blue in the forest—sometimes almost too blue to appear real. Though it's a big meaty mushroom with a strong flavor that can't be mistaken for anything else, I know only a few people who eat it, yet in my opinion, it's quite worthy of experimentation. Their size and meaty texture make them perfect for stuffing the way you might stuff a chicken breast or fish fillet. Boiling the mushrooms makes them a bit more pliable and stuffable (but still pleasantly firm), while preserving their big flavor and removing their occasional bitterness. After the boiling and stuffing, they still sear quite nicely. When finished, the mushrooms look almost like ravioli, and your diners might believe this to be an ultra-mushroomy ravioli dish. I like to serve this dish with roasted brussels sprouts.

TOMATO SAUCE

1 tablespoon extra virgin olive oil

1 small yellow onion, thinly sliced

1 garlic clove, chopped

One 28-ounce (830 ml) can diced tomatoes

1 tablespoon sugar

½ bunch fresh basil, leaves only

STUFFING

¼ cup (30 g) freshly grated aged Gouda or Parmesan

2 tablespoons unseasoned bread crumbs

2 tablespoons chopped fresh parsley

Zest of 2 lemons, plus juice from ½ lemon

1 tablespoon finely chopped walnuts

BLUE KNIGHT "RAVIOLI"

1.5 pounds (680 g) blue knights, stems removed

1 tablespoon oil

1. To make the tomato sauce, heat a saucepan over medium heat. Add the extra virgin olive oil, then add the onion and a pinch of salt. Sauté, stirring regularly, until the onion is softened and just beginning to brown, about 10 minutes. Add the garlic and cook for another 1 to 2 minutes, until fragrant. Reduce the heat to medium-low, then add the tomatoes, sugar, and another pinch of salt. Simmer until the liquid is reduced to only a few tablespoons, then remove from the heat, add the basil, and blend until smooth using a blender or immersion blender. Adjust the salt and sugar to taste. Keep the sauce warm over low heat. (The sauce can be refrigerated for up to 3 days and reheated just before use.)

2. To make the stuffing, mix the Gouda, bread crumbs, parsley, lemon zest, and lemon juice, and the chopped walnuts together in a bowl, with a pinch of salt and pepper, and set aside. (If not using within 1 hour, refrigerate until needed.)

3. To make the blue knight "ravioli," bring a pot of salted water to a boil over high heat. Add the mushrooms and cook for 5 minutes, until cooked through, then drain, and let cool slightly. When the mushrooms are cool enough to handle, use a sharp paring knife to cut an opening in the thickest part of the mushroom, where the stem was attached, carefully cutting parallel to the cap surface and as close to the edges as possible without breaking the top or bottom surface. You should be able to create a pouch that goes to within about ½ inch (1.25 cm) of the other edge, most of the way around the mushroom. The mouth of the pouch should be just wide enough to fit a small spoon. Repeat with all the mushrooms.

Mushroom Substitutions: Use any meaty *Albatrellus* or *Scutiger* species for this. You can also use this technique with young, tender pheasant backs (*Cerioporus squamosus*).

The beautiful blue knight, Albatrellopsis flettii

4. Carefully spoon the stuffing into each mushroom, using a finger to push it deeper into the pockets. Gently press down on the pore side of each stuffed mushroom to even out the filling and close the opening. Reserve the extra stuffing.

5. Heat a large, heavy-bottomed pan over medium heat. Add the oil, then add the mushrooms pore-side down, cooking in 2 or 3 batches to avoid crowding the pan. When lightly browned on the first side, flip the mushrooms and cook until the other side has browned, 3 to 5 minutes per side.

6. Add the sauce to the pan and gently mix with the mushrooms. To serve, spoon a little sauce into the bottom of individual bowls, arrange the mushrooms on top pore-side up, and garnish with extra stuffing.

Candy Cap Brined and Braised Pork Belly

Serves 8

I almost always serve this sinfully delicious recipe in some form at my formal mushroom dinners, and it always scores big with diners. Searing the pork perfumes the entire house or restaurant with the seductively sweet candy cap aroma, and nothing compares to the rich flavor and supple texture of pork belly. The prep is easy, but you need to plan a few days ahead to do the brining and braising. I strongly recommend weighing the salt and sugars that go into the brine to ensure that the flavor balance is right. These ingredients can vary a lot in volume and give poor results if the proportions are off.

¾ cup plus 2 tablespoons (175 g) kosher salt

¼ cup plus 2 tablespoons (75 g) granulated sugar

¼ cup (50 g) light brown sugar

1 ounce (28 g) dried candy caps

2 quarts (1.9 L) ice water

4-pound (1.8 kg) piece of pork belly, skin removed

1½ cups (360 ml) dry red wine

2 cups (480 ml) unsalted pork, beef, or veal stock

2 tablespoons cold, unsalted butter, cut into pieces

1. Combine the salt, granulated sugar, brown sugar, and 0.5 ounce (14 g) of the dried candy caps with 2 quarts (1.9 L) water in a large pot. Bring to a boil over high heat, then turn off the heat and add the ice water.

2. Submerge the pork belly in the brine. If necessary, place a weight on top of the pork to keep it submerged. Refrigerate, covered in the brine for 24 to 48 hours, then remove the pork and discard the brine. Pat the pork dry and let rest uncovered on a rack in the fridge for at least 2 hours or up to 24 hours to dry the surface.

3. Heat a large, heavy-bottomed pan over medium heat. If necessary, cut the pork into 2 or 3 pieces so it will fit in the pan. Place the pork fat-side down and sear until browned, 5 to 7 minutes, then flip the belly and cook it meat-side down until browned, about another 5 minutes. Transfer the pork to a 9-by-13-inch (23 by 33 cm) baking dish or roasting pan in a single layer (divide between two baking dishes if needed), discarding the rendered fat.

4. Preheat the oven to 350°F (180°C). Add the wine to the still-hot pan and scrape up any browned bits from the bottom. Add another 0.25 ounce (7 g) of the dried candy caps and bring to a simmer over medium-high heat. Simmer for about 3 minutes to cook off some of the alcohol, then add the stock and bring back to a simmer. Pour the liquid into the roasting pan with the pork belly and cover with parchment paper, then foil. Transfer to the oven and bake for 90 minutes, or until the meat is very tender but not falling apart.

5. Carefully remove the pork, straining and reserving the braising liquid separately. Refrigerate the braising liquid and pork belly for at least 4 hours or up to 24 hours, to allow the pork to firm up, then cut the meat into ½-inch (1.25 cm) slices.

6. Use a large spoon to carefully scoop off and discard the thick layer of fat from the top of the cooled braising liquid. Add the braising liquid to a small saucepan along with the remaining dried candy caps. Bring to a boil over high heat, then reduce the heat to simmer gently until the liquid reduces by about half. Adjust the salt to taste. Remove from the heat and swirl in the butter.

7. To finish, heat a heavy-bottomed pan over medium heat. Add the pork belly and cook until lightly browned on all sides, 2 to 3 minutes per side. Serve immediately, topped with the sauce.

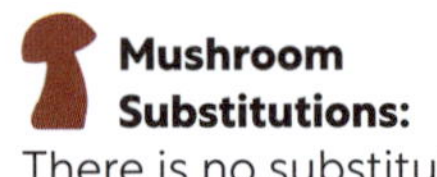

There is no substitute for candy caps in this recipe.

Pork Braciole Stuffed with Morels and Pecorino

Serves 2

If you grew up in an Italian American family or neighborhood, you know braciole—thin pieces of meat stuffed and rolled up like a roulade, then braised in a sauce (often tomato). In Italy, the word "braciole" refers to the thin pieces of meat themselves, while the rolled stuffed version is called *braciole ripiene* or *involtini*. There may be as many different braciole recipes as there are Italian grandmothers. In this one, the luxurious cheese and morel stuffing is brightened with lemon zest and spring onion. Braising with artichokes in a red wine sauce makes for an elegant and delicious dish that looks beautiful on the plate. The rich, meaty flavor of the morels comes through clearly, but you can serve more morels on the side to make this dish even more special.

1 ounce (28 g) dried morels or 6 ounces (170 g) fresh

2 cups (480 ml) Chianti or other dry red wine

3 tablespoons unsalted butter

1 small spring onion or 2 scallions, thinly sliced, white and green parts separated

Juice and zest of 1 lemon

4 small or 2 large artichokes

1.5 ounces (45 g) Pecorino Romano, grated

2 ounces (60 g) mozzarella or other mild melting cheese, shredded

Four 3.5- to 4-ounce (100–115 g) pork shoulder cutlets

1 tablespoon oil

1. Soak the dried morels in the wine until softened, about 30 minutes. Tear them into pieces, agitate a little in the wine to get rid of any dirt, and then remove them. Strain the wine and reserve separately. (If using fresh mushrooms, do not soak them; skip directly to Step 2.)

2. Wet sauté the morels, following the instructions on page 31, using 1½ tablespoons of the butter. Add the spring onion whites for the last couple minutes of cooking. Remove from the heat, let the mushrooms cool enough to handle, and then roughly chop and set aside in a bowl.

3. Fill a bowl three quarters of the way with water and add the lemon juice. One at a time, working as quickly as possible to prevent the artichokes from oxidizing, dip the artichokes into the lemon water, then place on your cutting board and use a sharp knife to cut off all the tough green outer leaves, exposing the edge of the tender yellow heart. Use a paring knife to peel away the green fibrous outer layer around the stem and base of the heart. Slice off the top half of the flowers to get rid of all the thorns at the top of the remaining leaves, then dip the artichokes back in the lemon water. Cut in half and use a spoon to carefully remove and discard the cottony "choke" at the center of each flower. Cut the hearts into wedges and place immediately in the lemon water.

4. Mix the two cheeses together with the lemon zest in a bowl and line up next to the bowl of morels and the spring onion greens.

5. On a clean surface, cover 1 cutlet with a piece of plastic wrap and use a meat mallet or small, heavy pan to pound it to about ⅛ inch (3 mm) thick. Be careful not to tear the meat while you pound it out, especially in fatty areas. Repeat with the other cutlets. (Note: If you gently roll up the cutlets after pounding them, they are much easier to move without tearing.)

continued ›

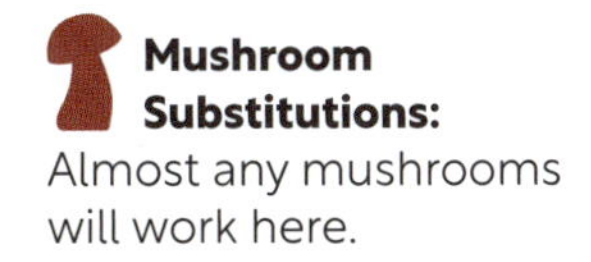
Mushroom Substitutions: Almost any mushrooms will work here.

6. Lay the cutlets out flat and season with salt and pepper. Top each with a thin layer of cheese, then a layer of morels, then a few of the onion greens. Starting from the longer end, roll them up around the filling, being careful not to tear the meat. Secure each end of the rolls with a toothpick. Reserve any extra morels.

7. Heat a large, heavy-bottomed pan over medium-high heat. Add the oil, then place the braciole in the pan, leaving space between them. After 1 minute, reduce the heat to medium so the meat doesn't burn. One the bottoms of the braciole have a good, dark brown sear, give them a quarter turn and repeat until all sides are seared, about 3 minutes per side. Be very careful not to tear them when turning, as they can stick to the pan.

8. Add the artichokes and let cook for about 2 minutes, until they begin to brown, then add the strained wine. Bring to a simmer, then reduce the heat to medium-low, cover, and continue cooking for 30 minutes, adjusting the heat as needed to keep the liquid at a gentle simmer, to tenderize the braciole. Transfer them to a plate to rest.

9. Taste the sauce. If your braciole were well-seasoned, the sauce may not need any adjustment, but add salt if necessary. Remove from the heat and swirl in the remaining butter.

10. To serve, remove the toothpicks from the braciole, slice if desired, then arrange on individual plates. Top with some of the artichokes, sauce, and any extra morels.

Braised Beef Tongue with Wrinkled Rozites

Serves 4 to 6

My first encounter with beef tongue was in my late teens, as a delicious taqueria staple for tacos and burritos. It soon became, and has since remained, one of my favorite meats. This recipe takes mild-flavored, luscious-textured tongue and turns it into a braised meat centerpiece. For a satisfying meal, serve alongside some good crusty bread and roasted potatoes. Wrinkled rozites (*Cortinarius caperatus*) have a pleasant texture and mild flavor, but sometimes leave a strange aftertaste that I am not a big fan of. In the context of this dish, though, that aftertaste becomes a pleasant note that helps them punch through the other big flavors.

BRAISED BEEF TONGUE

1 beef tongue (3 to 3.5 pounds/1.3–1.6 kg), rinsed under cold water for a few seconds to remove any scum

1 yellow or white onion, halved

1 tablespoon salt

3 garlic cloves, crushed

1 teaspoon whole black peppercorns

MUSHROOM SAUCE

1.5 ounces (40 g) dried mushrooms

1 pound (450 g) fresh wrinkled rozites, cut into ½-inch (1.25 cm) pieces

3 tablespoons oil

2 onions, finely diced

½ bunch fresh cilantro

4 garlic cloves

2 green bell peppers, cut into ¼-inch (6 mm) pieces

1 red bell pepper, cut into ¼-inch (6 mm) pieces

½ cup (120 ml) dry red wine

Extra virgin olive oil

1. To make the braised beef tongue, place the tongue, onion, salt, garlic, and peppercorns into a large, heavy-bottomed pot and cover with cold water. Bring to a boil over high heat, then reduce the heat to medium-low. Simmer, skimming and discarding any scum that collects on the surface, until the tongue is tender by not falling apart, 3 to 4 hours, testing for doneness by poking the tongue with a sharp paring knife. After the first 30 minutes or so, there should be little to no skimming required. Add water as needed during cooking to keep the tongue covered.

2. Remove the tongue from the pot and strain, reserving the cooking liquid, but discarding the remaining solids. When the tongue is cool enough to be handled, peel off the thick skin and discard. You can use a sharp paring knife to help remove the skin, but if the tongue is fully cooked, it should peel off fairly easily. Cut the tongue into 1-inch (2.5 cm) thick slices and set aside.

3. To make the mushroom sauce, cover the dried mushrooms with the tongue braising liquid and let soak for at least 10 minutes, until soft, then chop them into ½-inch (1.25 cm) pieces. Strain and reserve the liquid.

4. Dry sauté the wrinkled rozites, following the instructions on page 31, using 1 tablespoon of the oil. Cook until lightly browned, then season with salt, transfer to a bowl, and set aside.

5. Return the empty pan to medium heat, add the remaining oil, then add the onions. Sauté, stirring regularly, until soft and just barely starting to brown, about 7 to 10 minutes.

continued ›

Mushroom Substitutions: Almost any dried mushrooms will work here. For the fresh mushrooms, all of the usual suspects that do well stewed will work great, such as mild-flavored *Russula* and milk caps, hens (maitake), coccora, your local Caesar's Amanita, sweet tooth hedgehogs, hawk's wings, crimini, or any dense *Agaricus*.

The author with Wrinkled Rozites

6. While the onions cook, make a paste from half of the cilantro, the garlic, and a pinch of salt using a mortar and pestle or a small food processor. Roughly chop the remaining cilantro and set aside.

7. Add the peppers to the onions and continue to sauté until they are meltingly soft, 7 to 10 minutes. Add more oil as needed to prevent the vegetables from sticking. Season with salt, then add the rehydrated mushrooms and sauté for another 3 minutes, stirring a few times, to incorporate and lightly cook them. Stir in the cilantro paste and sauté for another 2 minutes to incorporate and bring out the fragrance, then add the cooked wrinkled rozites and cook for 1 more minute.

8. Increase the heat to medium-high, add the wine, and scrape up any browned bits from the bottom of the pan. When the wine has almost completely reduced, add the sliced tongue, the reserved mushroom soaking liquid, and enough of the reserved braising liquid to barely cover the contents of the pan. When the liquid begins to boil, reduce the heat to medium-low to keep at a simmer. Simmer until the liquid has reduced by about half, 5 to 10 minutes, stirring occasionally, being careful not to break up the tongue slices. Adjust the seasoning to taste.

9. To serve, arrange the tongue slices in a deep platter and carefully pour the mushrooms and sauce over the top. Garnish with a generous drizzle of extra virgin olive oil and the reserved chopped cilantro.

Venison Loin with Chanterelles, Dried Apricots, and Moroccan Spices

Serves 4

This recipe came about several years ago when a couple mushroom friends came to stay with Rosa and me right before New Year's Eve. Our fridge was overflowing from a bountiful chanterelle harvest, and I wanted to play with the mushrooms' fruity character. The sweet spices and dried apricots give this dish a North African feel, and stewing the mushrooms with the spices gives the sauce a great depth of flavor. Though the fruit and spices shine with venison, they also play very well alongside lamb or even chicken breast, so feel free to substitute whatever protein you have on hand.

1½ teaspoons whole coriander seeds

1 teaspoon whole black peppercorns

5 whole cloves

½ teaspoon whole cumin seeds

2 pounds (900 g) chanterelles, cut into ½-inch (1.25 cm) pieces

¼ cup (60 ml) oil

½ yellow onion, cut into ¼-inch (6 mm) pieces

1 small fennel bulb, cut into ¼-inch (6 mm) pieces

1 cinnamon stick

½ teaspoon minced fresh ginger

1 cup dried apricots, cut into ½-inch (1.25 cm) pieces

1 bottle (750 ml) dry red wine

1.5 pounds (680 g) venison loin or lamb loin

Juice of 1 Meyer lemon or regular lemon

1½ tablespoons unsalted butter, cut into pieces

1. Toast the coriander seeds in a dry pan over medium-high heat until very fragrant, being careful not to let them burn, 1 to 2 minutes, then immediately transfer to a mortar or spice grinder. Add the peppercorns, cloves, and cumin seeds to the empty pan together and toast until very fragrant, another 30 to 60 seconds, then transfer to the mortar or spice grinder with the coriander and grind the spices to a powder.

2. Dry sauté the chanterelles in 2 batches, following the instructions on page 31, using 1 tablespoon of the oil per batch, until lightly browned. Season lightly with salt, then remove from the pan and set aside.

3. Increase the heat to medium, then add 1 tablespoon of the remaining oil to the empty pan, then add the onion, fennel, cinnamon stick, and ginger. Cook until the vegetables start to soften, 5 minutes, then add the spice mix and season with salt. Continue sautéing gently until the vegetables are soft but not browned, another 5 minutes.

4. Stir in the apricots, chanterelles, and ½ cup (120 ml) of the wine and scrape any browned bits from the bottom of the pan, then add the rest of the wine, increase the heat to medium-high, and simmer until the wine has mostly reduced, 10 to 15 minutes.

5. Set a second large, heavy-bottomed pan over medium-high heat. Season the venison with salt and pepper, pour the remaining oil into the pan, then add the meat. When the first side is well browned, flip the meat and sear the other side, again until well browned, 4 to 5 minutes per side. At this point, the meat should be almost medium-rare (my preference). If you want to cook past medium-rare, preheat

continued ›

Mushroom Substitutions: This recipe was developed to showcase the fruity essence of an abundant chanterelle harvest, but you can experiment with just about any mushrooms you have on hand. Hedgehogs (*Hydnum* spp.) and crimini would both work well.

the oven to 375°F (190°C) and place the pan inside a for a few minutes to achieve your desired doneness. Remove the loin from the pan and let rest for 5 to 10 minutes before slicing, to keep the juices from running out everywhere. Slice ½ inch (1.25 cm) thick.

6. While the meat rests, finish the sauce. When the wine has reduced to about ¼ cup (60 ml), remove from the heat and stir in the lemon juice. Add the butter and let it melt while stirring or swirling constantly to emulsify the sauce. Adjust the seasoning to taste. If the sauce gets too thick to spread easily with a spoon, or if the emulsion breaks, stir in 1 to 2 tablespoons of warm water. Serve hot, spooning the sauce over the sliced venison.

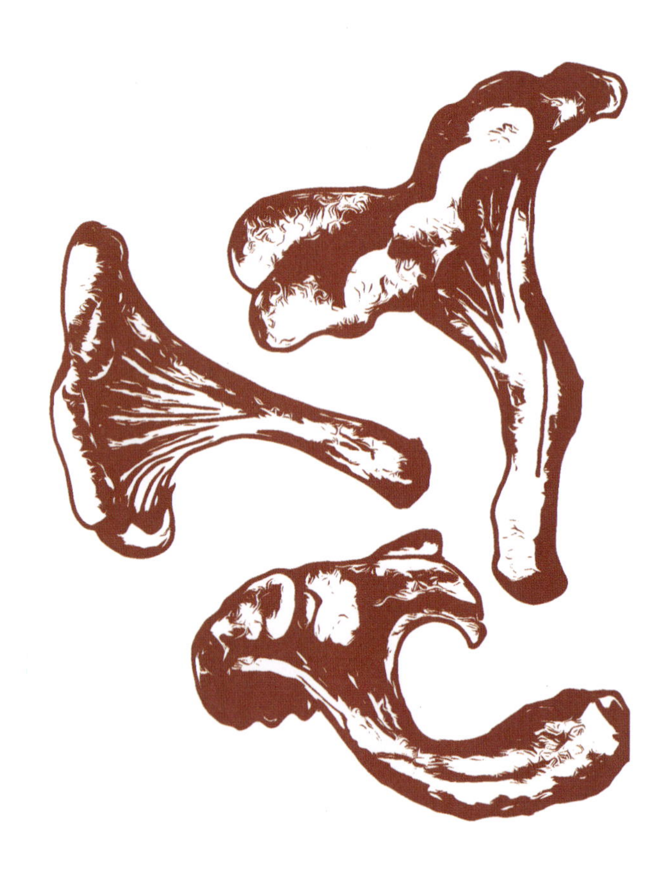

Sweetbreads with Sweetbreads and Sweet Breads

Serves 4

I must admit that the inspiration behind this recipe was the silly pun of putting together three very different items with the same name: mushrooms, meat, and challah. The sweetbread mushroom (*Clitopulus prunulus*) often pokes above the duff near well-hidden porcini, earning it another name, "the spy." It is a rather plain and somewhat small and fragile white mushroom that most hunters leave undisturbed. However, it's a good edible with a big flavor and texture. Challah croutons, our second sweet bread, add texture and a vehicle to soak up the sauce and the apple-chestnut purée. And finally, sweetbreads are an organ meat that is highly prized in many culinary traditions. They take a bit of extra prep and finesse to cook, but well-prepared sweetbreads are delicious, with a melt-in-your-mouth interior texture surrounded by a crispy seared exterior. Silliness aside, this is a deliciously complex, elegant dish with beautifully contrasting textures, meaty flavor, creaminess, sweetness, a sour tang, and nutty, earthy mushrooms to tie everything together. Roasted brussels sprouts would make a wonderful addition to the plate.

POACHED SWEETBREADS

One 1-pound (450 g) veal sweetbread lobe, trimmed of any thick pieces of fat or membrane

4 cups (960 ml) whole milk

5 black peppercorns

1 bay leaf

1 star anise

½ teaspoon coriander seeds

APPLE-CHESTNUT PURÉE

2 tart apples, peeled and diced

1 cup (150 g) roasted, peeled, roughly chopped chestnuts (about 18 chestnuts)

2 tablespoons cold unsalted butter, cut into pieces

APPLE CIDER GASTRIQUE

½ cup (120 ml) apple cider vinegar

2 tablespoons granulated sugar

1 cinnamon stick

MUSHROOMS

1 pound (450 g) sweetbread mushrooms, larger mushrooms halved or quartered, smaller mushrooms left whole

1 tablespoon oil

¼ cup (35 g) all-purpose flour

1 tablespoon plus 1 teaspoon oil

3 tablespoons unsalted butter

½ cup (120 ml) dry red wine

Challah, cut or torn in ½-inch (1.25 cm) pieces and toasted

Mushroom Substitutions: Almost any mushrooms will work here. Remember, though, that if you use a different mushroom, you'll have to change the name to the much less awesome "Sweetbreads with ____ Mushrooms and Sweet Breads."

1. To make the poached sweetbreads, place the sweetbreads in a bowl, cover with half of the milk, cover the bowl with plastic wrap, and let soak in the fridge overnight to remove impurities that could affect the flavor and appearance.

2. The next day, carefully drain and rinse the milk from the sweetbreads.

3. Add the peppercorns, bay leaf, star anise, and coriander seeds and the remaining milk to a heavy-bottomed saucepan and bring up to about 170°F (76°C)—a little bit below a simmer—over medium heat. Place the sweetbreads in the pan and poach until they've reached an internal temperature of 165°F (74°C), 35 to 40 minutes.

continued ›

4. Carefully drain and rinse the sweetbreads, discarding the milk and spices. Pat dry with a clean towel or paper towel, let cool completely, and then wrap tightly in plastic wrap and refrigerate until ready to use.

5. To make the apple-chestnut purée, add the apples, chestnuts, and a pinch of salt to a small saucepan and cover with water. Place over medium-low heat and cook, stirring regularly, until the apples start to disintegrate, about 15 minutes, adding a few tablespoons of water as needed if the pan starts to look dry, then transfer the mixture to a blender and purée until very smooth. With the blender running, add a few pieces of butter at a time, blending until well incorporated between each addition. Adjust the seasoning to taste. (The purée can be made ahead and refrigerated for up to 5 days.)

6. To make the apple cider gastrique, combine the vinegar, sugar, cinnamon stick, and a pinch of salt in a small saucepan and bring to a simmer over medium-high heat. Reduce the heat to medium-low to gently simmer until reduced to about 3 to 4 tablespoons and slightly thickened, then remove from the heat, remove the cinnamon stick, and set aside. (When cold, this sauce will be rather syrupy and thick. If needed, add a few drops of water to thin it out before using.)

7. To make the mushrooms, dry sauté the sweetbread mushrooms, following the instructions on page 31, using the oil. When lightly browned, season with salt and set aside. While the mushrooms cook, remove the sweetbreads from the fridge and cut into ¾-inch-thick (2 cm) medallions.

8. Spread the flour on a plate and season with a pinch of salt and pepper. Dredge the sweetbread medallions in the flour, coating on all sides and tapping to shake off any excess.

9. Heat a large, heavy-bottomed pan over medium-high heat. Add the oil, then add the sweetbread medallions. Do not overcrowd the pan, or the sweetbreads won't brown and crisp nicely; cook in batches if needed. Reduce the heat to medium and cook until the sweetbreads have lightly browned on the first side, about 3 minutes, then flip them, add 2 tablespoons of the butter to the pan, and as the butter starts to sizzle, use it to baste the sweetbreads by carefully tilting the pan toward you, using a spoon to scoop up the melted butter that pools at the bottom, and then spooning it over the sweetbreads on the other side of the pan. Line a cooling rack or plate with a clean kitchen towel or paper towel. Continue basting until the second side has browned, about 3 more minutes, then transfer the sweetbreads to the cooling rack or plate to drain.

10. Discard the remaining fat, then return the pan to the heat. Add the mushrooms and wine, scraping up any browned bits from the bottom. Cook until the wine has reduced by about two thirds, 3 to 5 minutes, then remove from the heat and stir in the gastrique and remaining 1 tablespoon of the butter until emulsified into the sauce. Add salt to taste.

11. To serve, spread the apple-chestnut purée across individual plates. Arrange the sweetbreads next to the purée. Top with the croutons and mushrooms, then spoon some of the pan sauce on top.

Tip: *I recommend cooking the sweetbreads through Step 4 the day before you plan to serve. Portioning the sweetbreads is infinitely easier when cold.*

9

Sweet Treats

My first time in Spain, Rosa and I drove hours out of our way to a restaurant called El Empalme, on a friend's insistence that they served the most memorable mushroom-themed meals around. We were so blown away that six years later, we took an overnight trip just to see if we had imagined the entire thing the first time. Somehow, the second experience wound up being even better than the first.

Each visit began the same, with Rosa and me parking at the restaurant in front of a mural of porcini and chanterelles. The restaurant is an old stone country house with mushroom photos adorning every wall and mushroom sculptures and art displayed everywhere. We sat in a side room with mushroom-patterned curtains covering the windows, myco-decorations all around, at a table with a mushroom-print tablecloth. We had the place all to ourselves; it was their day off, but the owners, the husband-and-wife team Elías Martín and Gloria Lucía, had opened just to serve us.

They opened El Empalme in the 1980s and have run it ever since with an evolving menu full of wild mushrooms that they collect. As we settled in, they chatted with us and poured wine. The conversation was immediately intense, direct, and honest, but deeply warm, and full of laughs—like old friends reconnecting.

Gloria suddenly decided the welcome was over, interrupting, "We'll see what I have for you to eat today," before disappearing into the kitchen. I still don't know if she had menus planned before either visit, but each time, one creative dish came after another, all featuring local wild mushrooms. All were hearty portions of reimagined, myco-centered, stick-to-your-ribs country food, not dainty bites masquerading as paintings on tiny plates. Gloria and Elías came to chat between each course.

At one point, Gloria disapprovingly said, "I'm too old to wash dishes, you need to do a better job cleaning that plate," handing me a piece of bread, while dramatically showing the proper technique for mopping up the sauce.

On our first visit, after eating our way through seven courses, we felt ready to burst when she asked, "Should I keep going? Or should we move to dessert?"

We chuckled, "We're sorry. We can't eat much more. Dessert, please!"

Rosa and I still tell people about that dessert course, which consisted of a cep (porcino) button poached and served in a local cream liquor called *crema de arroz con leche*. It was as memorable as it was simple and delicious, and it

Golden and ashen chanterelles in hand

inspired me to start playing with sweet-poaching mushrooms in all kinds of new ways, several of which appear in this chapter.

On our second visit, after eight courses, I tossed my napkin to the center of the table, saying, "I am throwing in the towel. I can't fit in another bite." Of course, dessert still followed.

At the end of our first visit, I proudly showed Gloria our first ever European chanterelles, which we had just picked that morning, and she shook her head with disapproval, disappearing again into the kitchen. She returned with a large bag of chanterelles from her personal stash, saying, "You can't show up to your family with that. It's not enough." The chanterelles were a gift, and she refused all attempts to pay for them.

After the second meal, they invited us to their home's back porch to hang out and talk over drinks. The warm hospitality both times was unlike anything I've ever experienced, permanently influencing how I approach food in general and how I strive to treat my diners.

Sweet Poached Mushrooms

Serves 6 to 8

I had already candied mushrooms for years when I first ate at El Empalme, but that experience opened my eyes to even more possibilities. When candying, I usually try to focus on the natural flavor and aroma of the mushrooms, but when sweet-poaching, I want to infuse interesting flavors into the mushrooms, opening them up to all kinds of uses. The original dish used a regional liquor called *licor de arroz con leche*, but almost any creamy liquor will do. While this recipe calls for Irish cream liquor and a couple recipes in the book require poaching mushrooms in grape juice, don't limit yourself. Experiment with fruity liquors, sweet wine, and other fruit juices. The porcini buttons here can be served as a statement dessert all on their own, but other poached mushrooms work well as a garnish for all sorts of desserts and salads.

1 pound (450 g) porcini buttons, left whole, or cut in half or quartered if large

2 cups (480 ml) Irish cream liquor

1. Cover the porcini with the liquor and bring to a boil over medium-high heat, then reduce the heat to keep the liquid at a gentle simmer. Continue simmering until the liquid reduces to a consistency like heavy cream, 60 to 90 minutes. Don't let the liquid get too thick.

2. Remove from the heat and let the mushrooms cool completely in the liquid. The mushrooms can be refrigerated in the poaching liquid for at least 1 week or frozen for several months. The sauce will be very thick when cold. To serve, gently warm over low heat to loosen the consistency, and serve the mushrooms with some of the poaching liquid.

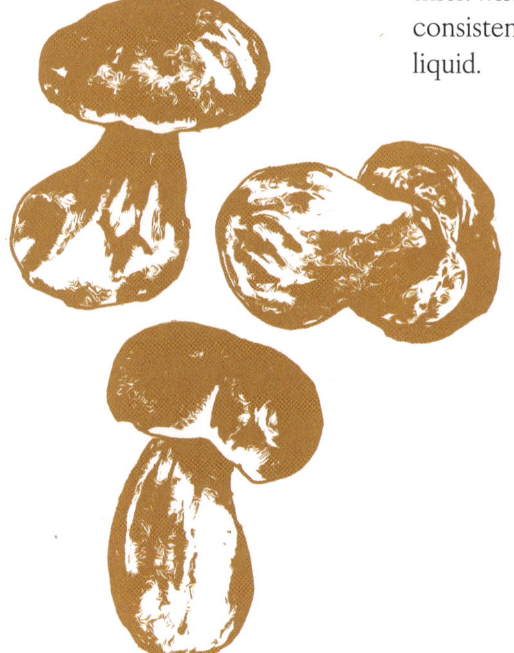

Mushroom Substitutions: White buttons, crimini, and most tight young *Agaricus* buttons work well in the creamy liquor. To poach in juice, beech (shimeji) work well, as do any jelly fungus, cultivated or wild. There's tons of room for experimenting with almost any mushrooms, especially as you start playing with different poaching liquids. Mild-flavored mushrooms, like cat's tongue, witch's butter, and even the cultivated white jelly mushroom (*Tremella* spp.) can be poached in just about anything with good results. If using mushrooms that need thorough cooking to make them safe to eat, cook them well before candying them.

Candied Mushrooms

Makes about 3 cups (675 g)

Candying preserves the distinctive flavors and aromas of most mushrooms almost indefinitely, while opening up all kinds of sweet possibilities. Candying also helps consolidate a large pile of mushrooms into a manageable size for easy long-term storage in the freezer, making it a favorite preservation method in my house. You can infuse an infinite number of flavors into mild-flavored mushrooms when candying. Add anything you like to the cooking liquid, from spices to fresh herbs to citrus juice and peels. I highly recommend weighing the ingredients in this recipe because it's the only way to ensure the ratios are accurate.

18 ounces (510 g) fresh mushrooms, cut to desired size if large or left whole if small

1½ cups plus 2 tablespoons (340 g) granulated sugar

1. Add the mushrooms and sugar to a heavy-bottomed pot that fits them somewhat snuggly. Add just enough water to cover the mushrooms. Bring to a boil over high heat, then reduce the heat to keep the liquid at a gentle simmer. The mushrooms usually release a lot of water as they start cooking, so they will be swimming in liquid for a while.

2. Keep simmering until the liquid reduces to a syrupy consistency, then remove from the heat and let cool completely. The candied mushrooms can be left in pieces or puréed before storage. Store in sealed containers in the fridge for 2 to 3 weeks or in the freezer for 6 months or longer.

Tip: *This ratio of sugar to mushrooms has worked well for me for various almondy* Agaricus, *chanterelles, and others. Unless a recipe specifically calls out a different ratio, I suggest using this as a starting point. You can add more sugar if you want things sweeter. For my taste, matsutake require a ratio closer to 1:1 of sugar to mushrooms.*

Mushroom Substitutions: Almost any mushrooms will work here, though you may have to experiment with the flavor of your candying syrup when working with stronger-flavored mushrooms. Mild-flavored, slimy-textured mushrooms like small waxy caps make a uniquely slippery and cute dessert garnish when candied and left whole. You can also dehydrate candied jelly-textured mushrooms like cat's tongue (*Pseudohydnum gelatinosum*) and witch's butter to make a gummy bear–like treat.

Mushroom Frangipane and Stone Fruit Tart

Serves 8

This elegant dessert evolved out of a frangipane fruit tart I saw from David Lebovitz. Frangipane is a classic almond filling for various pastries, and this updated version uses almondy *Agaricus* as part of the frangipane base, which adds almond extract flavor and a lot of moisture. It also uses an interesting, crumbly tart dough with egg yolks, milk, and a little almond flour, which is pressed into the pan instead of rolled. (You can use a premade crust if you prefer.) This is a great way to use stone fruit in the summer, but you can substitute almost any seasonal fruit to make this year-round. I highly recommend weighing the dry ingredients in this recipe for accuracy, to ensure a consistently good crust and filling.

CRUST

2½ cups plus 2 tablespoons (330 g) all-purpose flour

½ cup (60 g) powdered sugar

¼ cup (25 g) almond meal

½ cup plus 2½ tablespoons (150 g) cold unsalted butter, diced

4 egg yolks, lightly beaten

1 tablespoon plus 1½ teaspoons milk

FRANGIPANE FILLING AND FRUIT

½ cup (120 g) room-temperature unsalted butter

1 cup (225 g) puréed candied *Agaricus* (see page 243)

2 eggs

1½ cups (150 g) almond meal

3 plums or small peaches, pits removed, cut into ¼-inch (6 mm) slices

2 cups (365 g) cherries, pitted and halved

1. **To make the crust,** sift the flour, powdered sugar, almond meal, and a pinch of salt together into a bowl. Using a pastry cutter or your fingers, cut the butter into the flour mix until it is fairly homogeneous with a texture like sand.

2. Whisk the egg yolks with the milk in a small bowl, then drizzle it into the flour mix a little bit at a time, working in just enough to form a cohesive dough (you may not need the entire egg mixture). Press into a disk and wrap tightly in plastic wrap. Refrigerate for 45 to 60 minutes to allow the dough to fully and evenly hydrate and to relax the gluten.

3. Preheat the oven to 375°F (190°C). Place an 11-inch (28 cm) tart pan onto a rimmed baking sheet. Remove the dough from the fridge and press small pieces into the tart pan using your fingers, evenly lining the entire pan, including the edges. Gently press the dough using your fingers to form an even layer slightly more than ⅛-inch (3 mm) thick. Use a fork to poke holes into the bottom to prevent large air bubbles forming while it bakes.

4. Cut out a circle of parchment paper slightly larger than the diameter of the tart pan, place it on top of the dough, and then fill the tart with dried beans and transfer, still on the baking sheet, to the oven. Bake for 30 to 35 minutes, until the crust sets and just barely starts to brown. Check underneath the beans to be sure the crust looks dry and sandy. If necessary, return to the oven without the beans for another 5 to 10 minutes to finish cooking the bottom. Remove from the oven and let cool completely, then remove the beans. (The baked shell can be stored, covered, for up to 24 hours at room temperature.)

continued ›

Mushroom Substitutions: Any almondy *Agaricus* work great, and you can also get good results candying plain old store-bought button mushrooms and adding ½ teaspoon of almond extract when you purée them.

5. To make the frangipane filling and fruit, preheat the oven to 350°F (180°C). Use a stand mixer fitted with a paddle attachment to whip the butter on medium speed until it starts to get a bit airy and lighter in color, 1 to 2 minutes. Add the candied mushroom purée and a pinch of salt and continue beating on medium speed until the mixture is homogeneous and airy, about 30 seconds longer.

6. Add 1 egg, beat until well incorporated, then add the other, and beat again until well incorporated. Add the almond meal and beat on low speed until it is evenly distributed.

7. Spread the frangipane evenly into the tart shell, then arrange the plums and cherries on top, covering most or all of the frangipane.

8. Transfer to the oven and bake for 45 to 60 minutes, until the frangipane is set, and the fruit is beginning to lightly brown on top. If the tart begins to get too dark, you can cover it loosely with foil for the remaining time, being sure to not let the foil touch the sticky frangipane. Remove and let the tart rest until cooled enough to safely remove from the tart pan, 45 to 60 minutes. Gently separate the bottom from the tart pan, lift out the tart, and cut into wedges to serve. (The tart will keep for about 3 days covered in the fridge—if you can keep from eating it for that long.)

Tip: *You can bake the shell without filling it with dried beans if necessary. Just be aware that the dough can sometimes bow or bubble up during baking, and it might not come out quite as perfectly. The beans used for baking should be kept and reused for the same purpose or discarded. They're no longer good to eat.*

No-Bake Candy Cap Cookies

Makes about 20 cookies

These cookies are super easy and fast to make, as they are not even baked. It takes me longer to gather and measure the ingredients than it does to complete the rest of the process. They're also absolutely delicious, and dare I say, healthy. These cookies work just as well as a quick breakfast as they do for a lighter dessert or snack. Feel free to explore using different nuts and nut butters.

1 cup (170 g) pitted dates (about 13 dates)

½ cup (60 g) walnuts

¼ cup (25 g) shredded coconut

1 cup (90 g) rolled oats

3 tablespoons almond butter

½ teaspoon candy cap powder

1. Process the dates in a food processor to a paste-like consistency, then transfer to a large mixing bowl.

2. Pulse the walnuts and coconut in a clean food processor into very fine pieces. Add to the dates with the oats, almond butter, and candy cap powder and mix until homogeneous. I find this easiest to do with gloved hands.

3. Scoop or break off 1 to 2 tablespoons of the dough and roll the pieces into balls or press into cookie shapes. Serve immediately, or store in an airtight container in the fridge for several days.

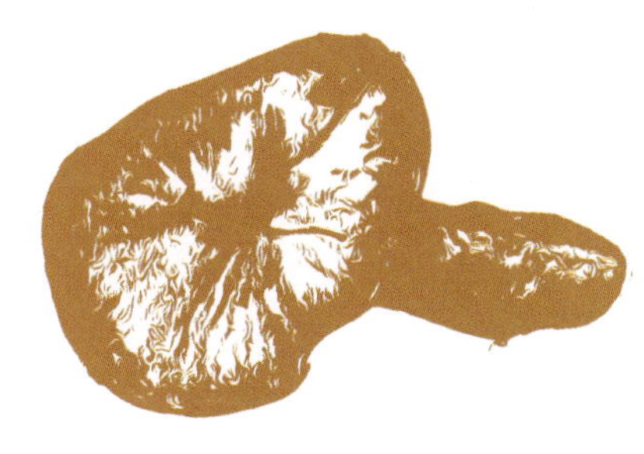

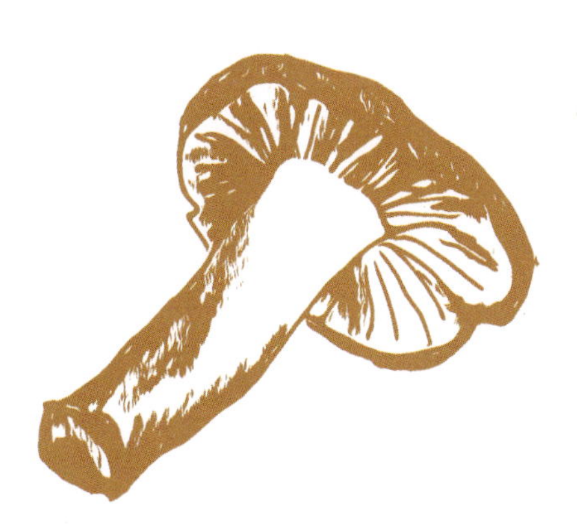

Mushroom Substitutions: Try dried almondy *Agaricus* to give the cookies an almond extract essence instead of the maple flavor from the candy caps.

Chanterelle and Persimmon Galette

Serves 4 to 6

The French word "galette" refers to a kind of rustic pie or tart in which the crust is folded up around the filling in a freeform manner, instead of the crust being molded into a pan and then filled. In this galette, the persimmons' mild, custardy sweetness provides an excellent platform to show off, but not overpower, the subtle aroma of the candied chanterelles, but you can substitute any mild, soft, sweet fruit. Don't be afraid to play with different mushroom and fruit combinations. Just be sure to assemble the fruit on top of the candied mushrooms, as otherwise the mushrooms' high sugar content can make them burn before the dough is cooked. This very quick dough recipe comes from my pastry chef friend Meredith Morris. If you don't have a food processor, you can make the dough by hand or in a stand mixer with a paddle attachment. I highly recommend weighing the dry ingredients in this recipe for accuracy, to ensure consistently good results.

SIMPLE CRUST

2 cups (250 g) all-purpose flour

½ teaspoon salt

¼ cup (60 ml) ice water

¾ cup plus 2 tablespoons (205 g) cold unsalted butter, cut into small pieces

GALETTE

2 cups (390 g) candied chanterelles, drained (see page 243)

2 persimmons, peeled and cut into ¼-inch (6 mm) slices

1 egg, beaten

1. To make the simple crust, combine the flour and salt in the bowl of a food processor. Add the butter and pulse until the mixture has the consistency of coarse sand (a few pea-size pieces are OK). With the processor running, stream in just enough of the ice water to form a dough. Flatten the dough into a disk, wrap in plastic, and refrigerate for 1 to 2 hours to allow the dough to fully and evenly hydrate and to relax the gluten.

2. Preheat the oven to 375°F (190°C). Line a rimmed baking sheet with parchment paper. Remove the dough from the fridge and roll it out into a 12-inch (30 cm) circle on a lightly floured surface, doing your best to work in as little extra flour as possible. Transfer the crust to the prepared baking sheet.

3. To make the galette, spread the candied chanterelles in an even layer in middle of the crust, leaving a 1½ inch (4 cm) border. Neatly arrange the persimmons on top of the candied chanterelles.

4. Starting from one side and working around the galette in a circle, fold the outer edge of the crust over the periphery of the filling, making a new fold or pleat about every 1 inch (2.5 cm) to create a rim. (Note that the crust should not fully cover the filling.) Brush the beaten egg over the crust.

5. Transfer to the oven and bake for about 40 minutes, until the crust is lightly browned and the persimmons look a bit dry and lightly browned.

6. The galette can be sliced into wedges and served hot from the oven or after cooling completely. It will keep for about 3 days covered in the fridge.

Mushroom Substitutions: Almost any candied mushrooms can work, but you may need to experiment with different fruits to find a great pairing.

Black Trumpet Brownies

Makes about 24 brownies

The black trumpets add earthy undertones that help balance the sweet richness of these almost fudge-like brownies. Chopping (instead of powdering) the mushrooms ensures that they don't get lost behind the big chocolate flavor. I highly recommend weighing the sugar, flour, and cocoa powder for this recipe to ensure that you get the right ratios and proper fudgy consistency.

1 ounce (28 g) dried black trumpets

1 teaspoon neutral oil

2¾ cups (550 g) granulated sugar

1¾ cups (210 g) cocoa powder

1¼ cup plus 2 tablespoons (305 g) unsalted butter

5 eggs

1¼ cups plus 1 tablespoon (170 g) all-purpose flour

¾ cup (90 g) walnuts, toasted and roughly chopped

1. Cover the dried black trumpets with warm water and let soak until soft, about 15 minutes, then drain, straining the grit out of the soaking liquid with a fine-mesh strainer. Reserve the liquid separately. Make sure that the mushrooms are well-cleaned before proceeding.

2. Heat a large, heavy-bottomed pan over medium-high heat. Add the oil and black trumpets and sauté until they barely begin to brown, 2 to 3 minutes. Season with salt, then add the reserved soaking liquid and cook until the liquid has completely reduced, 5 to 7 minutes. Remove from the heat and let cool enough to handle, then chop the mushrooms into very small pieces.

3. Preheat the oven to 325°F (160°C). Grease a 13-by-18-inch (33 by 45 cm) rimmed baking sheet, then line it with parchment paper. Combine the sugar, cocoa powder, and a generous pinch of salt in the bowl of a stand mixer fitted with a paddle attachment. Mix on slow speed until thoroughly and evenly combined.

4. Melt the butter in a small pan. While still warm, add to the sugar and cocoa with the mixer running on low speed. Mix until homogeneous, then add the eggs and again mix until homogeneous.

5. With the mixer off, add the flour, walnuts, and mushrooms. Mix on low speed until the flour is fully incorporated, then increase the speed to medium for about 10 seconds to ensure the mixture is evenly combined.

6. Spread the batter evenly into the prepared baking sheet and then bake for 15 to 18 minutes, until set, rotating the baking sheet 180 degrees about halfway through baking. When the brownies are done, a knife or cake tester inserted into the middle will come out clean.

7. Let cool completely, then run a knife around the edge of the pan to release the brownies and carefully flip it onto a clean surface. Remove the parchment and cut the brownies into 24 pieces. Serve warm or at room temperature. The brownies will keep for a few days in a covered container in the fridge.

Mushroom Substitutions: You can experiment with other dried mushrooms to give an interesting earthy contrast to the fudgy brownies, but you'll lose the trumpets' chocolaty notes.

Princely Panellets

Makes about 50 cookies

Panellets are soft, mildly sweet, easy-to-make little cookies originating in Catalonia, where they traditionally appear on All Saints Day, November 1. Pine nuts adorn the most popular variety, though chocolate, coconut, coffee, and other versions are all quite common. Marzipan, which is not only expensive, but extremely sweet and rich, traditionally comprises the cookie base. Though the marzipan versions remain quite popular and are still widely sold, home cooks typically use boiled potato or sweet potato instead. The boiled potato produces a lighter, less sweet, but equally delicious and, dare I say, more irresistible treat which costs a lot less to produce. Here, the addition of the almond-flavored mushrooms, in this case prince mushrooms (*Agaricus augustus*), gently perfumes the cookies while playing beautifully with the pine nuts. I highly recommend weighing the ingredients in this recipe to ensure the proportions are right.

1 russet potato (about 9 ounces/255 g)

5 cups (500 g) almond flour

2½ cups (500 g) granulated sugar

0.25 ounce (7 g) prince mushroom powder

2 eggs, beaten separately

1 cup (140 g) pine nuts

1. Cover the potato with cold water in a saucepan and bring to a boil over high heat, then reduce the heat to gently simmer until the potato is soft all the way through when pierced with a sharp knife or skewer, 10 to 15 minutes. Drain and let cool enough to handle, then peel. Weigh out and separate 7 ounces (200 g) of the potato and mash until smooth. Reserve the rest for another purpose, or discard.

2. Mix the almond flour, sugar, prince mushroom powder, and a pinch of salt together in a large bowl. Add the potato, kneading with your hands until well combined, then add 1 of the beaten eggs and continue kneading until the dough has a very smooth, even texture.

3. Preheat the oven to 350°F (180°C) and line a cookie sheet with parchment paper. Pour the pine nuts into a small bowl. Roll a 1- to 2-tablespoon portion of the dough into a ball, then gently press and roll in the pine nuts to cover. Place the ball on the cookie sheet, and repeat until all the dough is gone.

4. Brush the panellets with the remaining beaten egg, then bake for 20 to 30 minutes, until lightly browned. Let cool completely before handling. The cookies will keep for several days in a covered container at room temperature.

Tip: *Traditionally, the panellets get completely coated with pine nuts, but in my house, we usually coat half of the ball, and then press the other side slightly down to form a flat base. This way you get plenty of pine nuts in each bite and save a little money on an expensive ingredient. If you prefer your panellets slightly less sweet, reduce the sugar to 2 cups (400 g).*

Mushroom Substitutions: Candy caps or any almondy *Agaricus* make lovely panellets.

Sweet Cauliflower Mushroom "Noodle" Kugel

Serves 6 to 8

Noodle kugel is a traditional Ashkenazi sweet noodle casserole. My grandmother made a version regularly when I was growing up that my whole family loved. I have always felt that "egg noodle mushroom" would be a much more appropriate name than "cauliflower mushroom" for *Sparassis*, so why not use it instead of egg noodles in this comforting sweet treat from my youth? This kugel is great on its own, but it's even better served with poached pears or garnished with fresh berries.

1½ tablespoons unsalted butter, melted, plus extra to grease the baking dish

1 pound (450 g) cauliflower mushroom, torn into "noodles"

2 cups (450 g) cottage cheese

1 cup (230 g) sour cream

4 eggs plus 1 yolk

½ cup (80 g) raisins

¼ cup plus 2 tablespoons (75 g) granulated sugar

1½ teaspoons ground cinnamon

1. Preheat the oven to 375°F (190°C). Butter the inside of a 7-by-10-inch (18 by 25 cm) casserole dish.

2. Bring a pot of water to a boil over high heat, add the cauliflower mushroom "noodles," and boil for 5 minutes, until cooked through. Drain and let cool completely.

3. Mix the butter, mushroom "noodles," cottage cheese, sour cream, eggs and yolk, raisins, sugar, cinnamon, and a pinch of salt in a large bowl until thoroughly combined, then pour into the casserole dish and bake for about 45 minutes, until set and lightly browned on top.

4. The kugel can be served hot directly from the oven, but I much prefer it cold the next day. It is also much easier to cut clean portions when cold. The kugel will keep, covered in the fridge, for up to 4 days.

Mushroom Substitutions: There is no substitute for the special shape and texture of the cauliflower mushrooms here.

Candy Cap Flan

Serves 6

Flan is a deceptively simple dessert that appears in most cultures that were part of the Spanish Empire. In basic terms, flan is a baked custard with a bit of caramel on top, oozing over the edge to sauce the dish. The luscious but simply flavored custard base provides a perfect canvas to savor the earthy maple and butterscotch notes that you can get only from candy caps. I can't think of a better way to introduce a neophyte to these sweet-smelling mushrooms.

CARAMEL

½ cup (100 g) granulated sugar

A few drops of fresh lemon juice

FLAN

3 cups (720 ml) heavy cream

¾ cup plus 2 tablespoons (180 g) granulated sugar

5 dried candy caps

6 eggs

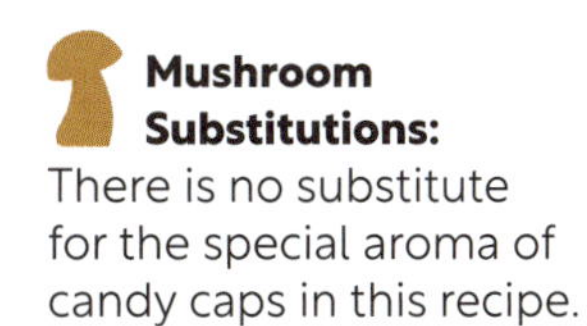
Mushroom Substitutions: There is no substitute for the special aroma of candy caps in this recipe.

1. To make the caramel, place the sugar, lemon juice, and 1 tablespoon water in a small saucepan over medium heat. (It's best not to use nonstick here, as the darker surface will make it much harder to see the caramel change color.) Tilt the pan to move the sugar around until it begins to melt. At the first sign of melting, swirl gently to melt the sugar evenly. Keep the sides of the pan clean, as any stuck sugar is likely to burn. (Use a moistened pastry brush to clean sugar splatters from the sides.) When the caramel turns a golden-brown color, usually 1 to 2 minutes, immediately remove from the heat and pour into the bottom of a *flanera*, pie pan, or six 4-ounce ramekins. Gently swirl the vessel(s) to make sure the entire bottom is coated with caramel. Work quickly, as the caramel will begin to harden in only a few seconds. (Be sure to give the caramel your full attention until you completely finish this step. Getting distracted for even a few seconds can result in burnt caramel, even if the pan is off the heat.)

2. To make the flan, preheat the oven to 350°F (180°C). Place the cream, sugar, and dried candy caps in a saucepan. Warm over medium heat, stirring gently, until the mixture barely shows signs of starting to simmer, then immediately remove from the heat. Let rest for 5 minutes, then blend using a blender or immersion blender until smooth.

3. Beat the eggs in a large bowl. While the cream is still hot, slowly pour about one quarter of it into the eggs while whisking to combine thoroughly. Pour in the rest while still whisking, then pour the custard directly on top of the caramel in each of your chosen vessels, filling to within about ¼ inch (6 mm) of the rim.

4. Place your flan vessels in a large casserole or baking dish and then transfer that larger dish to the oven. Once in the oven, use a pitcher or measuring cup to carefully fill the baking dish with 1 to 3 quarts (1–2.8 L) hot water, as much as needed to reach at least halfway up the sides of your flan vessels. Bake for 45 to 60 minutes, until the flan is set. Test by inserting a toothpick or cake tester in the center; if it comes out clean, the flan is done.

continued ›

5. Carefully remove the flan from the oven and the water bath, and let cool completely, then cover and refrigerate for at least 3 to 4 hours to finish setting. (The flan will keep in the fridge, covered, for up to 4 days.)

6. Remove from the fridge 20 to 30 minutes before serving. Run a small knife all the way around the edge of the vessel(s), then carefully invert the flan onto a plate, giving the vessel a tap or gentle shake to help release the flan. If the flan doesn't slide easily out of the dish, place the vessel into a hot water bath for 20 to 30 seconds, then try again. Serve.

Tip: *There is a pan called a flanera with fluted sides that is traditionally used for making flan, but a pie pan works just as well. My preference is to make flan in individual ramekins, which can make for a much more elegant single-serving presentation. The recipe can easily be adjusted to fit any vessel. If you aren't sure how much custard you'll need, fill your vessel(s) with water and then pour the water into a measuring cup. Just make sure to use a vessel with a flat bottom.*

Waxy Cap and Plum Bread Pudding with Waxy Cap-Whisky Caramel Sauce

Serves 6

Bread pudding is an easy and hearty dessert that adapts well to just about any available ingredients. Many people pair bourbon sauces with sweet bread puddings, which taste great, but using a smoky Scotch gives the sauce a surprisingly satisfying complexity. Use whatever fruit is in season; apples, persimmons, figs, and any stone fruit will all work well in place of the plums. The candied mushrooms add fun texture and visual appeal to the bread pudding and the sauce.

3 plums, pitted and cut into ½-inch (1.25 cm) pieces

1¼ cups (250 g) plus 1 tablespoon granulated sugar

½ cup (120 ml) peaty (smoky) Scotch whisky

10 ounces (280 g) small mild waxy caps (about 2 cups)

1¼ cups (300 ml) milk

3 eggs

½ teaspoon ground nutmeg

3 cups (300 g) crusty bread, cut into ½-inch (1.25 cm) pieces and left out for at least a few hours or overnight to stale

½ cup (45 g) roasted, salted pecan pieces

2 tablespoons unsalted butter, cut into pieces, plus extra to grease the baking dish

1. Toss the diced plums with 1 tablespoon of the sugar in a small bowl and set aside.

2. Pour the whisky over the waxy caps in a saucepan and cook over medium-high heat until the whisky is reduced by about three quarters of its volume, 3 to 5 minutes, then quickly add 1 cup (200 g) of the sugar and ½ cup (120 ml) water. Bring to a boil, then reduce the heat to simmer gently, uncovered, until the liquid has reduced to a light syrupy consistency, 10 to 15 minutes. Remove from heat and set aside to cool.

3. Whisk together the milk, eggs, ground nutmeg, a pinch of salt, and the remaining sugar in a bowl.

4. Remove about half of the candied waxy caps from the syrup, cut them into large pieces, and mix them with the bread, pecans, plums, and any liquid the plums have released. Mix into the egg mixture and let sit for 30 minutes to allow the flavors to meld and the bread to get fully saturated.

5. Preheat the oven to 325°F (160°C) and grease a 7-inch (18 cm) square baking dish or 8-inch (20 cm) cast-iron pan with butter.

6. After 30 minutes of soaking, pour the bread pudding evenly into the baking dish. Arrange 1 tablespoon of the butter over the top of the bread pudding. Bake uncovered for 40 to 45 minutes, until the custard sets and the top is lightly browned.

7. When nearly ready to serve, reheat the remaining waxy caps in their syrup over medium heat. When the waxy caps are hot, turn off the heat and whisk in the remaining butter until melted and emulsified.

8. The bread pudding can be cooled, then portioned and warmed up to serve, or served hot, straight out of the oven. To serve, spoon some of the sauce over each portion of the bread pudding, being sure that each portion gets some of the whole candied mushrooms.

Mushroom Substitutions: Beech (shimeji), pioppini (*Cyclocybe aegerita*), and nameko (*Pholiota nameko*) mushrooms are great store-bought choices, but mild-flavored, slimy waxy caps (*Hygrophorus* spp.) are my favorite here, especially the larch waxy cap (*H. speciosus*). You can substitute just about any mild-flavored mushroom you like candied, though that slippery texture brings something special to this dessert sauce.

Chanterelle Jelly Roll

Serves 12

A homemade jelly roll is always an attention grabber. The chanterelles star in this surprisingly easy cake without being too overpowering, both in the cake batter and making up the jelly filling. Because the recipe is not overly sweet, the cake can be enjoyed either as a light dessert or a treat with late morning or afternoon tea. I highly recommend weighing the dry ingredients in the cake batter to ensure you use the right proportions for a properly textured cake.

Nonstick cooking spray

5 eggs, whites and yolks separated

3 tablespoons granulated sugar

¼ teaspoon salt

1 cup (225 g) puréed candied chanterelles (see page 243)

1 tablespoon unsalted butter, melted

½ cup plus 1 tablespoon (75 g) all-purpose flour

1. Preheat the oven to 400°F (200°C). Grease a 12-inch (30 cm) square rimmed baking sheet with the nonstick cooking spray, line it with a sheet of parchment paper, then grease the paper with the nonstick cooking spray.

2. Combine the egg yolks, 1½ tablespoons of the sugar, and salt in the bowl of a stand mixer fitted with a whisk attachment. Whisk on medium-high speed for 1 to 2 minutes, stopping occasionally to scrape down the sides of the bowl with a spatula, until the mixture is much lighter in color and more viscous (called the "ribbon stage" because the texture can support "ribbons" of trailing mixture).

3. Add ½ cup (110 g) of the puréed candied chanterelles to the egg yolk mixture and continue mixing until homogeneous. Add the melted butter and again mix until evenly combined. Sift in the flour and whisk slowly until thoroughly incorporated.

4. With a clean bowl and whisk, whip the egg whites with the stand mixer on high speed to just before the soft peak stage, 1 to 2 minutes. Reduce the speed to medium and slowly add the remaining sugar while whisking. Continue whisking until you have medium-stiff peaks, which will look somewhat shiny and moist and will stand almost straight up, another 1 to 2 minutes.

5. Add about one quarter of the egg whites to the egg yolk mix. Using a spatula, fold in the egg whites until homogenous to help loosen the batter. Add another quarter of the egg whites, again folding in with a spatula, trying not to deflate the batter too much. Add the last half of the egg whites in the same fashion, again trying to not deflate the batter too much.

6. Pour the batter over the prepared baking sheet and use an offset spatula to gently spread it evenly. Transfer to the oven and bake for 8 to 10 minutes, until risen, firm, and a toothpick inserted into the center of the cake comes out clean. Remove from the oven, set on a rack,

continued ❯

Mushroom Substitutions: Candied yellow foots make a somewhat similarly flavored cake. Candied black trumpets will give an almost chocolaty result, and a stunning dark-colored cake and jelly. Various *Agaricus* also are worth exploring.

and let cool in the pan for about 2 minutes. Lay out a large piece of parchment paper on the work surface.

7. While still very warm, run a knife around the edge of the cake, to separate it from the edge of the pan. Invert the cake onto the piece of parchment paper, removing the paper it baked on, then use the fresh paper to roll up the cake into a tight spiral. The paper should be rolled up with the cake, inside the spiral, to keep the layers of the cake from sticking to each other. Let the cake cool completely while rolled up like this, 10 or 15 minutes.

8. Unroll the cake, leaving it on top of the parchment paper. Spread the remaining chanterelle purée in an even layer across the whole cake, leaving about 1 inch (2.5 cm) clean on the far edge.

9. Starting with the edge closest to you, roll the cake into a tight spiral as evenly as possible. If any of the purée leaks out, wipe it off with a damp towel. Roll the cake tightly in the parchment paper and either tape it closed to keep the roll tight, or prop it against something heavy so it can't unroll. Let it rest in the fridge for at least 4 hours before serving. After resting, the tight spiral should hold on its own.

10. To serve, remove the parchment paper and cut crosswise into 1-inch (2.5 cm) slices. Covered in the fridge, the cake will keep for about 4 days.

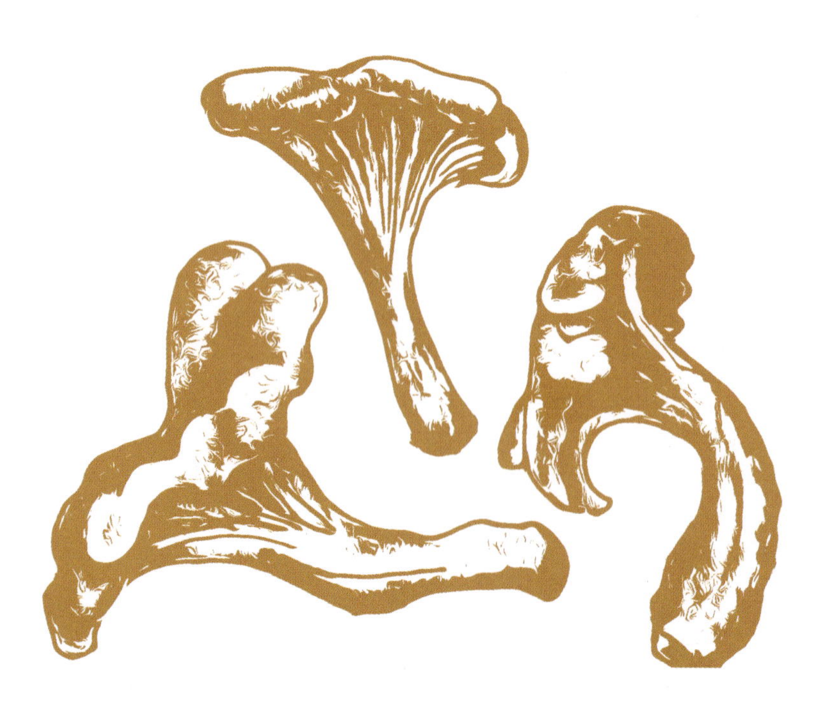

Crimini Cream Pie

Serves 8 to 10

Well-known mycologist and myco-educator Christian Schwarz suggested I come up with a recipe for banana cream pie with chanterelles all the way back in 2017, but although I loved the idea, I didn't get around to playing with it until years later. After a few iterations, I realized that the bananas were unnecessary, detracting from the mushroom flavor. Without the fruit, this pie becomes a great vehicle for just about any candied mushrooms, from chanterelles to black trumpets, yellow foots to crimini. The crimini give the pie an almost chocolaty flavor. Using a classic pie crust keeps the focus on the flavor of the mushrooms, but you can use a graham cracker crust if you prefer.

1 recipe Simple Crust from the Chanterelle and Persimmon Galette (page 249)

2 cups plus 2 tablespoons (500 ml) milk

1 cup (225 g) candied crimini mushrooms, puréed with their syrup (see page 243)

5 egg yolks

¼ cup (32 g) cornstarch

1 tablespoon sugar

2 tablespoons unsalted butter, cut into small pieces

1 cup (195 g) candied crimini mushrooms, well drained and cut into pieces (see page 243), plus extra for garnish

Fresh whipped cream

1. Preheat the oven to 375°F (190°C). Roll the dough into a circle about ⅛-inch (3 mm) thick, then carefully transfer into a 9-inch (23 cm) pie dish. Trim off and discard any excess dough. Use a fork to poke a few holes into the bottom. If desired, use your fingers to crimp the crust around the rim.

2. Cut out a circle of parchment paper about the diameter of the pie dish or slightly larger, place it on top of the dough, and then fill the pie with dried beans. This will keep the dough from puffing up too much while it bakes. Transfer to the oven and bake for 15 to 20 minutes, until the edge looks dry and sandy and begins to brown lightly. Remove the beans and parchment and return to the oven to bake for another 10 to 15 minutes, until the bottom of the crust is lightly browned. Let cool completely.

3. Add the milk and puréed candied crimini mushrooms to a saucepan and bring to a simmer over medium-high heat, stirring occasionally to prevent burning. While the milk is heating up, add the egg yolks, cornstarch, sugar, and a pinch of salt to a large bowl and whisk until thoroughly combined. When the milk reaches a simmer, pour about one quarter into the yolk mixture while whisking constantly. Once thoroughly combined, pour the yolk and milk mixture back into the milk and return to the stove, whisking constantly. Keep whisking until the mix is very thick, then for about 10 more seconds. Remove from the heat and stir in the butter until melted and combined.

4. Arrange the candied crimini mushroom pieces on the cooled crust in an even layer. Then, working quickly, pour the custard into the crust, using a spatula to even it out. Refrigerate for at least 2 hours before serving to allow the custard to set. The pie will keep for about 3 days in the fridge.

5. To serve, cut into wedges and top with freshly whipped cream and the extra candied mushrooms.

Mushroom Substitutions: Almost any candied mushrooms you like are worth experimenting with here.

Matsutake, Pear, and Chestnut Strudel

Serves 6 to 8

The cinnamon essence of the matsutake is a great accompaniment to the pears, while the nutty sweetness of the chestnuts ties this strudel together. Save any extra liquid from the filling to use as an accompanying sauce. I use soy sauce not just to provide a lightly salty background flavor, but because it helps tame the musky notes of the matsutake. Phyllo dough generally comes frozen, folded, or rolled up in a box. Be as gentle as possible when handling it, as it can tear very easily. Handle it no more than necessary, and make sure it is fully thawed before attempting to unfold or separate the sheets.

1 cup (225 g) candied matsutake, including the syrup, mushrooms cut into ¼-inch (6 mm) slices (see page 243)

2 large, ripe, sweet pears, peeled, cored and cut into ¼-inch (6 mm) slices

2 tablespoons light brown sugar

½ teaspoon soy sauce

7 sheets phyllo dough

3 tablespoons unsalted butter, melted, plus 1 tablespoon cold unsalted butter

1 cup (150 g) roasted, peeled, and chopped chestnuts (about 18 chestnuts)

1. Preheat the oven to 350°F (180°C). Line a rimmed baking sheet with parchment paper. Add the candied matsutake and their syrup, pears, brown sugar, and soy sauce to a large bowl and mix well to combine. Set aside to macerate.

2. Lay 1 sheet of phyllo dough flat on a clean work surface and brush a thin layer of melted butter across the entire sheet. Carefully place another sheet of phyllo on top and gently press it down, lining it up perfectly on top of the first. Repeat until all 7 sheets of phyllo have been layered and buttered.

3. Strain the mushroom-pear mixture, reserving the liquid separately. Spread the filling in an even line, a couple of inches wide, lengthwise across the phyllo, leaving about a 1-inch (2.5 cm) border at the ends. Spread the chestnuts evenly across the filling. Carefully roll the phyllo lengthwise over the filling and into a cylinder, rolling as tightly as possible without tearing.

4. Place the strudel on the prepared baking sheet and brush the top with more melted butter. Cut three small diagonal slits across the top to allow ventilation during baking. Bake for 20 to 30 minutes, until golden brown.

5. While the strudel bakes, place the reserved liquid from the filling in a small pan and bring to a boil over medium-high heat. Reduce the heat to medium-low to simmer, and when reduced by about half, about 10 minutes, remove from the heat and swirl in the cold butter to emulsify.

6. The strudel can be sliced and served straight from the oven, or cooled completely, covered, and refrigerated, where it will keep for 2 or 3 days. It is a great treat eaten cold, but even better warmed up in the toaster oven for a few minutes and served with your morning coffee. Just before serving, cover slices of the strudel with the sauce.

Mushroom Substitutions: Any mushrooms you like candied will work here, but if using other mushrooms, add ½ teaspoon of cinnamon to the filling.

An Ice Cream Primer

Before getting into ice cream recipes, let's talk briefly about ice cream making. The traditional custard ice-cream base that most cooks know provides a richly flavored and textured ice cream that keeps well in the freezer. It has some limitations, though, as the egg yolks contribute their flavor to the ice cream and can mute certain other flavors—like those of mushrooms!—while also making the ice cream feel heavy. While the Yellow Foot Eggnog Ice Cream on page 267 uses a traditional custard base, the other ice creams in this section use a much lighter base without sacrificing the rich, creamy mouthfeel that any good ice cream should have.

The most important thing in making good ice cream is to avoid forming ice crystals, which ruin an ice cream's texture. To that end, I almost always use dried instead of fresh mushrooms for ice creams, because fresh mushrooms contain a lot of water, and I don't want to add any extra moisture that can lead to ice crystals. As a bonus, dried mushrooms also have more concentrated flavor and aroma. Using an ice cream machine also helps to prevent crystals by rapidly freezing the ice cream.

I also use stabilizers to take the place of the eggs in emulsifying the ice cream and tying up free water. Unflavored, powdered gelatin is inexpensive, easy to use, and readily available at any supermarket. The proteins from the gelatin help create structure in the ice cream and bind up water, making it an ideal stabilizer. Gelatin creates a noticeably better, richer mouthfeel, while not changing the flavor at all.

Konjac flour is a natural starch from a Japanese yam that has been dried and powdered. It's extremely powerful at thickening liquids and binding up water, so you only need a tiny amount, which won't affect the flavor at all. I use it to help the gelatin coagulate the ice cream base before freezing. It's easy to use, easy to find and purchase online, and one small bag will last years of regular use if stored properly. You will still get good results with gelatin alone if you omit the konjac flour. If you are vegetarian and cannot use gelatin, then double, or even triple, the amount of konjac flour in the recipes.

Finally, I highly recommend eating ice cream within a few days of making it, as the texture will always degrade over time.

Blueberry-Porcini Ice Cream

Makes about 1 quart (about 1 L)

I have served this ice cream at a number of different events, and it has generally been a big hit. The blueberry porcini connection works on a few different levels for me. Over the years, many folks have spoken of the virtues of combining ingredients that grow together, and on more than one occasion, I've picked porcini in wild blueberry patches in the Sierra Nevada. In one of my early line cook jobs, I had a vegetarian entrée on my station that used a few wild mushrooms, including porcini, with a blueberry sage sauce. The popular dish was beautiful and interesting. The seemingly improbable combination has since remained in the back of my mind, and helped inspire this ice cream. Note that the sugar required will depend on the ripeness and sweetness of the blueberries. If your blueberries aren't at peak ripeness, you may need a bit more sugar. Taste the base when you blend everything together in Step 4 and decide then if you need to adjust the sugar.

2 cups (480 ml) half-and-half

1 cup (200 g) granulated sugar

1 cup (160 g) blueberries

0.5 ounce (14 g) dried porcini

⅛ teaspoon konjac flour

½ teaspoon unflavored powdered gelatin

3 large fresh sage leaves

1. Combine 1 cup (240 ml) of the half-and-half, ¾ cup plus 2 tablespoons (175 g) sugar, and a pinch of salt in a saucepan and bring to a simmer over medium-high heat, stirring regularly so the bottom does not burn. As soon as it comes to a simmer, remove from the heat, add the blueberries and dried porcini, and let cool.

2. Combine the konjac flour with the remaining sugar and set aside.

3. In another saucepan, stir the powdered gelatin into the remaining half-and-half. Let stand for 5 to 10 minutes, then place over medium-high heat and bring to a boil, stirring constantly. Immediately reduce the heat to gently simmer and slowly whisk in the konjac-sugar mix. Continue whisking to avoid any lumps and simmer for another 15 seconds, until noticeably thickened but still very smooth, then remove from the heat.

4. Combine the two mixtures in a blender and blend until very smooth. Pour the ice cream base into a container, then add the sage leaves, and let cool completely, preferably in an ice bath. Cover the container and refrigerate for at least 4 hours or up to 24 hours.

5. Remove the sage leaves, then follow your ice cream machine's instructions for freezing the ice cream. Transfer to an airtight container and freeze until fully set, at least 2 hours.

Tip: *For a different flavor profile, substitute huckleberries for the blueberries and increase the sugar by 1 to 2 tablespoons, since huckleberries can be slightly less sweet than commercially grown blueberries.*

Mushroom Substitutions: There is no substitute for porcini in this recipe.

Turkey Tail Sorbet

Makes about 1 quart (about 1 L)

The flavor of this sorbet is, by far, the most subtle of the frozen desserts in this section. Serve it simply on its own to savor the turkey tail flavor, which reminds me of a pleasantly earthy black tea. Besides being a light dessert, it also could be served as a small intermezzo or palate cleanser between courses at a dinner party.

0.75 ounce (21 g) dried turkey tails

1 cup (200 g) granulated sugar

½ teaspoon konjac flour

1¼ cups (300 ml) cold water

1½ teaspoons unflavored powdered gelatin

Juice of ½ lime

1. Cover the dried turkey tails with about 3 cups (720 ml) water in a saucepan. Add ¾ cups plus 2 tablespoons (175 g) of the sugar. Bring to a simmer over medium-high heat, then reduce the heat to low, cover to keep the water from reducing too much, and simmer gently for 30 minutes to infuse the mushroom's flavor into the liquid. You should be left with at least 2½ cups (600 ml) of liquid. If you don't have enough, you can add a little more water to make up the difference. Turn off the heat, keeping the lid on the pan, and set aside for at least 1 to 2 hours to give the turkey tails time to release their aroma and flavor.

2. Mix the konjac flour into the remaining sugar.

3. Add the cold water and gelatin to another saucepan and let sit for 5 to 10 minutes. Place the pan over medium-high heat, and bring to a boil while stirring constantly. Immediately reduce the heat to gently simmer and slowly whisk in the konjac-sugar mixture. Continue whisking to avoid any lumps while simmering for another 15 seconds, then remove from the heat. Whisk this thoroughly into the liquid with the turkey tails, along with the lime juice.

4. Pour the sorbet base into a container and let cool completely, preferably in an ice bath. Cover the container and refrigerate for at least 4 hours or up to 24 hours.

5. Stir to loosen, then strain out the turkey tails and follow your ice cream maker's instructions to freeze the sorbet. Transfer to an airtight container and freeze until fully set, at least 2 hours.

Tip: *The same method used in Step 1 can be used to make turkey tail tea, a warm drink my wife and I consume almost every day in cold weather. Besides tasting great, it contains compounds from the turkey tails that have immune-boosting and cancer-fighting properties. Just strain the mixture before drinking, saving the turkey tails if desired to re-simmer to make more tea another couple of times before discarding.*

Mushroom Substitutions: There isn't any substitute for the mild tea-like flavor of turkey tails (*Trametes versicolor*).

Butternut Squash Ice Cream with Black Trumpet Chocolate Chunks

Makes about 1.5 quarts (about 1.4 L)

This ice cream started as a joke after I'd been making ice creams for weeks on end, trying to hash out recipes for this book. I made an offhand comment to Rosa about a butternut squash sitting in the kitchen, but quickly realized that the idea had merit, and made a batch of it into ice cream. After one spoonful, planning for a follow-up batch ensued in earnest, because we both loved it. The trumpets have a deep, dark, earthy, and slightly bitter flavor that plays wonderfully with chocolate. Sugar pumpkin or red kuri squash would be great substitutes for the butternut.

BLACK TRUMPET CHOCOLATE CHUNKS

0.75 ounce (21 g) dried black trumpets

1 teaspoon neutral oil

1 cup (170 g) coarsely chopped bittersweet chocolate

BUTTERNUT SQUASH ICE CREAM BASE

1 butternut squash (about 2 pounds/900 g), peeled, halved, and seeded

1 teaspoon neutral oil

1 teaspoon light brown sugar

3 cups (720 ml) half-and-half

1½ cups (300 g) granulated sugar

¼ teaspoon konjac flour

2 teaspoons unflavored powdered gelatin

1. To make the black trumpet chocolate chunks, add the black trumpets to a bowl with the half-and-half and soak until softened, about 20 minutes. Squeeze the liquid out of the trumpets back into the bowl and set the mushrooms aside, then strain the half-and-half and reserve separately. Split and clean the trumpets under running water to remove any remaining dirt and grit.

2. Heat a large pan over medium-high heat. Add the oil, then the trumpets, season with a pinch of salt, and sauté for 2 to 3 minutes to cook through. Remove from the heat, and when cool enough to handle, mince the mushrooms.

3. Fill a saucepan with about 1 inch (2.5 cm) of water and bring to a simmer. Place a glass or metal mixing bowl on top of the pan, above the level of the water. Add the chocolate to the bowl and use a spoon or silicone spatula to stir occasionally until melted. Line a small cookie sheet with parchment paper or a nonstick silicone pad. When the chocolate is melted, stir in the mushrooms until evenly coated with chocolate. Pour the chocolate out onto the lined cookie sheet, and spread into a thin layer. Refrigerate for 1 hour to set.

4. Transfer the chocolate-trumpet bark to a cutting board and use a knife to cut it into rough ¼-inch (6 mm) pieces. If your kitchen is warm, store covered in the fridge until ready to use, or the chocolate chunks will melt.

5. To make the butternut squash ice cream base, preheat the oven to 350°F (180°C). Lay the squash halves cut-side up on a rimmed baking sheet, drizzle with oil, season with a pinch of salt, and sprinkle with the brown sugar. Once the oven is hot, bake for 30 to 45 minutes, until soft all the way through. Check by poking with a paring knife. (Getting some color on the squash during the bake is OK.) Remove from the oven, poke a few large holes in the flesh with a knife to allow

continued ›

Mushroom Substitutions: There is no substitute for the black trumpets in this recipe.

moisture to escape, and let cool enough to handle. When cool, cut or break it into chunks, add to a blender, and purée until very smooth. Set aside 1¼ cups (280 g) of the purée for the ice cream base, reserving the rest for another use. (The purée can be made up to 3 days in advance and stored, covered, in the fridge. Extra purée is excellent in various savory applications as a substitute for puréed or mashed sweet potatoes.)

6. Mix 2 tablespoons of the granulated sugar with the konjac flour and set aside.

7. Combine the squash purée, 2 cups (480 ml) of the half-and-half, the remaining sugar, and a pinch of salt in a saucepan and bring to a simmer over medium-high heat, whisking regularly so the bottom does not burn. As soon as the mixture comes to a simmer, remove from the heat and let cool.

8. Add the gelatin to another saucepan along with the remaining half-and-half and let sit for 5 to 10 minutes. Place the pan over medium-high heat and bring to a boil while stirring constantly. Immediately reduce the heat to gently simmer, then slowly whisk in the konjac-sugar mixture. Continue whisking to avoid any lumps while simmering for another 15 seconds, then remove from the heat. Immediately whisk the konjac-sugar mixture into the squash mixture until smooth and homogeneous. Pour into a container and let cool completely, preferably in an ice bath. Cover the container and refrigerate for at least 4 hours or up to 24 hours.

9. Freeze the ice cream following your ice cream maker's instructions. Stir in the black trumpet chocolate chunks, being sure to disperse them evenly throughout the ice cream, transfer to an airtight container, and freeze until fully set, at least 2 hours.

Tip: *If you don't want to go to the effort of making ice cream, the chocolate-trumpet bark makes a delicious treat on its own.*

Yellow Foot Eggnog Ice Cream

Makes about 1 quart (about 1 L)

This is an example of a traditional stirred-custard ice cream base. The technique takes a bit of care and attention to detail, but the resultant ice cream is impossibly rich in taste and texture. I love eggnog as a fun way to exploit the strong flavor that eggs impart to this type of base. Dried yellow foots contribute a mild but full-flavored earthy background, and leaving them chopped instead of ground adds to the textural interest, especially with the contrast of the crunchy hazelnut pieces.

3 cups (720 ml) half-and-half

1 ounce (28 g) dried yellow foots

½ clove of nutmeg, freshly grated

7 egg yolks

½ cup plus 3 tablespoons (130 g) packed light brown sugar

¼ cup plus 3 tablespoons (85 g) granulated sugar

½ cup (60 g) toasted, chopped hazelnuts

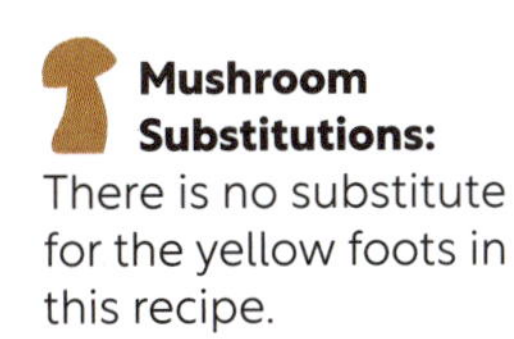

Mushroom Substitutions: There is no substitute for the yellow foots in this recipe.

1. Add the half-and-half and dried yellow foots to a bowl and soak for 20 minutes, until softened, then remove the mushrooms, chop them into small pieces, and return them to the half-and-half. Stir in the nutmeg.

2. Add the egg yolks, brown sugar, granulated sugar, and a pinch of salt to a large mixing bowl. Whisk carefully to combine without sending the sugar flying out of the bowl, then whisk more vigorously until homogeneous, creamy, smooth, and lightened in color, about 1 minute. Stop a couple times to scrape down the side of the bowl with a spatula to make sure all of the sugar and eggs are well incorporated.

3. Pour the half-and-half mixture into a pot and place over medium heat. Bring to a boil, stirring regularly so the bottom does not burn. As soon as it reaches a boil, remove from the heat. At the same time, fill a large pot with about 1 inch (2.5 cm) of water and bring to a simmer over medium heat.

4. Carefully pour about one quarter of the hot half-and-half mixture into the bowl of egg and sugar, whisking constantly. Beat together for about 10 seconds, then add another quarter of the hot liquid and beat for another 10 seconds. Finally, add the remaining liquid, and beat for another 15 seconds to thoroughly incorporate. (Be sure not to pour all of the hot liquid into the egg mix at once, or you'll end up with scrambled eggs, ruining your ice cream base and requiring you to start from scratch.)

5. Set this bowl of custard on top of the pot of simmering water. Whisk, making sure to continually scrape the sides and bottom of the bowl. Keep the bottom of the bowl at least 1½ inches (4 cm) above the surface of the simmering water. Continue whisking constantly until the custard thickens, 5 to 10 minutes.

6. Pour into a container and let the custard base cool completely, preferably in an ice bath. Cover the container and refrigerate for at least 4 hours or up to 24 hours.

7. Freeze the ice cream following your ice cream maker's instructions. Transfer to an airtight container, stir in the hazelnuts, being sure to disperse them evenly throughout the ice cream, and freeze until fully set, at least 2 hours.

Flourless Agaricus Almond Cake

Serves 8

Tarta de Santiago is a round, flourless cake made from only almonds, eggs, sugar, and citrus zest. It is typically garnished with powdered sugar in the stenciled shape of the cross of St. James. This cake is a popular prize for pilgrims as they finish the well-known Camino de Santiago, and it's one of the most famous foods from the Galician region of Spain. In this version, candied almondy *Agaricus* are added to the classic recipe. The mushroom flavor and almond extract aroma impart real depth while also making the cake moister. I have several Galician friends who insist that the mushrooms make this cake better than the original! The classic cake features a dusting of powdered sugar in the shape of a cross, but I like to use a homemade stencil to dust the sugar in the shape of a mushroom (obviously!). This cake is terrific on its own, though serving with fresh berries will add a bright punch. I highly recommend weighing the dry ingredients in this recipe to ensure you get accurate proportions and the best possible cake.

Butter or nonstick cooking spray

6 eggs, whites and yolks separated

¼ cup plus 2 tablespoons (75 g) granulated sugar

1¼ cups (275 g) puréed candied almondy *Agaricus* (see page 243)

Zest of 1 lemon

3 cups (300 g) almond meal

15 coarsely chopped almonds, optional

Powdered sugar

Mushroom Substitutions: Any almondy *Agaricus* will work well here. Young, immature mushrooms provide more sweet almond extract flavor and produce a lighter colored cake. More mature mushrooms give a deep earthiness and a darker colored cake. If you like the darker, more earthy flavor, you can try using candied white buttons or crimini and adding ½ teaspoon almond extract.

1. Preheat the oven to 325°F (160°C). Grease a 9-inch (23 cm) cake, pie, or tart pan with butter. Cut a piece of parchment paper into a 9-inch round and place inside the pan, then grease the parchment paper with butter.

2. Whip the egg yolks, sugar, and a pinch of salt on high speed in the bowl of a stand mixer fitted with a whisk attachment, stopping to scrape the bowl down with a spatula a couple of times, until the eggs lighten in color and slightly thicken, 1 to 2 minutes.

3. With the mixer off, add the candied mushroom purée and lemon zest, then mix on low speed until homogeneous. Turn the mixer off, then add the almond meal and chopped almonds, if using. Mix on low speed until evenly incorporated.

4. With a clean bowl and whisk in the stand mixer, whip the egg whites to stiff peaks. Fold one third of the egg whites into the batter to loosen it up a bit. When thoroughly mixed in, fold in another third of the egg whites, trying not to deflate the batter too much. Repeat with the final third of the whipped egg whites, being careful to deflate the batter as little as possible. Pour the batter into the prepared cake pan and spread out evenly, again being careful not to press too much air out of the batter.

5. Bake for 35 to 45 minutes, until slightly firm, lightly browned, and a toothpick inserted in the center comes out clean. Remove from oven and let cool in the pan on a rack. When cool enough to handle, run a knife around the edge of the pan to release the cake, and invert onto a plate or cutting board. Remove the parchment paper and let cool completely.

6. When cool, place the stencil, if desired, in the center of the cake and sift the powdered sugar generously over the top. Remove the stencil, slice, and serve. The cake will keep for 2 days at room temperature or 4 or 5 days in the fridge.

Tip: *See page 270 for a traceable stencil for the top of your cake.*

Stencil for Agaricus Almond Cake

Trace this drawing to make a stencil for applying powdered sugar to the Agaricus almond cake on page 268.

Further Reading and Mushrooming Resources

One of the best ways to learn about mushrooms and mushroom hunting is to find a mushroom club in your area. Start with the North American Mycological Association's list of affiliated local and regional clubs: namyco.org/clubs.

Resources for Identifying Mushrooms

A good field guide for the region where you live is absolutely essential for learning to identify mushrooms. Talk to people at your local clubs to find out which books are best for where you live.

For identifying mushrooms in the Western US, where I live, I highly recommend ***Mushrooms of the Redwood Coast*** and ***Mushrooms of Cascadia***, both coauthored by Noah Siegel and Christian Schwarz.

For a more general pocket-size, beginner-friendly book that you can bring with you in the field, nothing beats David Arora's ***All That the Rain Promises and More***.

While Arora's ***Mushrooms Demystified*** is now nearly four decades old, I still regularly refer to it for general info and lore about countless mushrooms. I also still think it's the best way to learn the basics about splitting *Agaricus* into easy-to-identify groups.

I don't recommend apps for identifying mushrooms you want to eat. Though some apps are improving, they are still unreliable, and when it comes to eating mushrooms, a wrong ID can have severe consequences.

inaturalist.org offers a free, easy-to-use app, but it's not like other apps. The citizen science community identifies your finds, and your finds help the scientific community understand what grows when and where. This platform also covers plants, animals, and even microscopic organisms, all over the world.

mushroomexpert.com: The specifics are more thorough in eastern North America, but it's full of excellent resources for anyone.

mushroomobserver.org: Post any of your finds and get help with identification. Search the database for any mushrooms or geographic areas that interest you.

mykoweb.com/CAF/index.html: This site includes tons of resources, pictures, descriptions, and cross references focused on California mushrooms, but the information is highly useful throughout Western North America.

Educational Articles

fungimag.com/spring-2012-articles/LR_Agaricidal.pdf: This article from the Spring 2012 edition of *Fungi Magazine* summarizes the scientific consensus about the sustainability of wild mushroom harvesting over time, and also cutting versus plucking. The article references a number of papers worthy of exploration.

williamrubel.com/william-rubels-books-and-articles/rubel_arora_muscaria_economic_botany: This article by William Rubel and David Arora was first published in *Economic Botany* in 2008. It's a very fun and interesting read about the history and process of detoxifying *Amanita muscaria* for use as an edible, including a "recipe" for detoxifying them that served as the basis for the technique on page 34.

The Ultimate Mushroom Resource List is an aptly named document created and maintained by Sigrid Jakob. It is a well-curated collection of links to online resources on all sorts of mushroom-related topics. If you can't directly find what you're looking for there, this collection will help you find alternatives. I have created a link to this fantastic online document on my webpage: themushroomhunterskitchen.com/mushrooms/ultimate-list.

To contact Chad Hyatt or find out about his events, where to see him, hear him, or eat his food, check out his webpages at catalego.net and themushroomhunterskitchen.com.

Image Credits

Photographs on pages ii–v, 10–12, 14–15, 19, 21, 24, 26–27, 66, 169, 183, and 189 © Adobe Stock

Photographs on pages vi–vii, 40–41, 46–47, 50, 53, 65, 68, 73, 78–79, 82–83, 86–87, 90–91, 93, 98–99, 103, 107, 112, 116, 120, 123, 124–25, 131, 134–35, 138–39, 143, 144, 154–55, 159, 167, 170, 174–75, 176, 178, 187, 190, 195, 202–3, 204–5, 208, 212, 215, 222, 227, 228, 236, 238–39, 244, 252, 256, 261, 263, 269, and 273 © 2018, 2025 by Elena Feldbaum

Photographs on pages 34, 57, 141, 150–51, 184 (top), 193, and 225 © 2018 by Noah Siegel

Acknowledgments

Anyone who has been around me over the last decade knows Rosa. Besides offering her tireless support, she has helped me collect countless mushrooms, been the chief taste-tester for almost every recipe in this book, and helped at most demos and classes I have done. She has also cleaned more mushrooms than anyone can imagine, and stayed up late, clearing up a million messes after the fun was over. Several of her family recipes even made it into this book. I cannot thank her enough for her constant help and positivity as I fought through various stages of this project. I do not exaggerate when saying that without Rosa, this book could never have come into being.

Thank you to Michael Miller, for your patience while I endlessly bounced ideas off you, your support, and your belief in me have all been immensely valuable; Noah Siegel, for much needed support, encouragement, and advice along the way; Christian Schwarz, for offering up a lot of help, encouragement, and endless patience; Phyllis Peterson, for guiding me through how to turn a bunch of words and ideas into an actual book; Elena Feldbaum, for bringing these recipes to life with your photography; William Rubel, for steering me in the right direction and getting my head on straight early in the process of creating this book, making the whole process go infinitely smoother; Jill Nussinow, for showing me the way and getting me going when I was stuck and spinning my wheels; "Missy Over There," Meredith Morris, for helping me sift through my baking and pastry issues; Leah Meyers for her help editing, proofreading, and generally cleaning up the text the first time around; Thea Chesney, for helping to check my myco-info, and much more; Eric Tucker from Millennium, for convincing me that pressing and searing mushrooms is a useful and fun technique; and Eugenia Bone, for her guidance, advice, and general help.

David Arora, the events you have included me in have introduced me to most of my best friends within the mushroom community. I don't think I could've done half of what I did in this book without the support and knowledge you have shared, and all of your answers to my random mushroom questions.

Thank you also to Todd Spanier, Jerry Kharitonov, Tatyana Vinogradov-Nurenberg, Denis Benjamin, Wendy So, Christopher Hodge, Mayumi Fujio, James Edmunds, Carter Jessop, Jonathan Frank, Dylan Taube, Tavis Lynch, Britt Bunyard, Raymond So, the Garrone family, everyone at Far West Fungi, all of the mushroom clubs that I've worked with, and all of my friends in the mushroom community, around the country and beyond. Though I can't call out every deserving person, please know that I am grateful to all of you who have helped me along the way.

Finally, I want to thank the entire team at The Experiment for taking on my crazy mushroom book, turning it into something we all can be proud of, and bringing it to a wider audience. Thank you to Matthew Lore for believing in me and this book, and to all the talented people who have worked so hard behind the scenes. Special thanks go to Beth Bugler, Zach Pace, and Ally Mitchell. Last, and certainly not least, thank you to my editor, Sara Zatopek, for her patience, guidance, and endless work in bringing this book to life.

Index

NOTE: Page references in *italics* identify mushroom types and recipe preparation.

D

E

F

G

H

I

R

S

About the Author

CHAD HYATT is an expert forager and classically trained chef who has made a name for himself in Northern California and beyond, sharing his delicious spin on wild mushroom cookery. He has cooked in a variety of restaurants and private clubs around the San Francisco Bay area, where he can often be found foraging for mushrooms, putting on wild mushroom-themed dinners, teaching mushroom-related classes, and attending mushroom festivals. He is passionate about cooking approachable comfort food based on local, seasonal ingredients, and, of course, wild mushrooms.

themushroomhunterskitchen.com
catalego.net | chadateit